ANGORA NAPKIN™

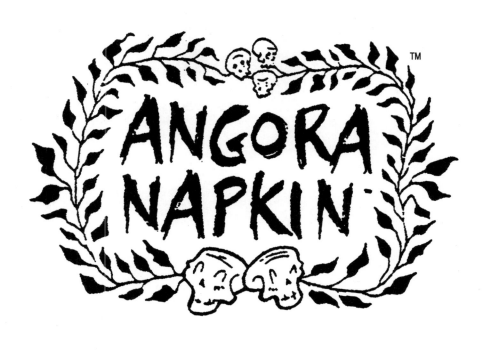

Meanwhile...

For Dad,
This is all your fault.

Operations:
Moshe Berger, Chairman
Ted Adams, Chief Executive Officer
Greg Goldstein, Chief Operating Officer
Matthew Ruzicka, CPA, Chief Financial Officer
Alan Payne, VP of Sales
Lorelei Bunjes, Dir. of Digital Services
Marci Hubbard, Executive Assistant
Alonzo Simon, Shipping Manager

Editorial:
Chris Ryall, Publisher/Editor-in-Chief
Scott Dunbier, Editor, Special Projects
Andy Schmidt, Senior Editor
Justin Eisinger, Editor
Kris Oprisko, Editor/Foreign Lic.
Denton J. Tipton, Editor
Tom Waltz, Editor
Mariah Huehner, Assistant Editor

Design:
Robbie Robbins, EVP/Sr. Graphic Artist
Ben Templesmith, Artist/Designer
Neil Uyetake, Art Director
Chris Mowry, Graphic Artist
Amauri Osorio, Graphic Artist

www.idwpublishing.com
ISBN: 978-1-60010-339-1
11 10 09 08   1 2 3 4

www.angoranapkin.com
www.meanwhilestudios.com
email: troy@meanwhilestudios.com

ANGORA
NAPKIN

by

TROY LITTLE

Edited by

CAROL LITTLE

Angora Napkin created by

TROY LITTLE & NICK CROSS

Introduction

"In an age when so much cartoon and comic art seems mechanized and created by computers, it's great to see a comic fully hand-drawn, hand-inked and hand-lettered in a cartoony custom-made style.

Angora Napkin is full of dynamic layouts, funny situations, individual, funny characters and varied pacing in the continuity. It plays like it's happening in real time. The style is unique and fun and is what I love to see in cartoon art—a sincere and observant unique look at the world. It's graphic yet still organic and alive—no easy feat to combine these two elements.

Troy worked for me on *Ripping Friends* and helped design backgrounds and layouts for the Spike TV *Ren and Stimpy* cartoons. I am always on the hunt for artists that have their own individual styles and this comic is a perfect demonstration of Troy's own stamp.

I hope you enjoy *Angora Napkin* as much as I do."

- John Kricfalusi

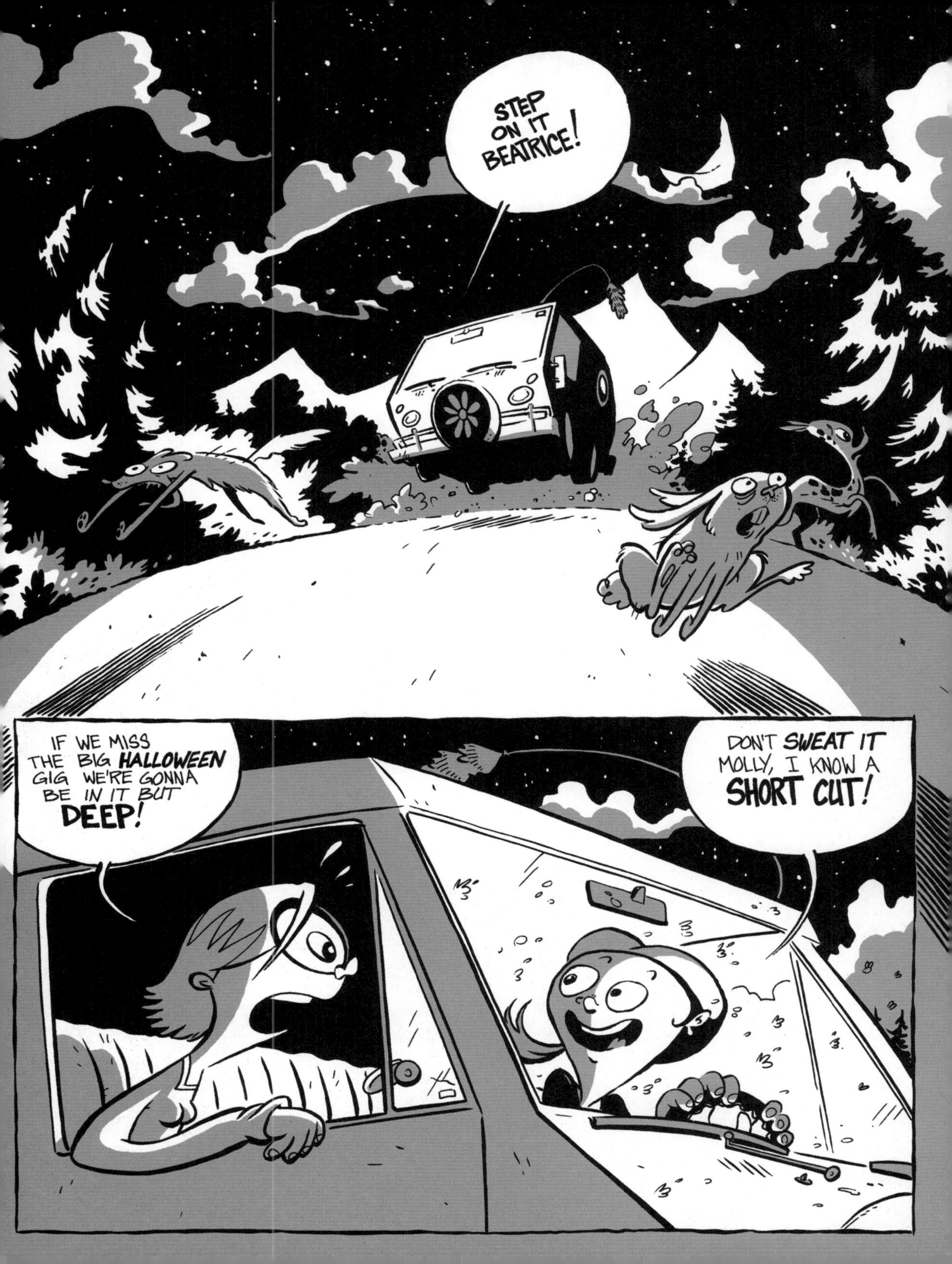
STEP ON IT BEATRICE!
IF WE MISS THE BIG HALLOWEEN GIG WE'RE GONNA BE IN IT BUT DEEP!
DON'T SWEAT IT MOLLY, I KNOW A SHORT CUT!

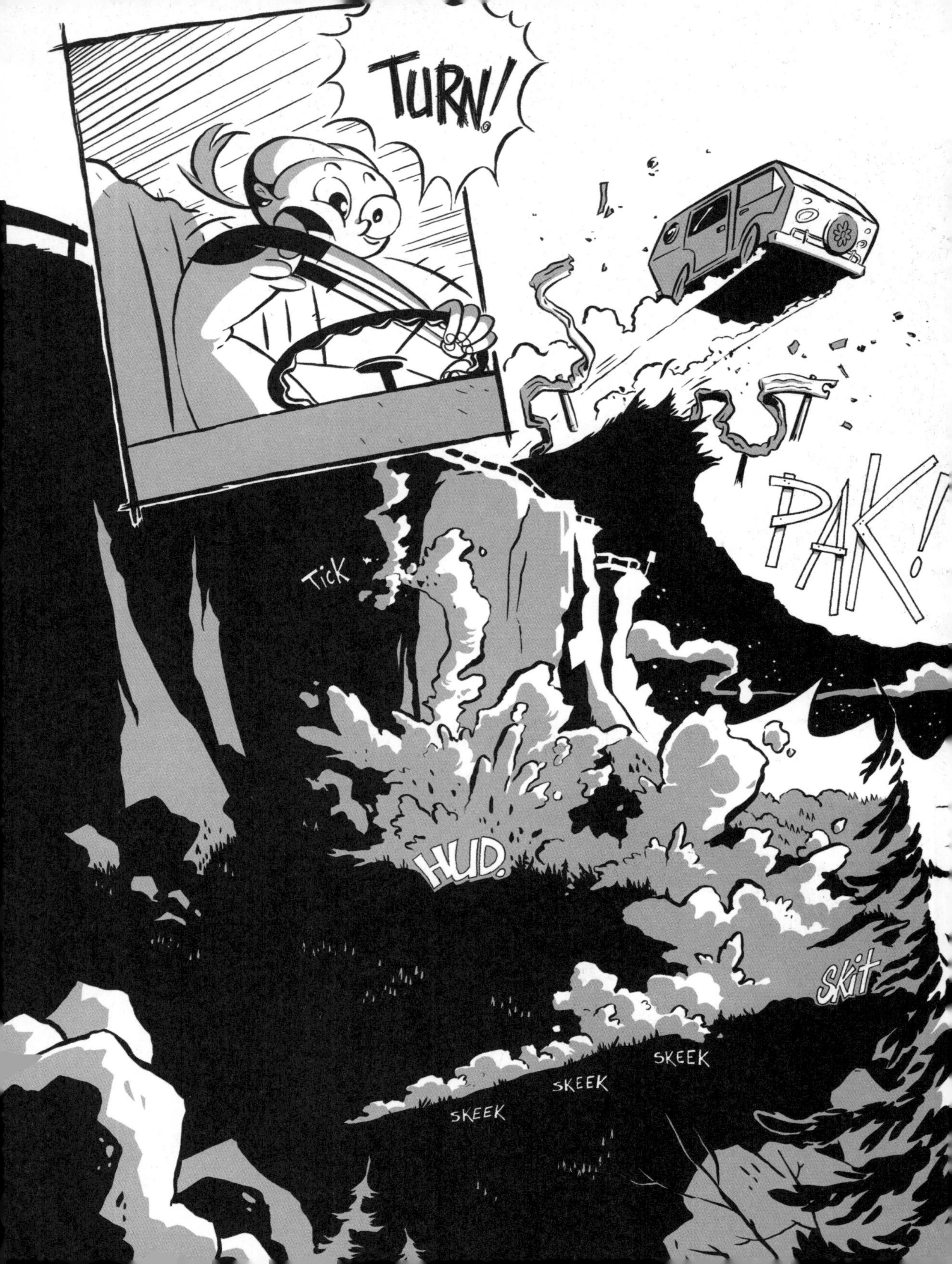

TURN!
PAK!
Tick
HUD.
Skit
SKEEK
SKEEK
SKEEK

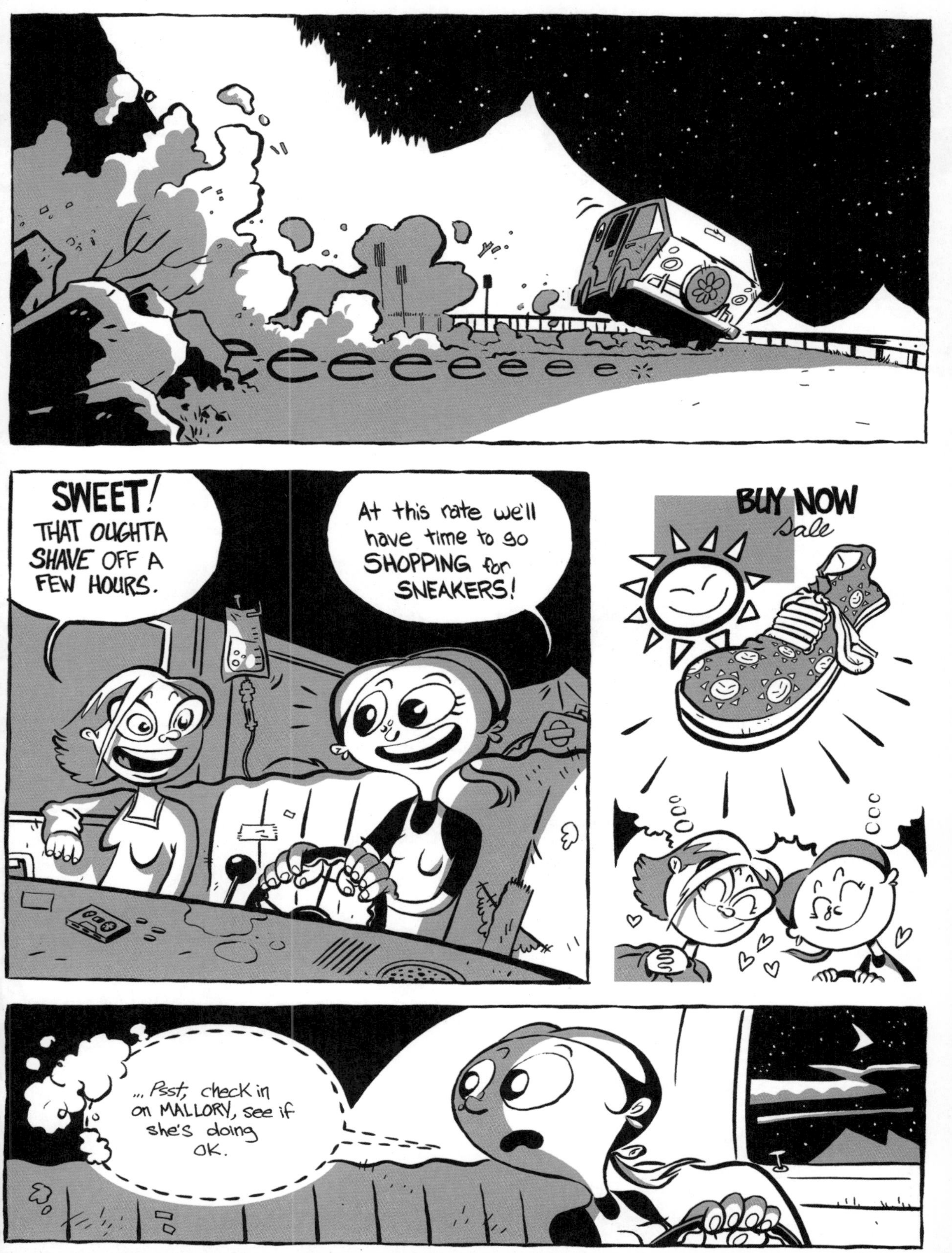
EEEEEEEEEE
SWEET! THAT OUGHTA SHAVE OFF A FEW HOURS.
At this rate we'll have time to go SHOPPING for SNEAKERS!
BUY NOW
Sale
... Psst, check in on MALLORY, see if she's doing OK.

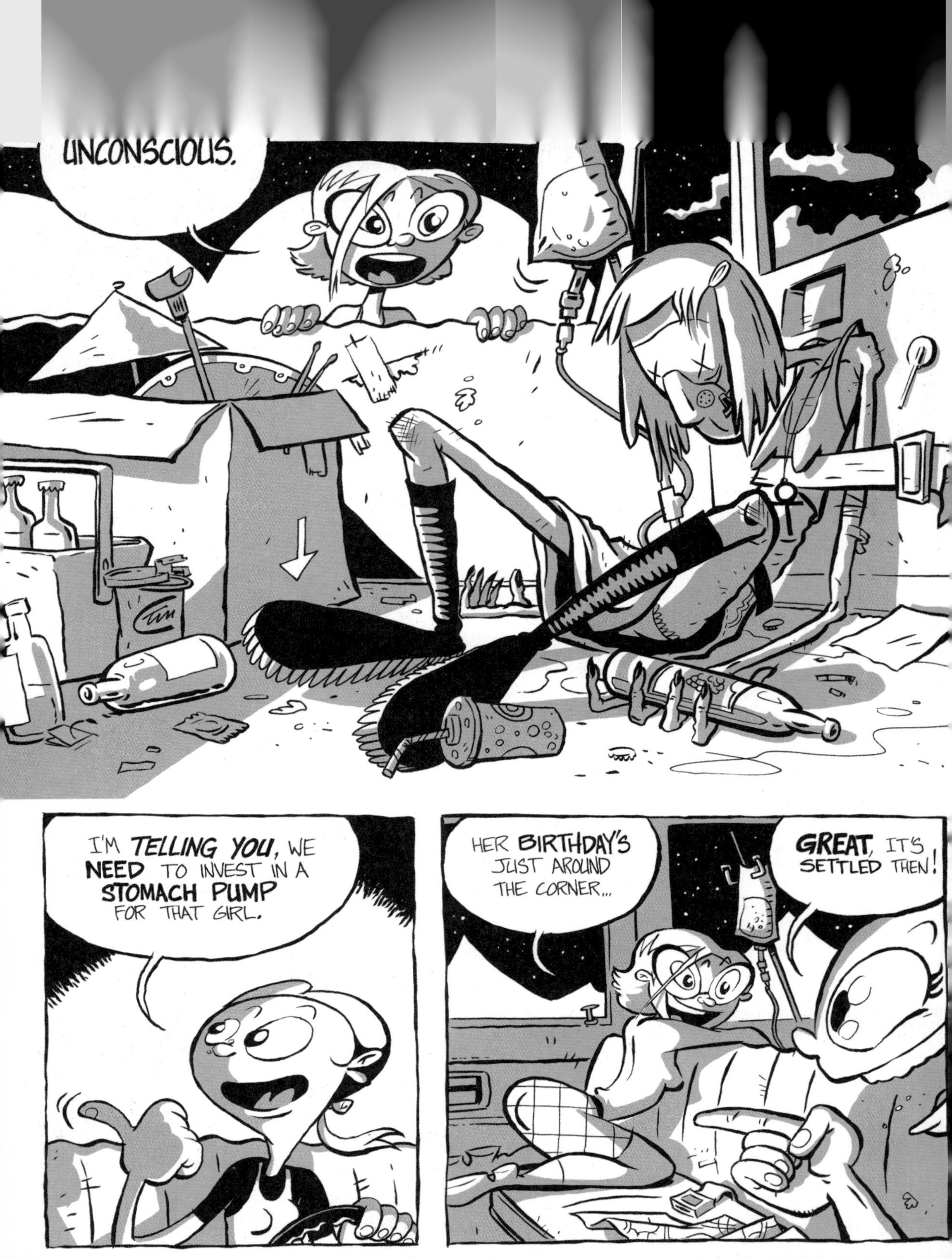
UNCONSCIOUS.
I'M TELLING YOU, WE NEED TO INVEST IN A STOMACH PUMP FOR THAT GIRL.
HER BIRTHDAY'S JUST AROUND THE CORNER...
GREAT, IT'S SETTLED THEN!

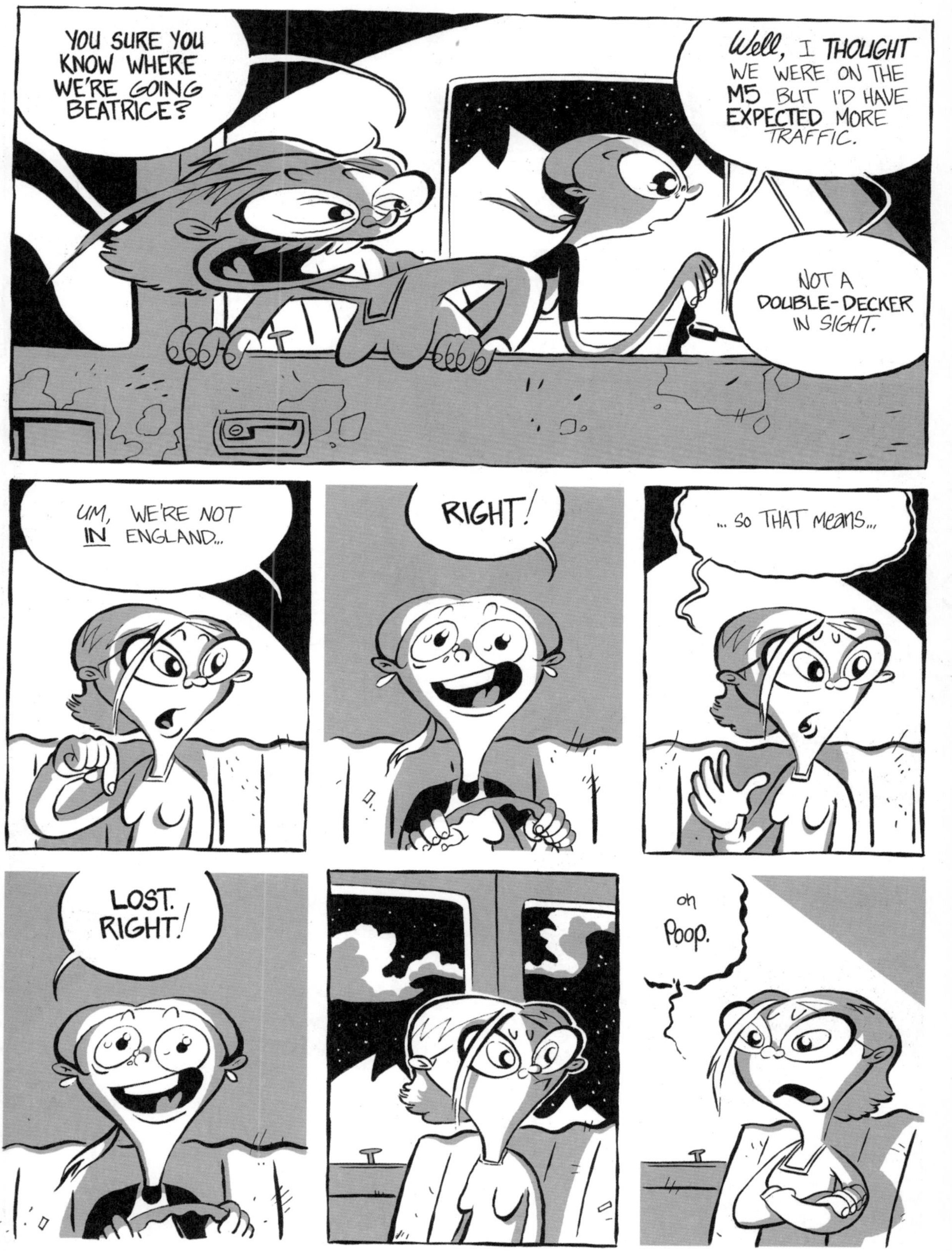
YOU SURE YOU KNOW WHERE WE'RE GOING BEATRICE?
Well, I THOUGHT WE WERE ON THE M5 BUT I'D HAVE EXPECTED MORE TRAFFIC.
NOT A DOUBLE-DECKER IN SIGHT.
UM, WE'RE NOT IN ENGLAND...
RIGHT!
... SO THAT means...
LOST. RIGHT!
oh Poop.

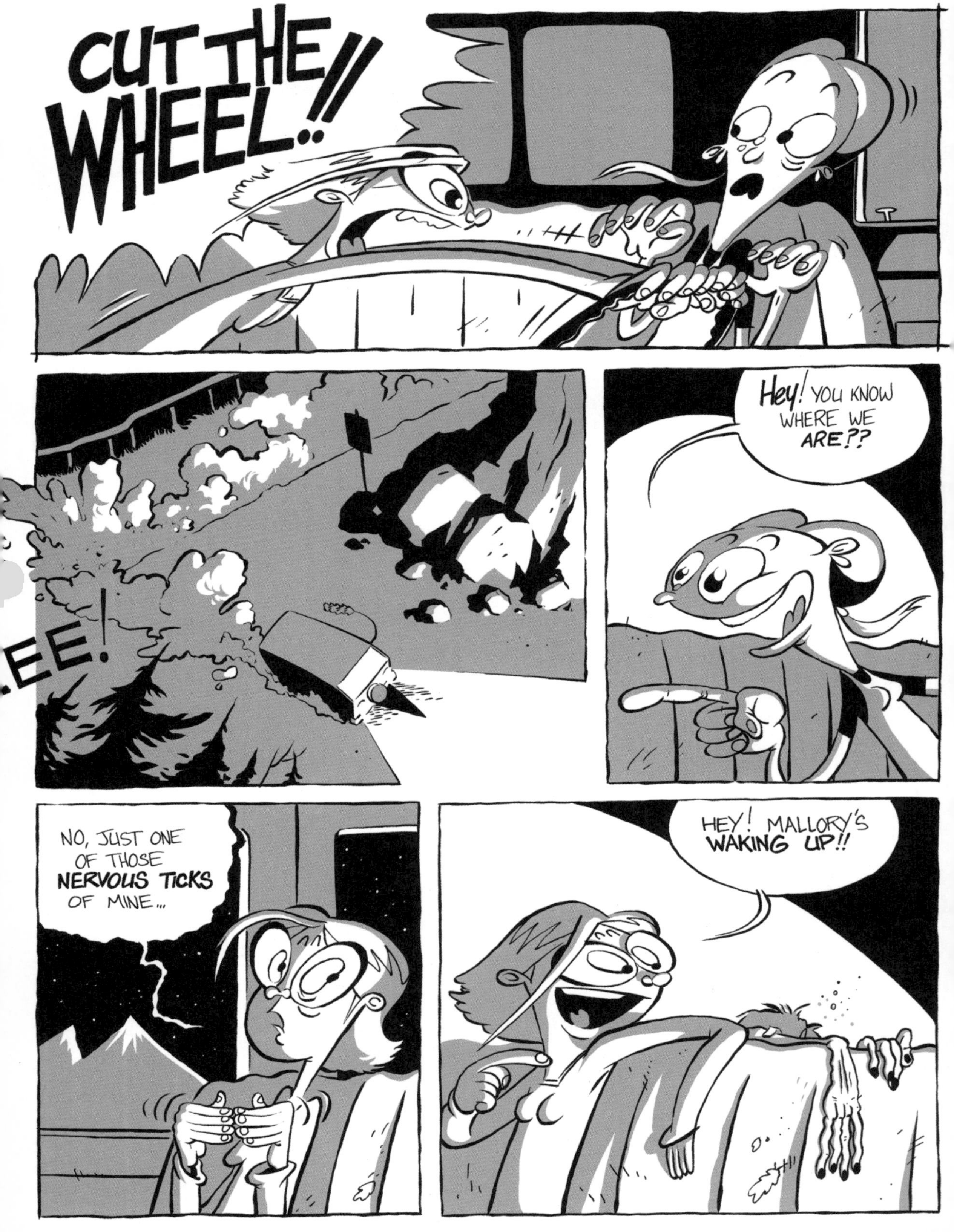
CUT THE WHEEL!!
..EE!
Hey! YOU KNOW WHERE WE ARE??
NO, JUST ONE OF THOSE NERVOUS TICKS OF MINE...
HEY! MALLORY'S WAKING UP!!

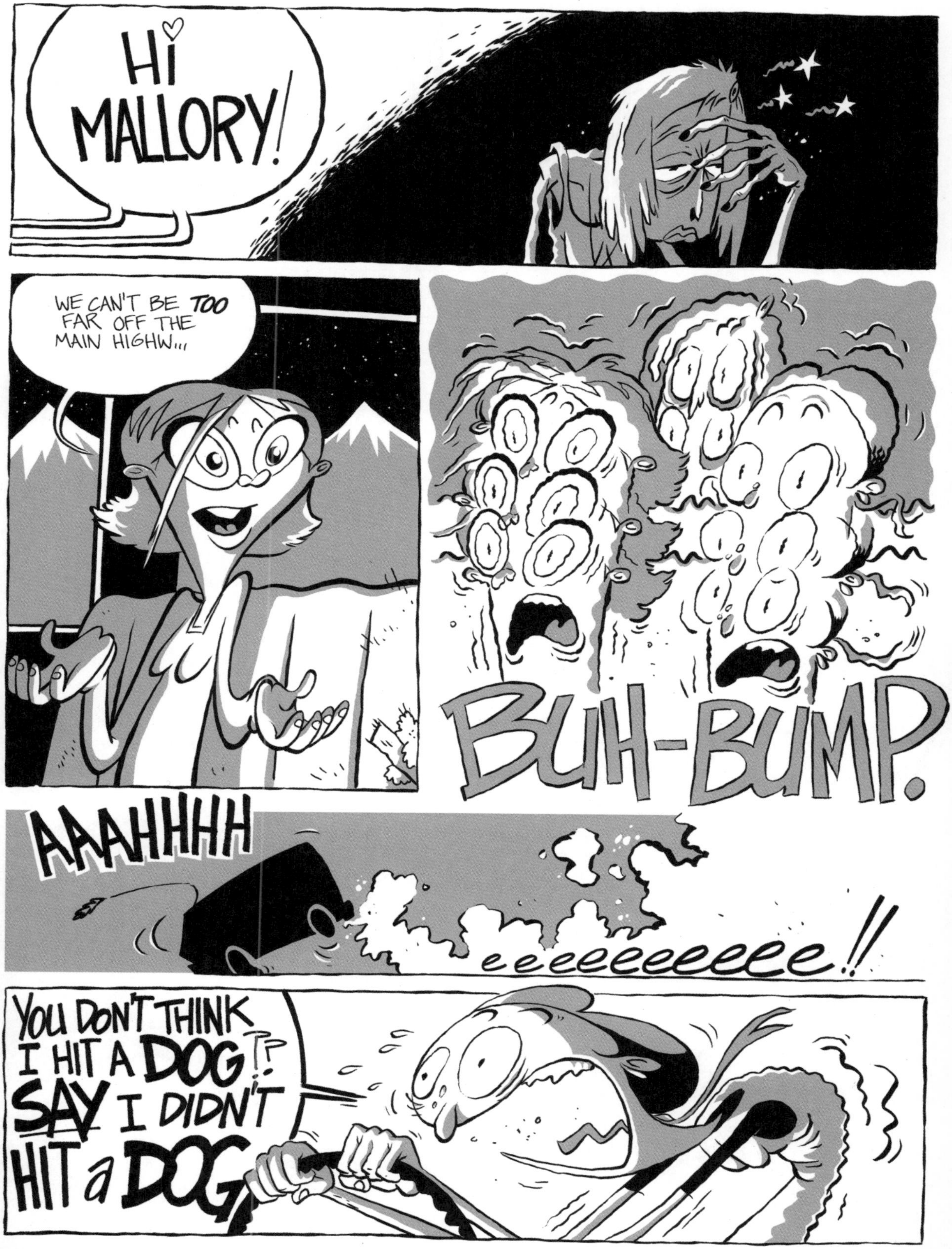
Hi MALLORY!
WE CAN'T BE TOO FAR OFF THE MAIN HIGHW...
BUH-BUMP.
AAAHHHH
eeeeeeeeeee!!
YOU DON'T THINK I HIT A DOG?! SAY I DIDN'T HIT a DOG

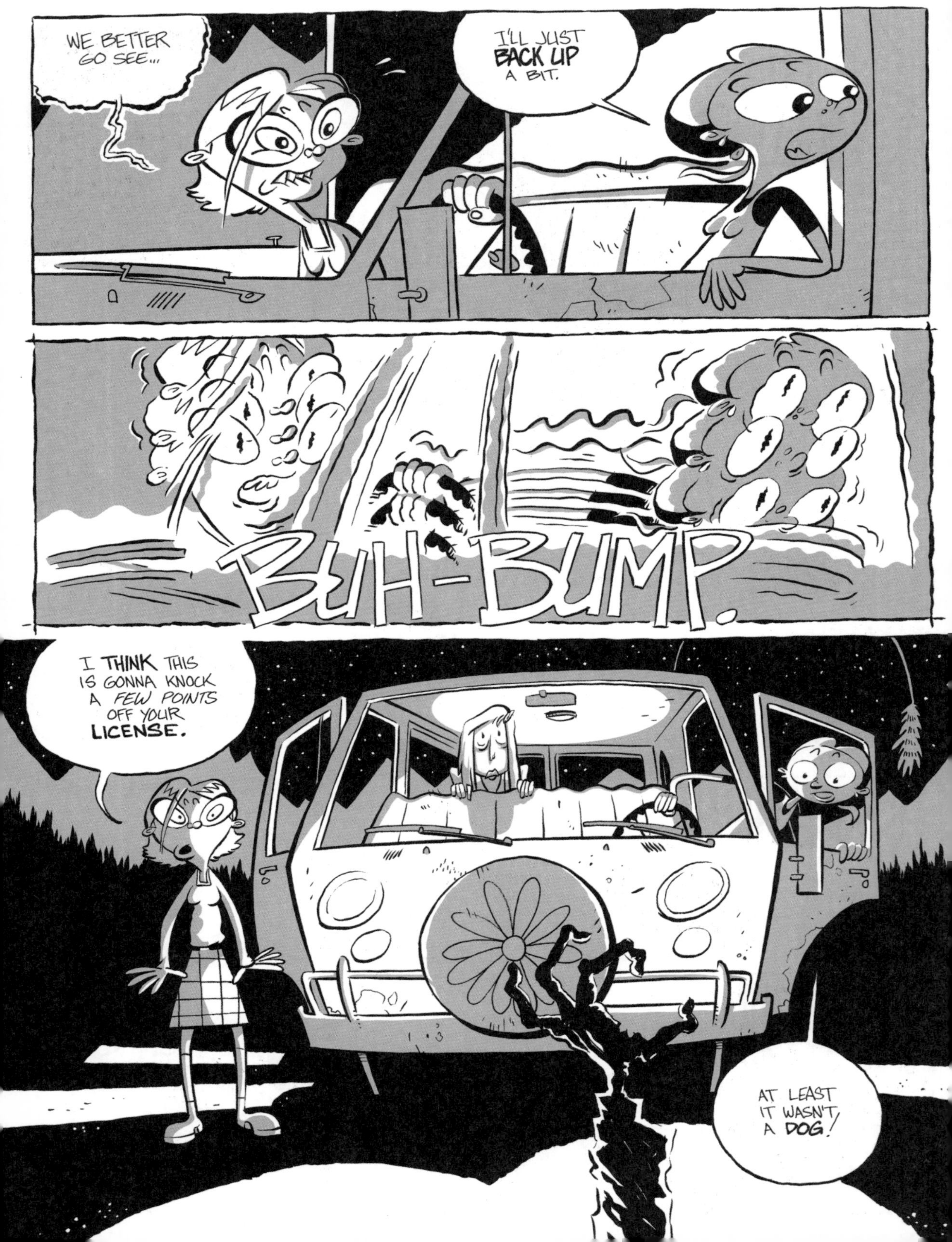
WE BETTER GO SEE...
I'LL JUST BACK UP A BIT.
BUH-BUMP.
I THINK THIS IS GONNA KNOCK A FEW POINTS OFF YOUR LICENSE.
AT LEAST IT WASN'T A DOG!

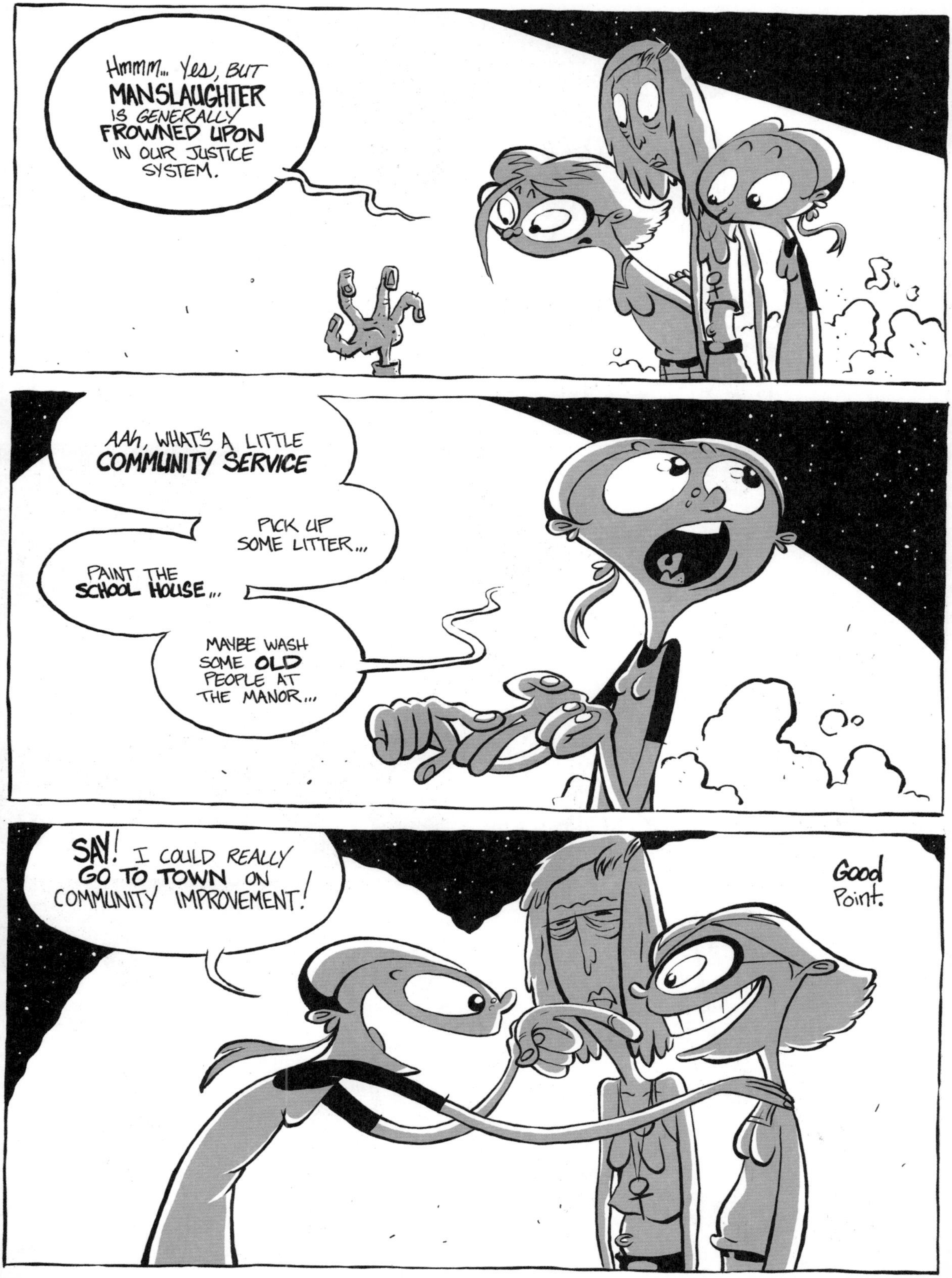

Hmmm... Yes, BUT MANSLAUGHTER IS GENERALLY FROWNED UPON IN OUR JUSTICE SYSTEM.
AAh, WHAT'S A LITTLE COMMUNITY SERVICE
PICK UP SOME LITTER...
PAINT THE SCHOOL HOUSE...
MAYBE WASH SOME OLD PEOPLE AT THE MANOR...
SAY! I COULD REALLY GO TO TOWN ON COMMUNITY IMPROVEMENT!
Good Point.

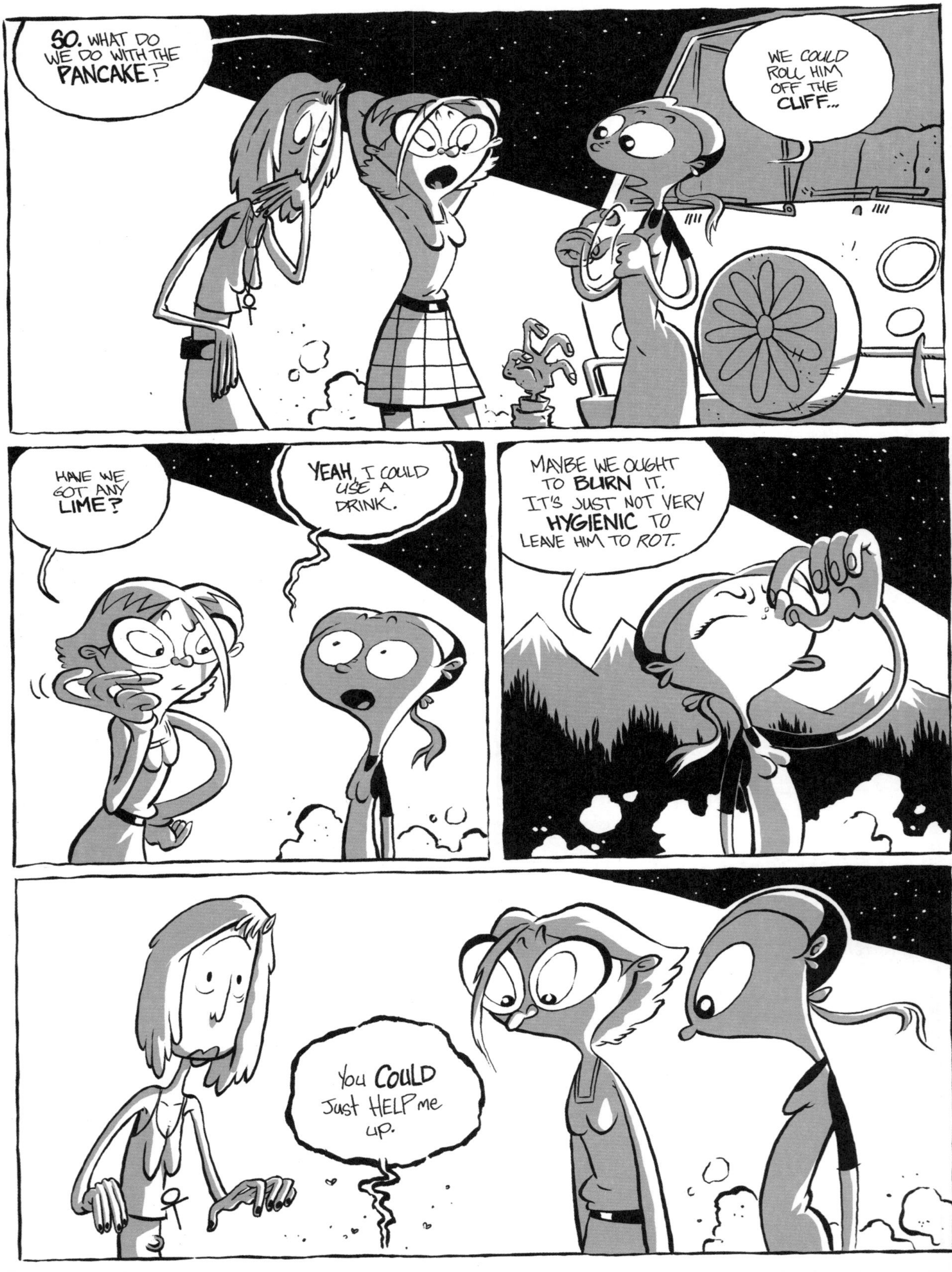

SO. WHAT DO WE DO WITH THE PANCAKE?
WE COULD ROLL HIM OFF THE CLIFF...
HAVE WE GOT ANY LIME?
YEAH, I COULD USE A DRINK.
MAYBE WE OUGHT TO BURN IT. IT'S JUST NOT VERY HYGIENIC TO LEAVE HIM TO ROT.
You COULD Just HELP me up.

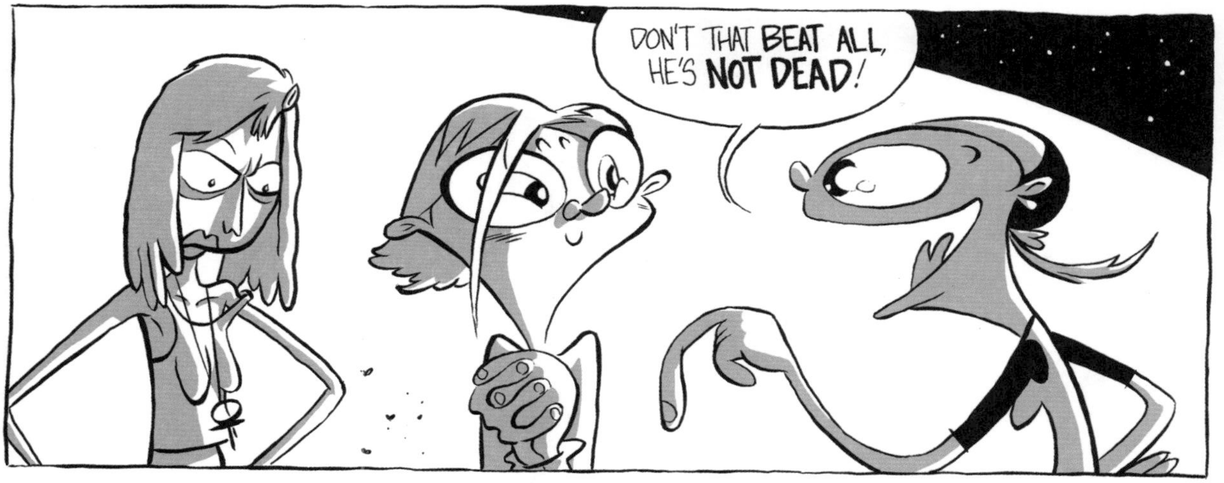
DON'T THAT BEAT ALL, HE'S NOT DEAD!

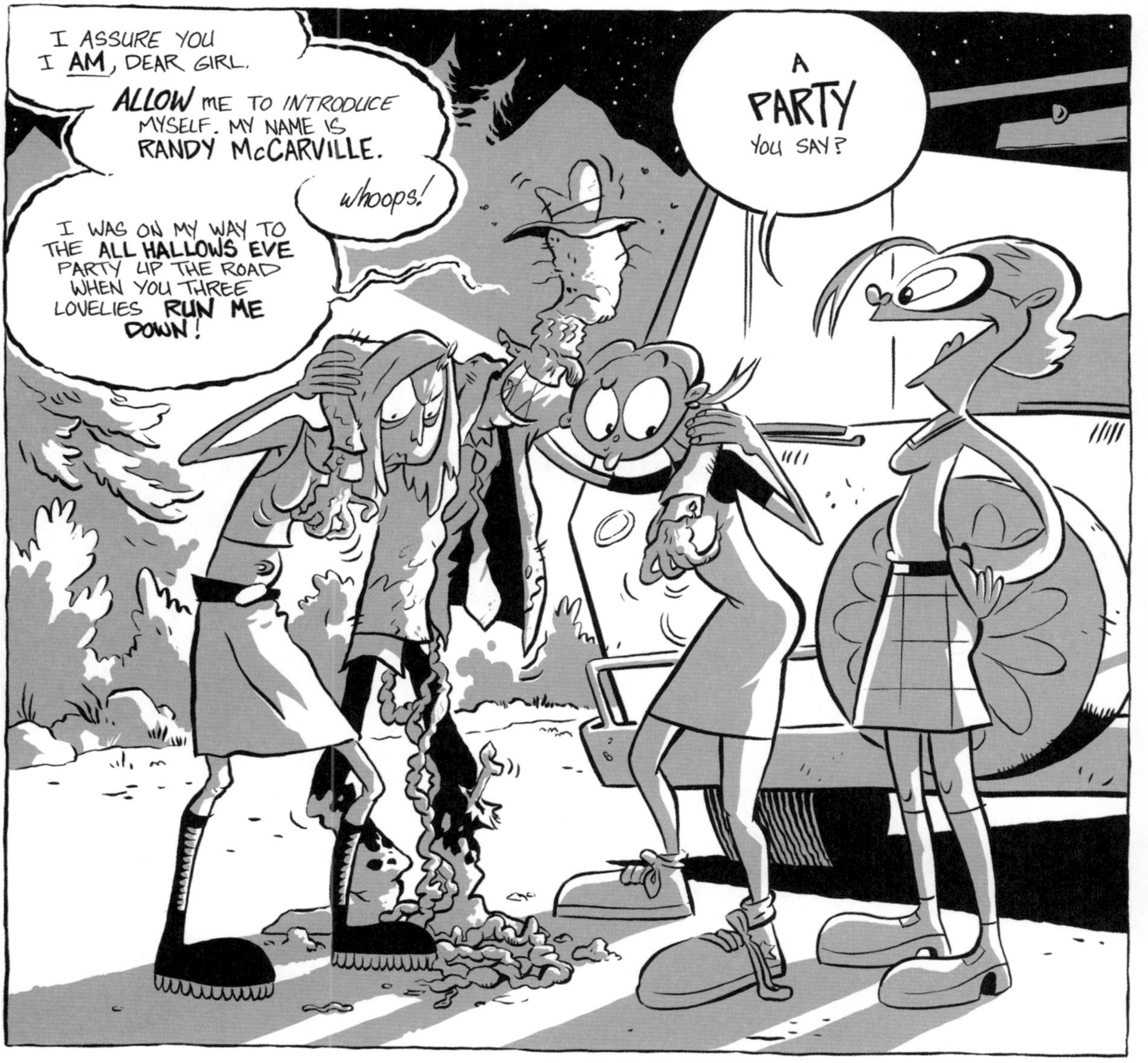
I ASSURE YOU I AM, DEAR GIRL.
ALLOW ME TO INTRODUCE MYSELF. MY NAME IS RANDY McCARVILLE.
whoops!
I WAS ON MY WAY TO THE ALL HALLOWS EVE PARTY UP THE ROAD WHEN YOU THREE LOVELIES RUN ME DOWN!
A PARTY YOU SAY?

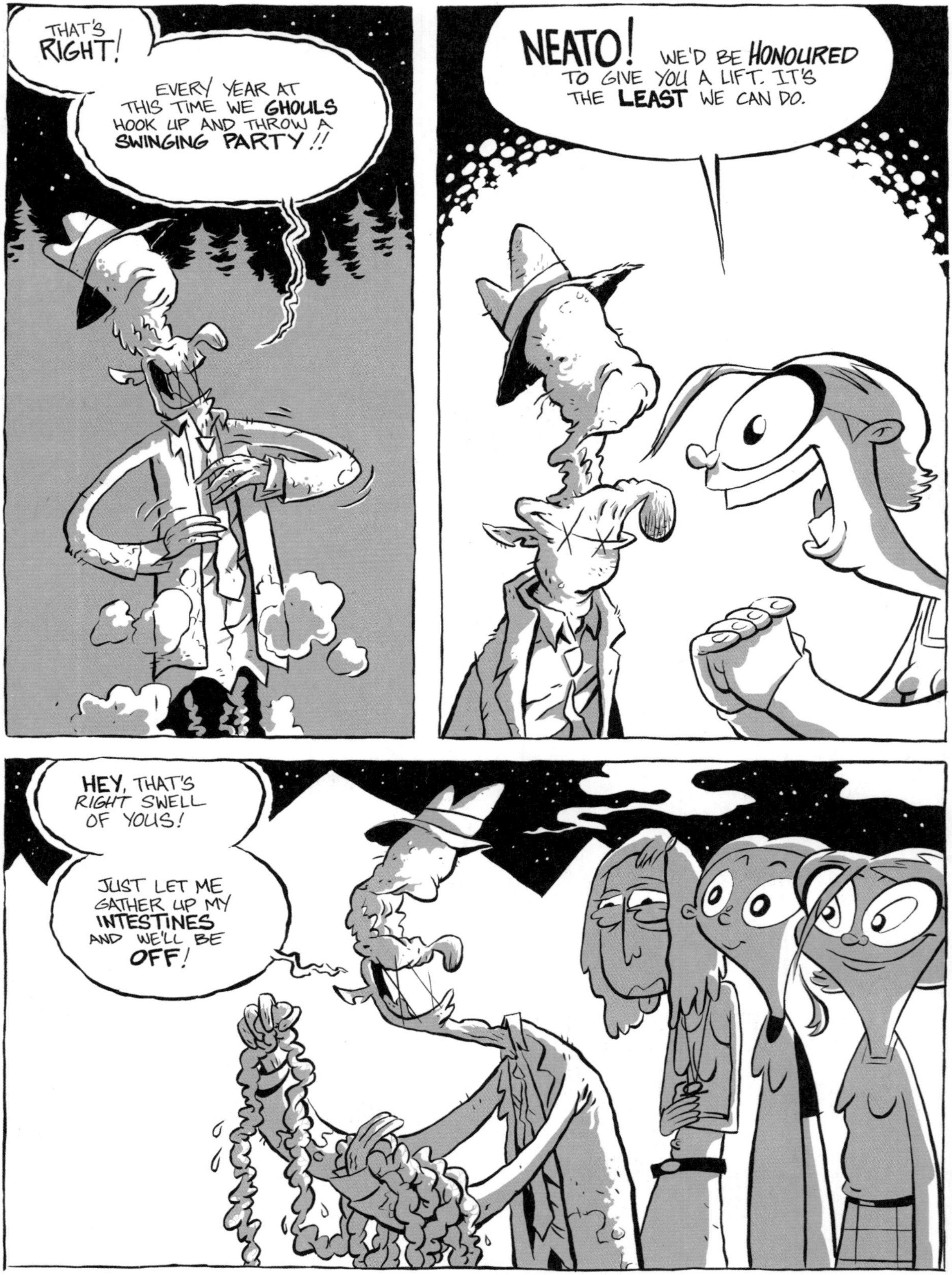
THAT'S RIGHT!
EVERY YEAR AT THIS TIME WE GHOULS HOOK UP AND THROW A SWINGING PARTY!!
NEATO! WE'D BE HONOURED TO GIVE YOU A LIFT. IT'S THE LEAST WE CAN DO.
HEY, THAT'S RIGHT SWELL OF YOUS!
JUST LET ME GATHER UP MY INTESTINES AND WE'LL BE OFF!

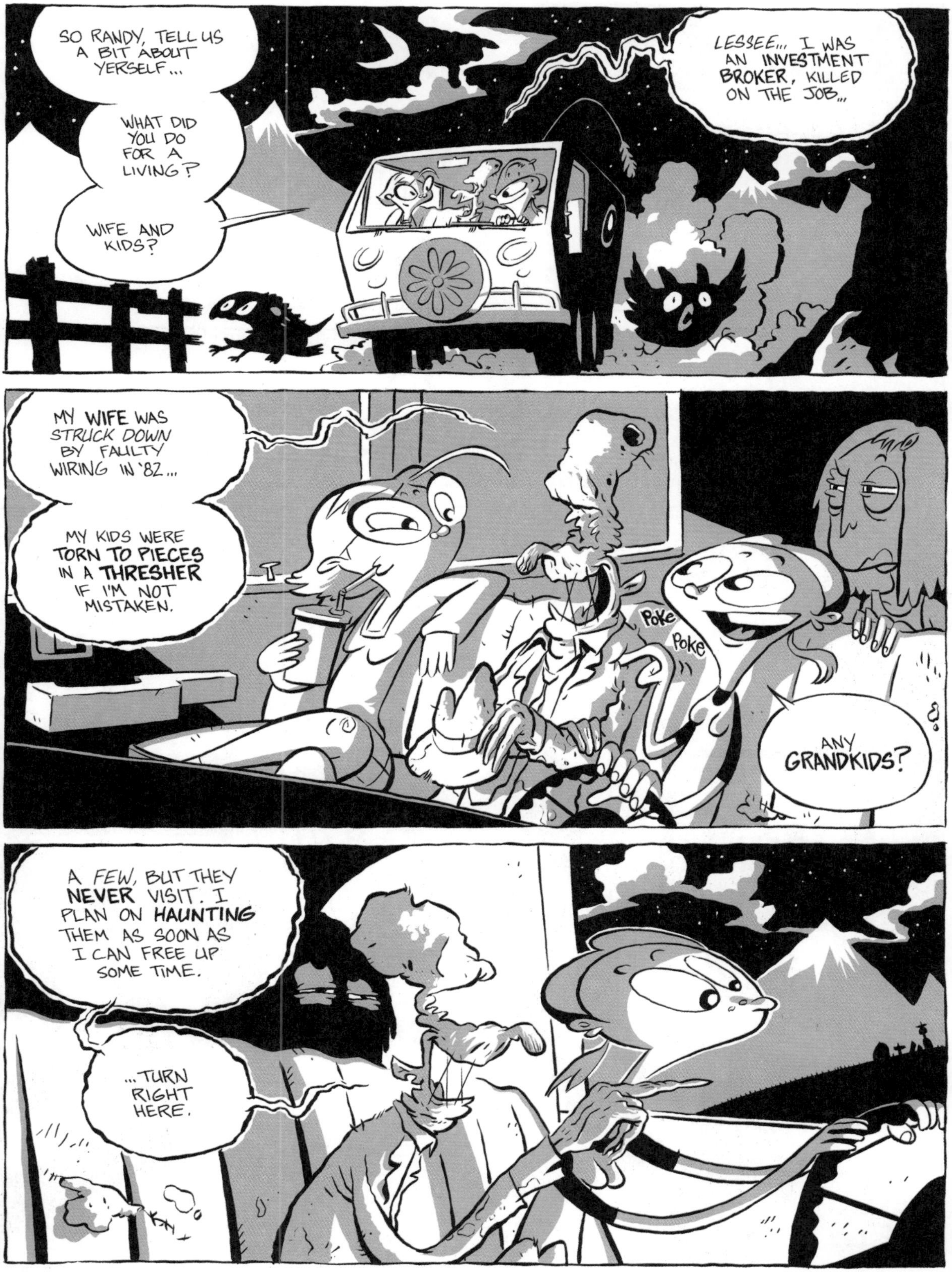
SO RANDY, TELL US A BIT ABOUT YERSELF...
WHAT DID YOU DO FOR A LIVING?
WIFE AND KIDS?
LESSEE... I WAS AN INVESTMENT BROKER, KILLED ON THE JOB...
MY WIFE WAS STRUCK DOWN BY FAULTY WIRING IN '82...
MY KIDS WERE TORN TO PIECES IN A THRESHER IF I'M NOT MISTAKEN.
POKE
POKE
ANY GRANDKIDS?
A FEW, BUT THEY NEVER VISIT. I PLAN ON HAUNTING THEM AS SOON AS I CAN FREE UP SOME TIME.
...TURN RIGHT HERE.

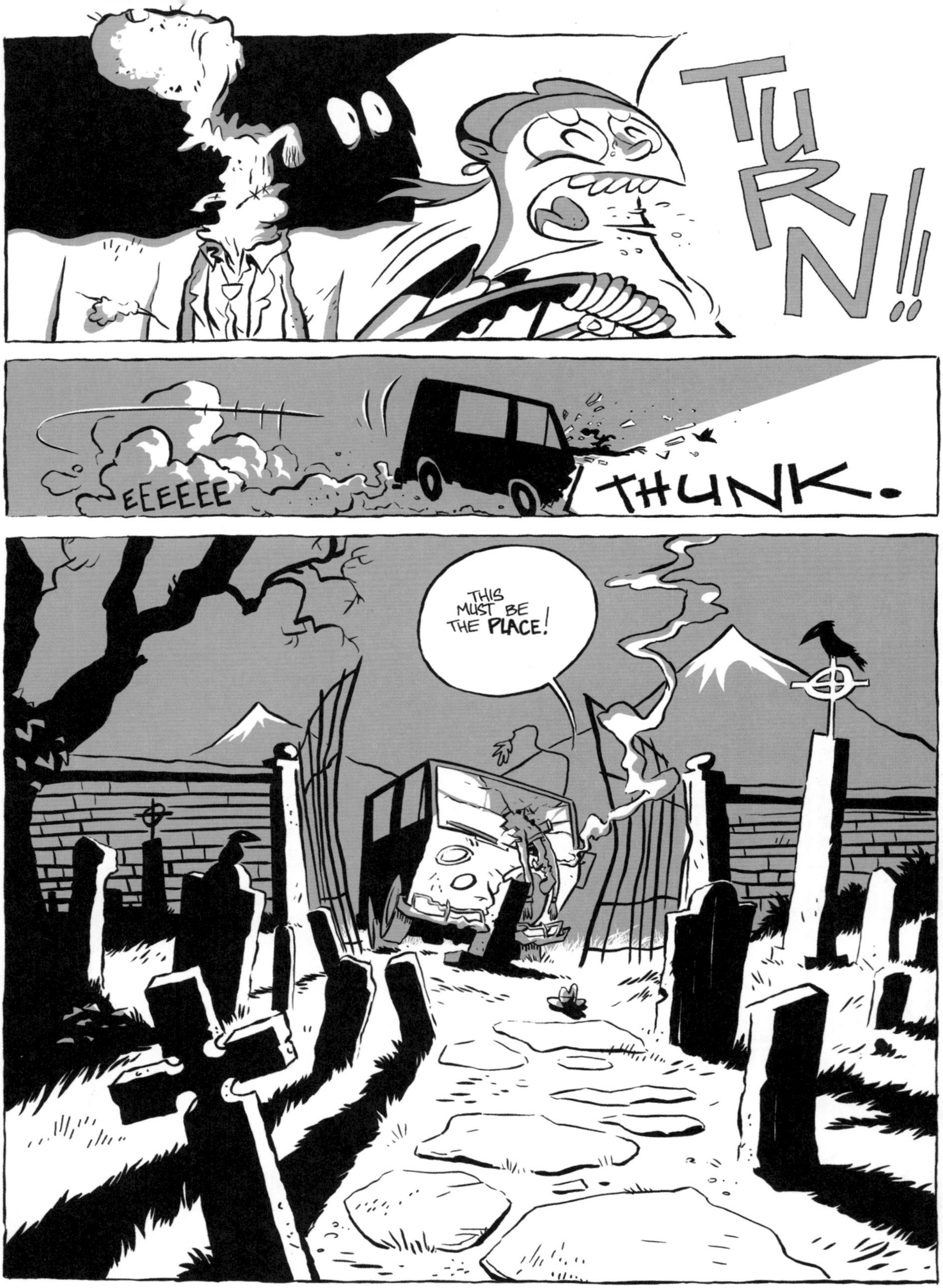
TURN!!
EEEEEE
THUNK.
THIS MUST BE THE PLACE!

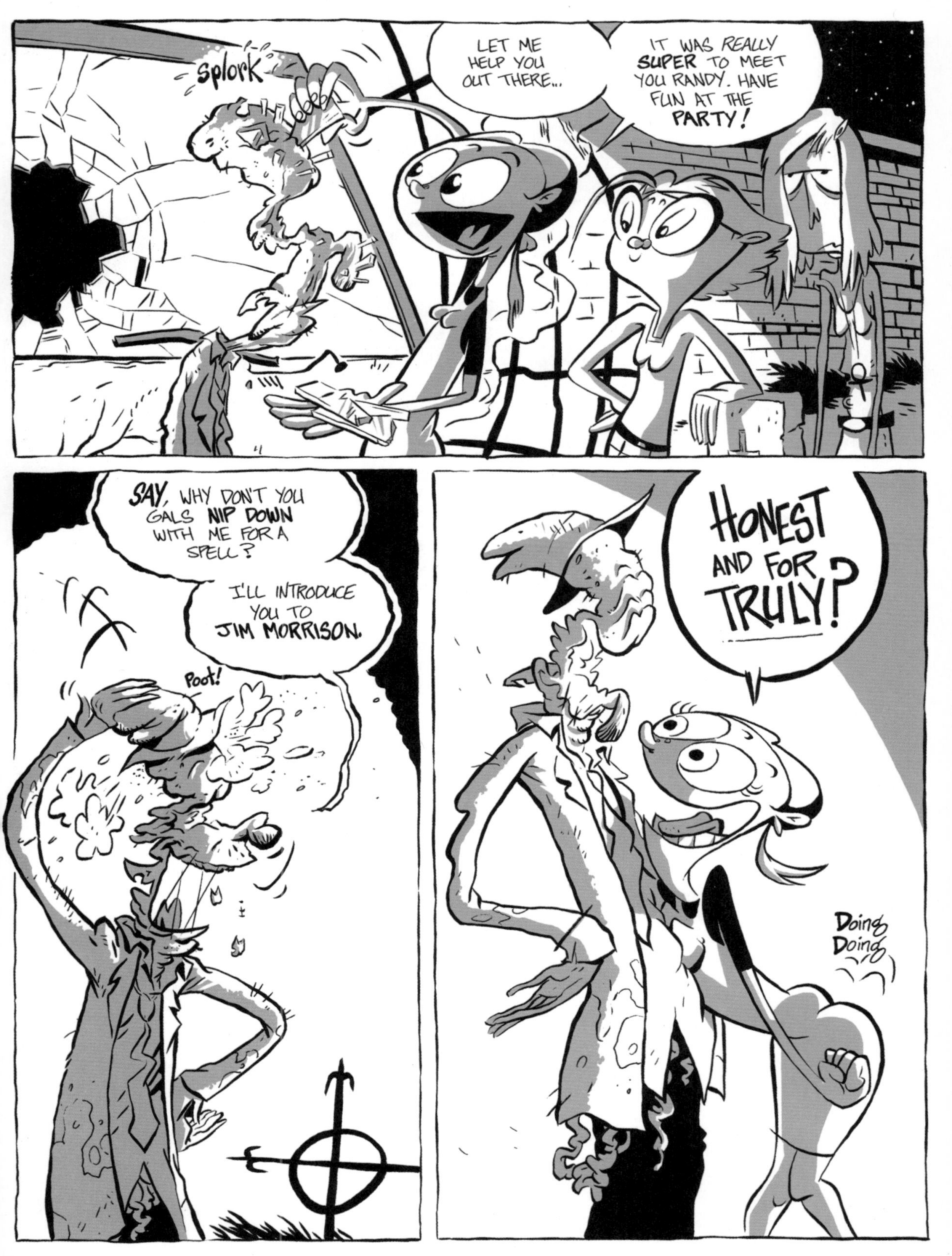
Splork
LET ME HELP YOU OUT THERE...
IT WAS REALLY SUPER TO MEET YOU RANDY. HAVE FUN AT THE PARTY!
SAY, WHY DON'T YOU GALS NIP DOWN WITH ME FOR A SPELL?
I'LL INTRODUCE YOU TO JIM MORRISON.
Poot!
HONEST AND FOR TRULY?
Doing Doing

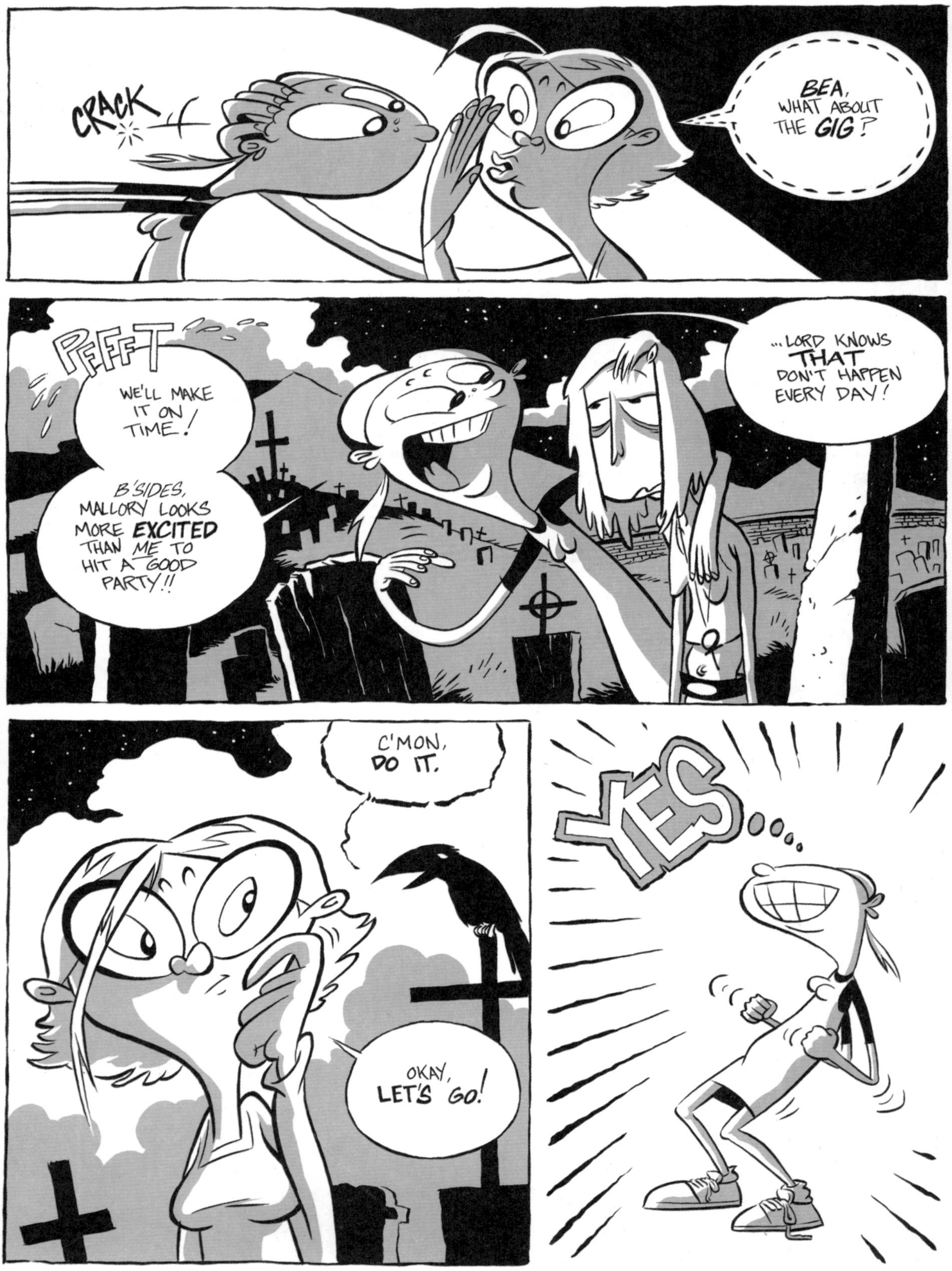
CRACK
BEA, WHAT ABOUT THE GIG?
PFFFFT
WE'LL MAKE IT ON TIME!
B'SIDES, MALLORY LOOKS MORE EXCITED THAN ME TO HIT A GOOD PARTY!!
...LORD KNOWS THAT DON'T HAPPEN EVERY DAY!
C'MON, DO IT.
OKAY, LET'S GO!
YES

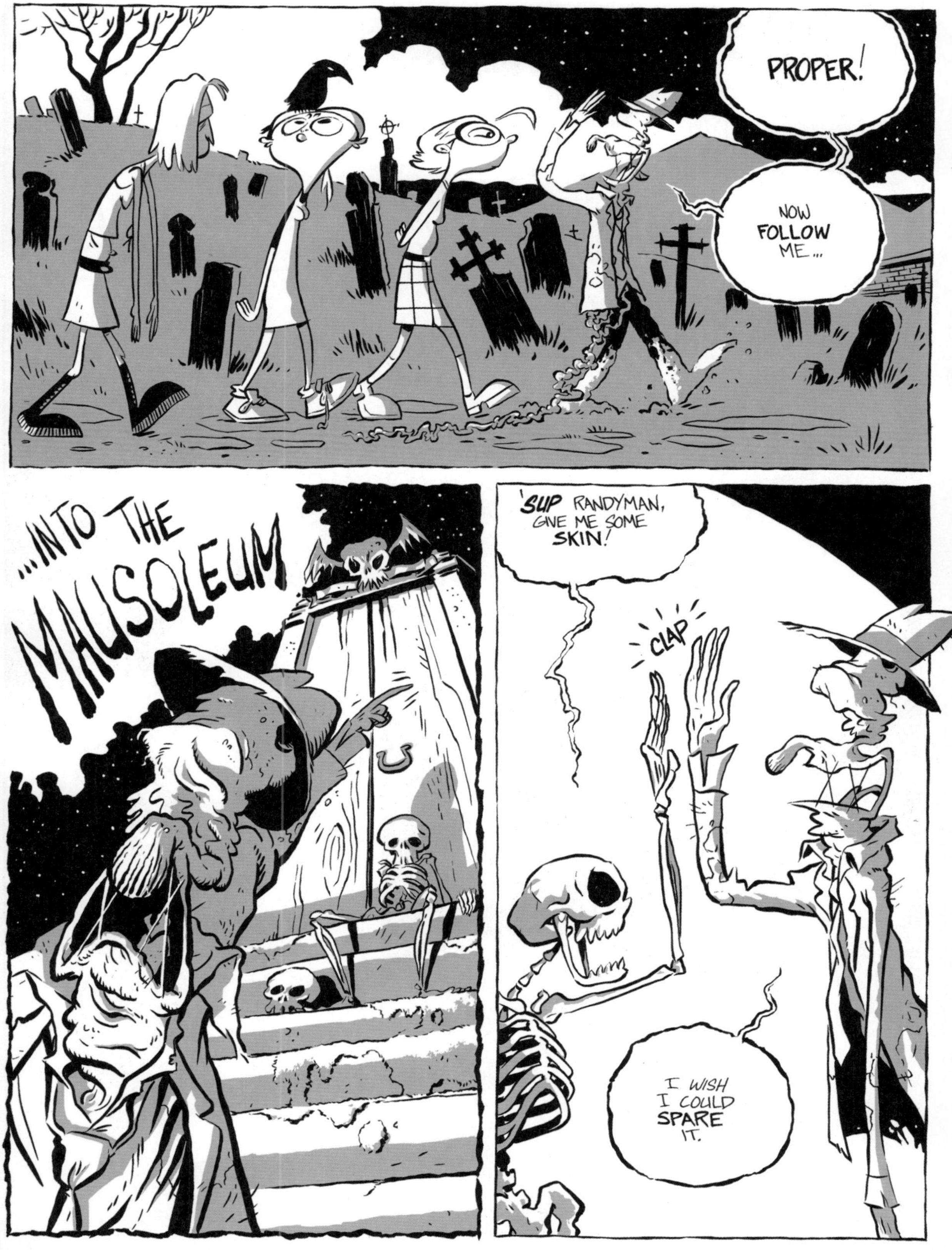
PROPER!
NOW FOLLOW ME...
...INTO THE MAUSOLEUM
'SUP RANDYMAN, GIVE ME SOME SKIN!
CLAP
I WISH I COULD SPARE IT.

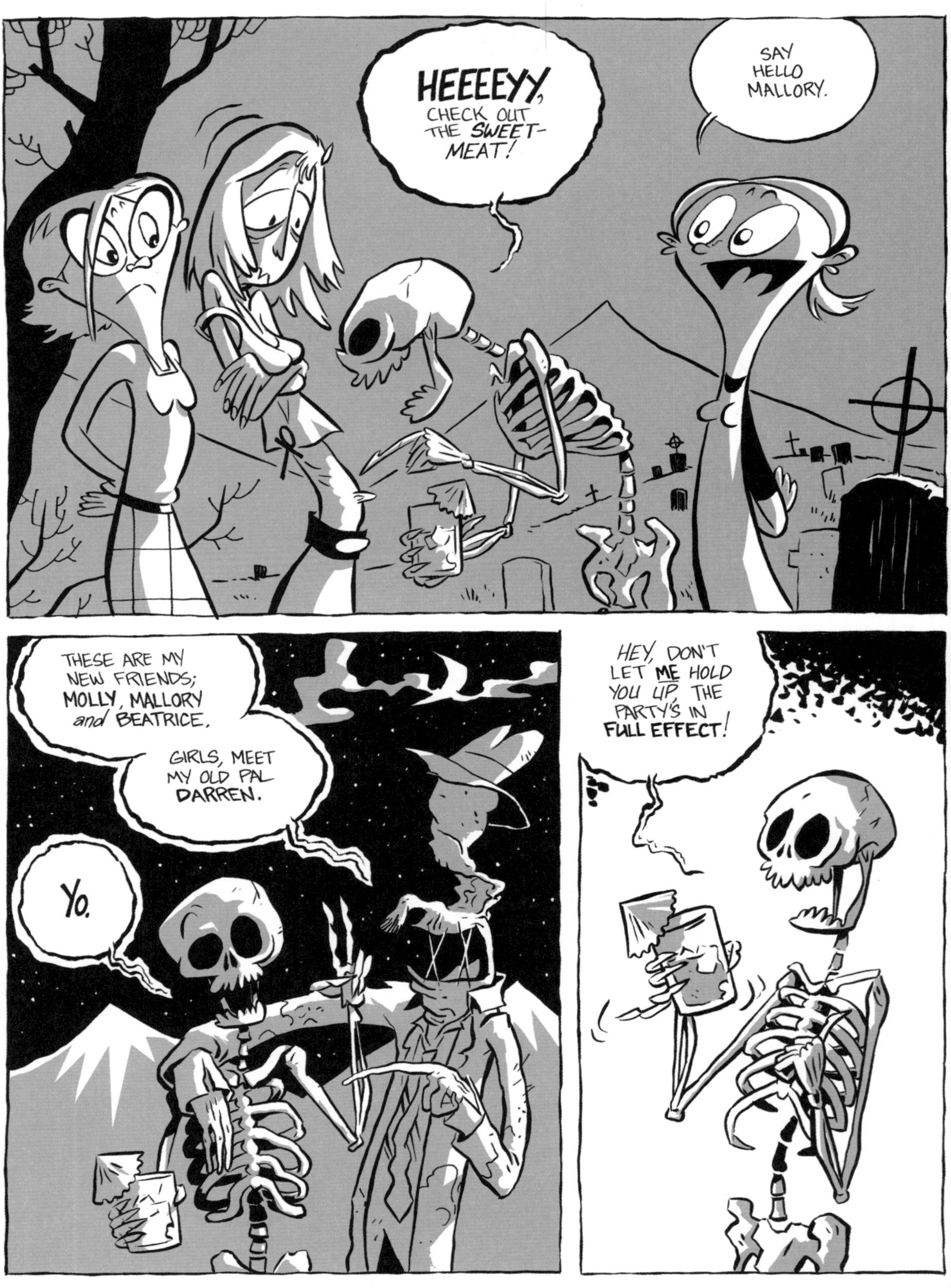
HEEEEYY, CHECK OUT THE SWEET-MEAT!
SAY HELLO MALLORY.
THESE ARE MY NEW FRIENDS; MOLLY, MALLORY and BEATRICE.
GIRLS, MEET MY OLD PAL DARREN.
YO.
HEY, DON'T LET ME HOLD YOU UP, THE PARTY'S IN FULL EFFECT!

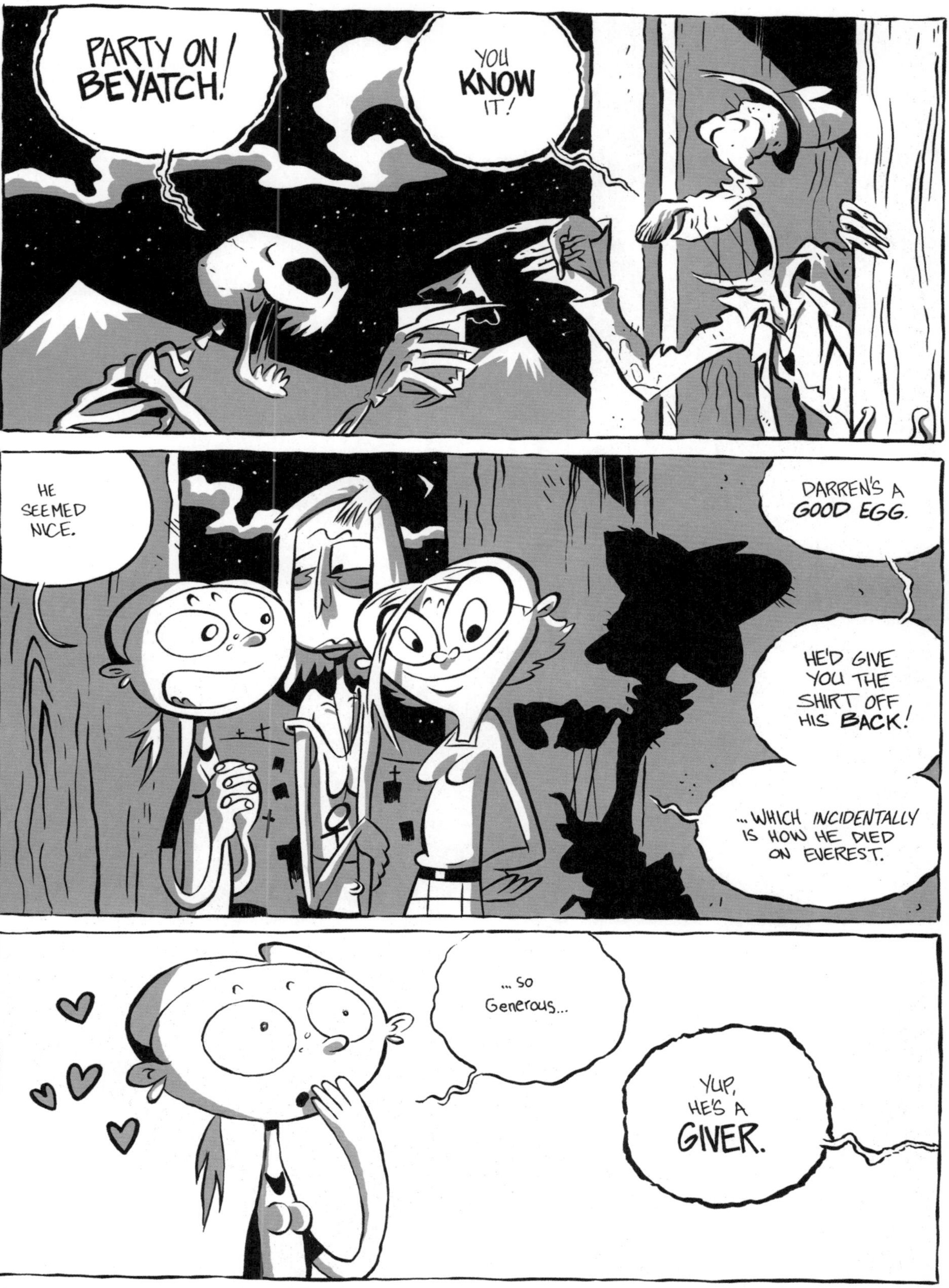
PARTY ON! BEYATCH!
YOU KNOW IT!
HE SEEMED NICE.
DARREN'S A GOOD EGG.
HE'D GIVE YOU THE SHIRT OFF HIS BACK!
...WHICH INCIDENTALLY IS HOW HE DIED ON EVEREST.
...SO Generous...
YUP, HE'S A GIVER.

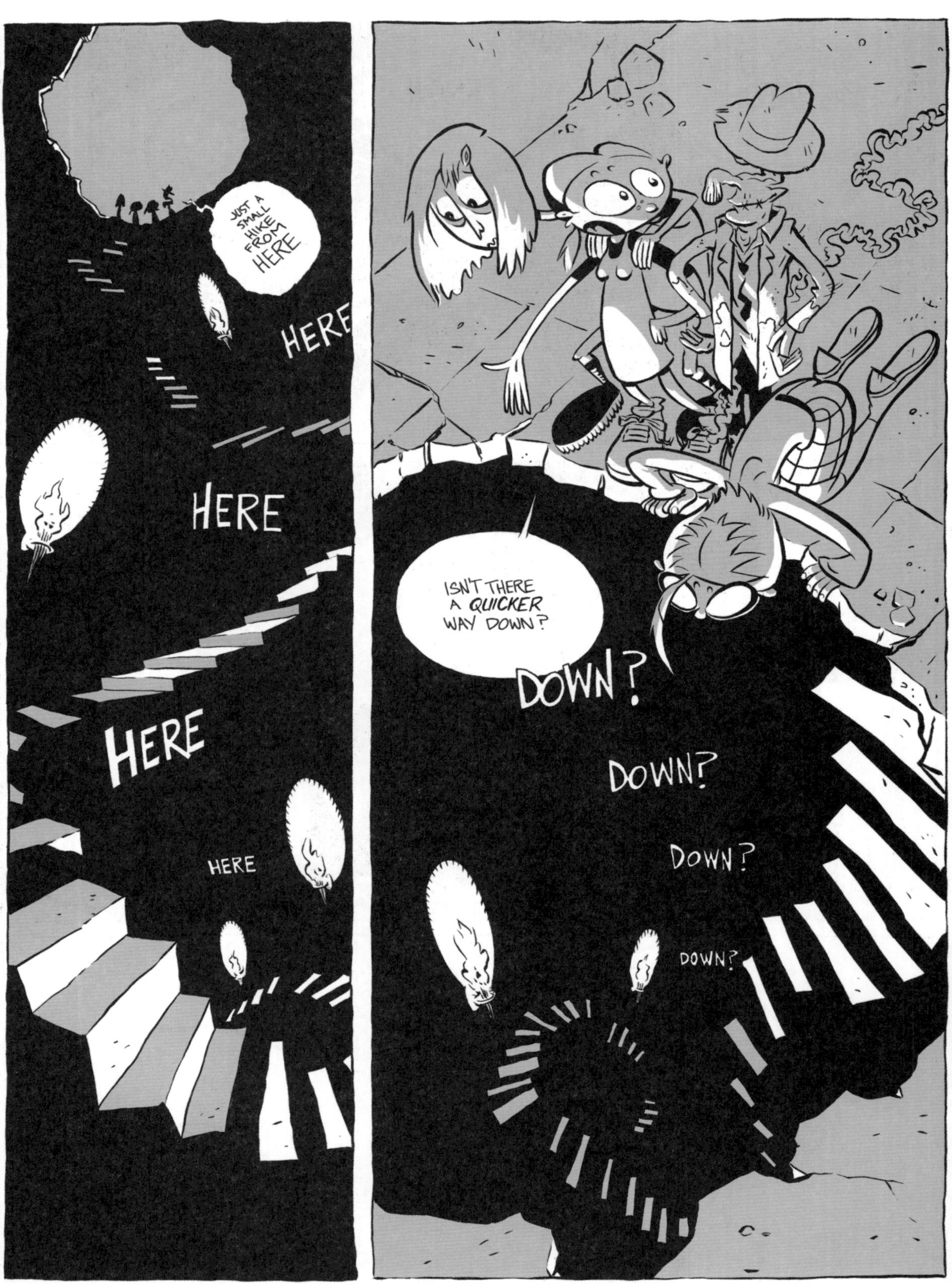
JUST A SMALL HIKE FROM HERE
HERE
HERE
HERE
HERE
ISN'T THERE A QUICKER WAY DOWN?
DOWN?
DOWN?
DOWN?
DOWN?

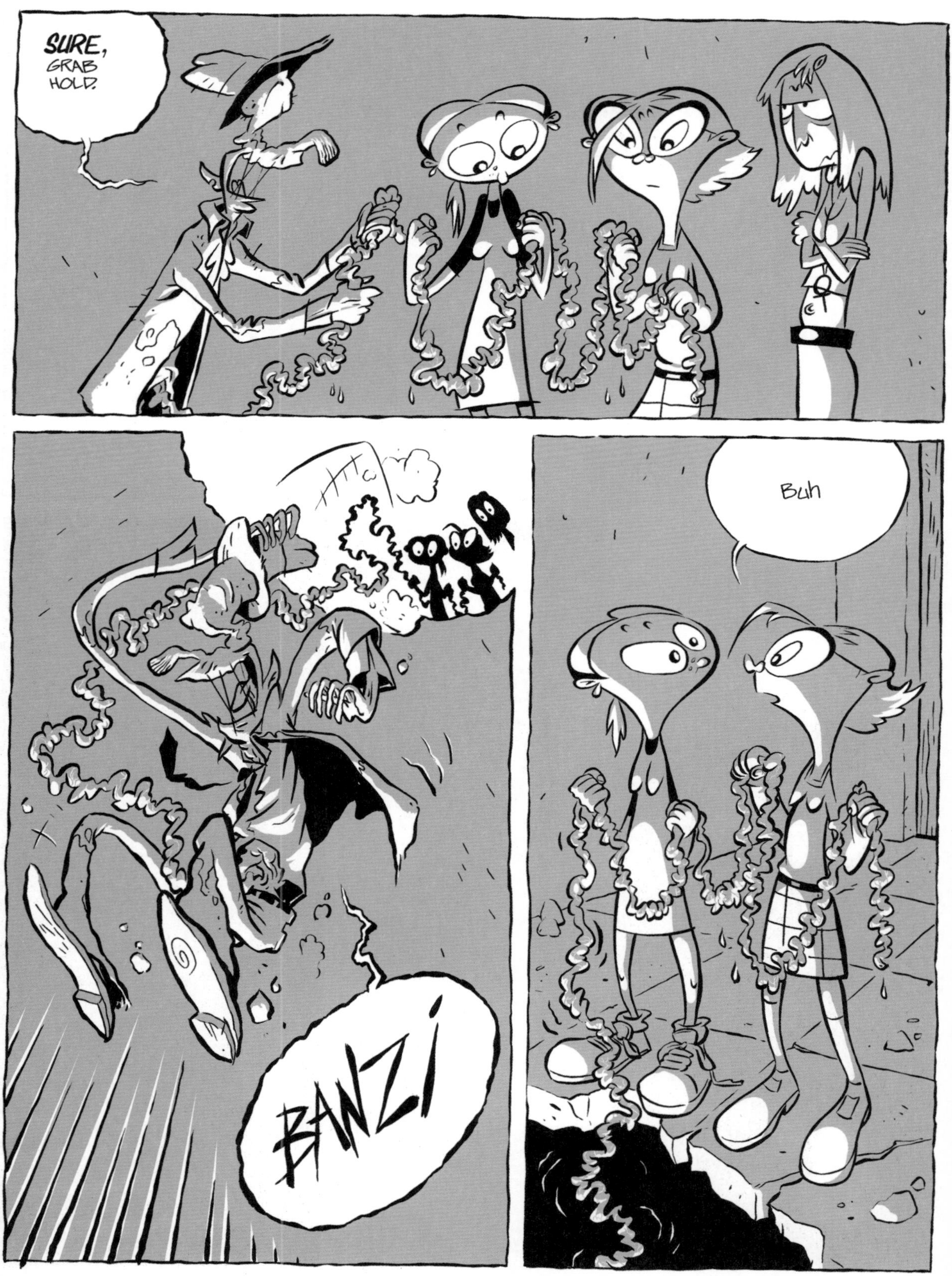
SURE, GRAB HOLD.
BANZI
Buh

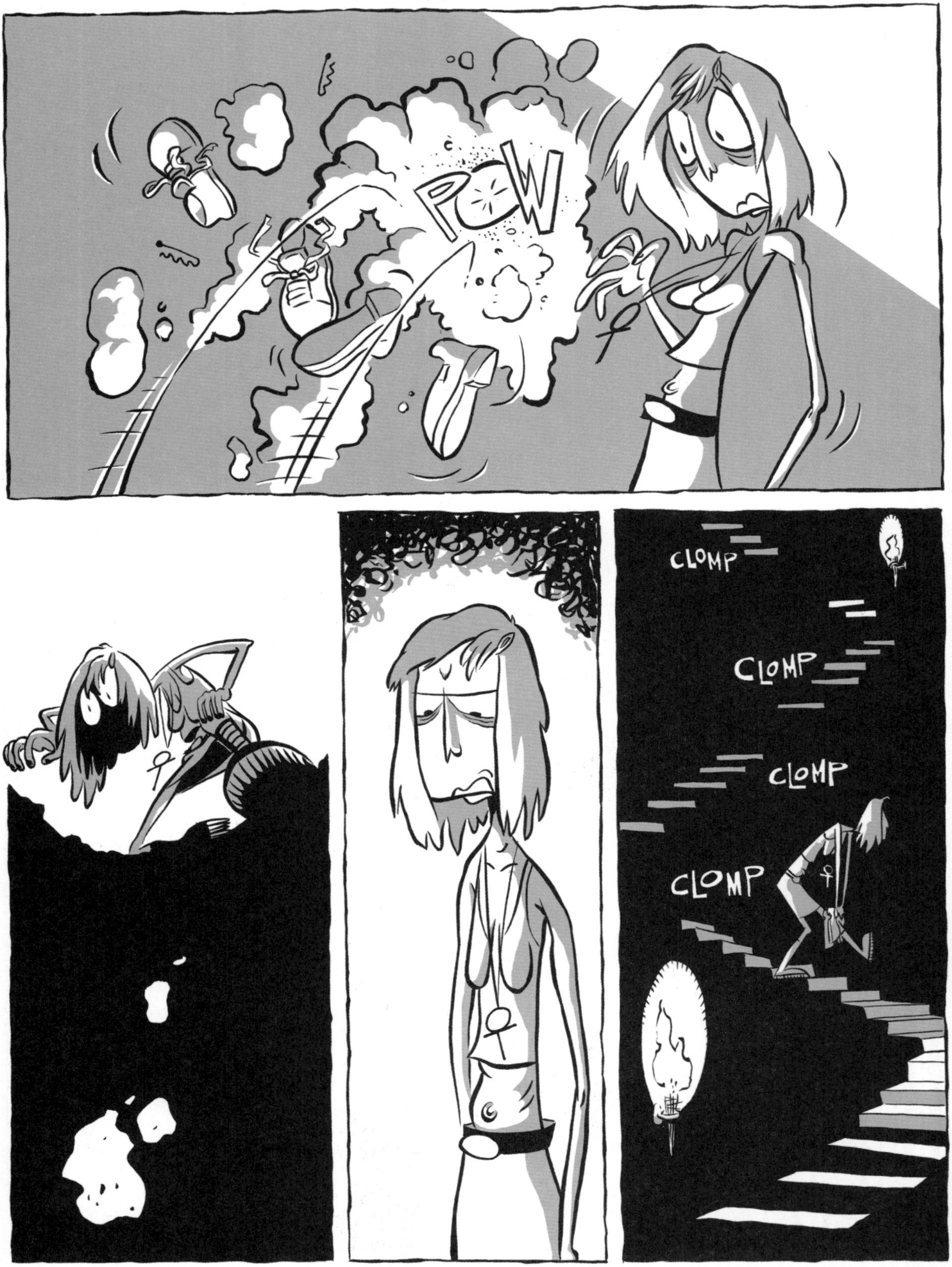
POW
CLOMP
CLOMP
CLOMP
CLOMP

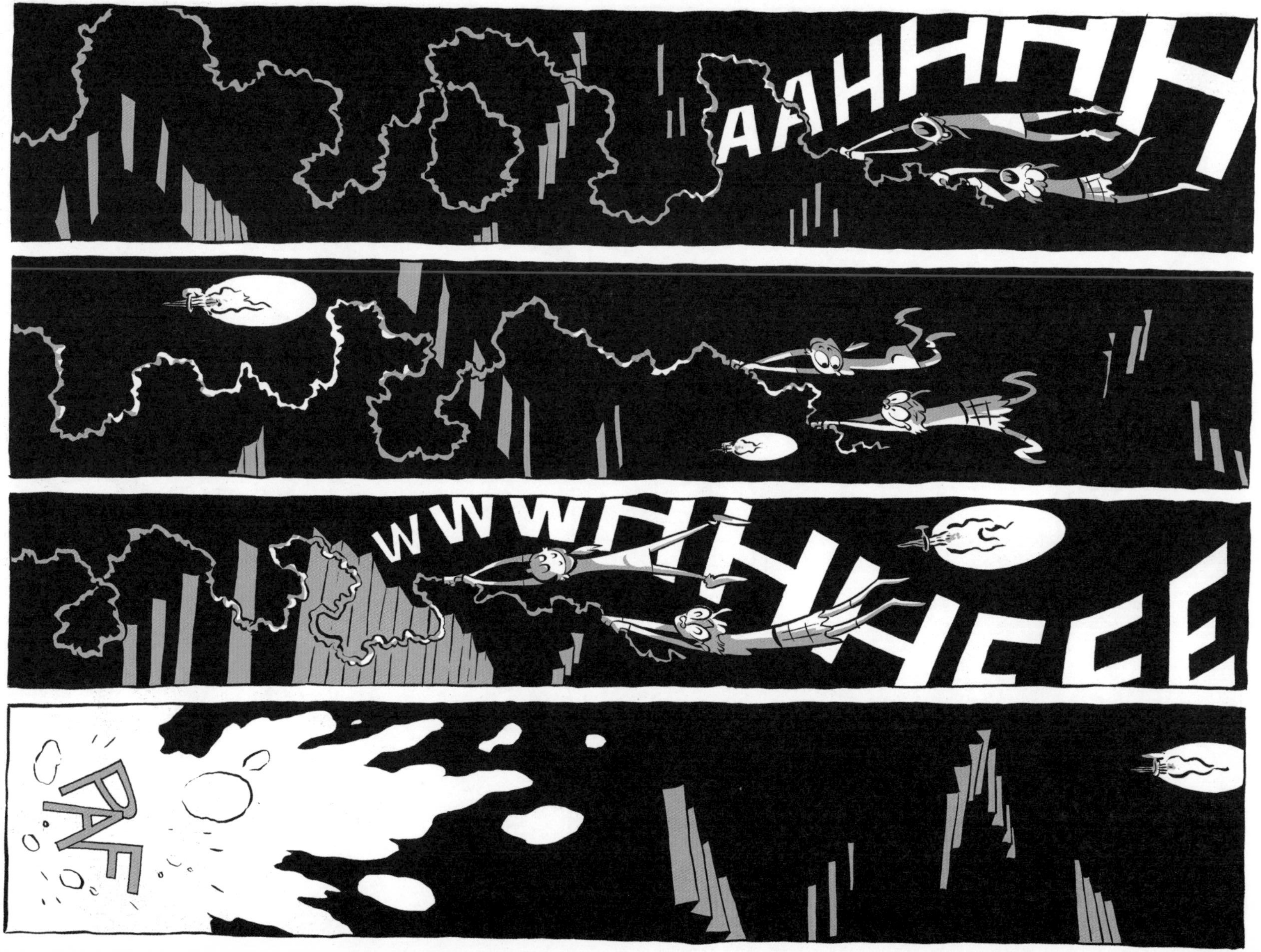
AAHHHHHH
WWWHHHHEEE
PAF

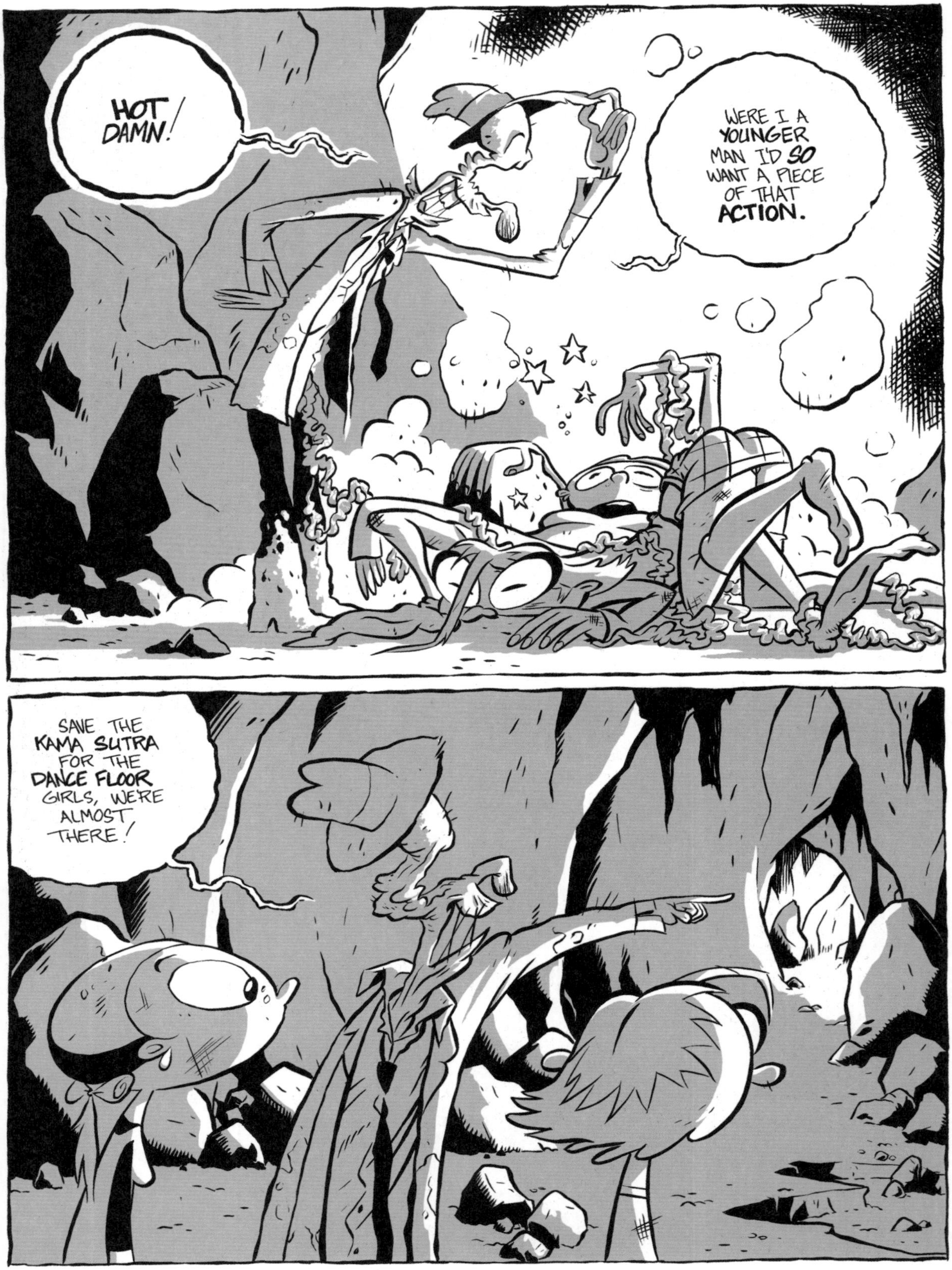
HOT DAMN!
WERE I A YOUNGER MAN I'D SO WANT A PIECE OF THAT ACTION.
SAVE THE KAMA SUTRA FOR THE DANCE FLOOR GIRLS, WE'RE ALMOST THERE!

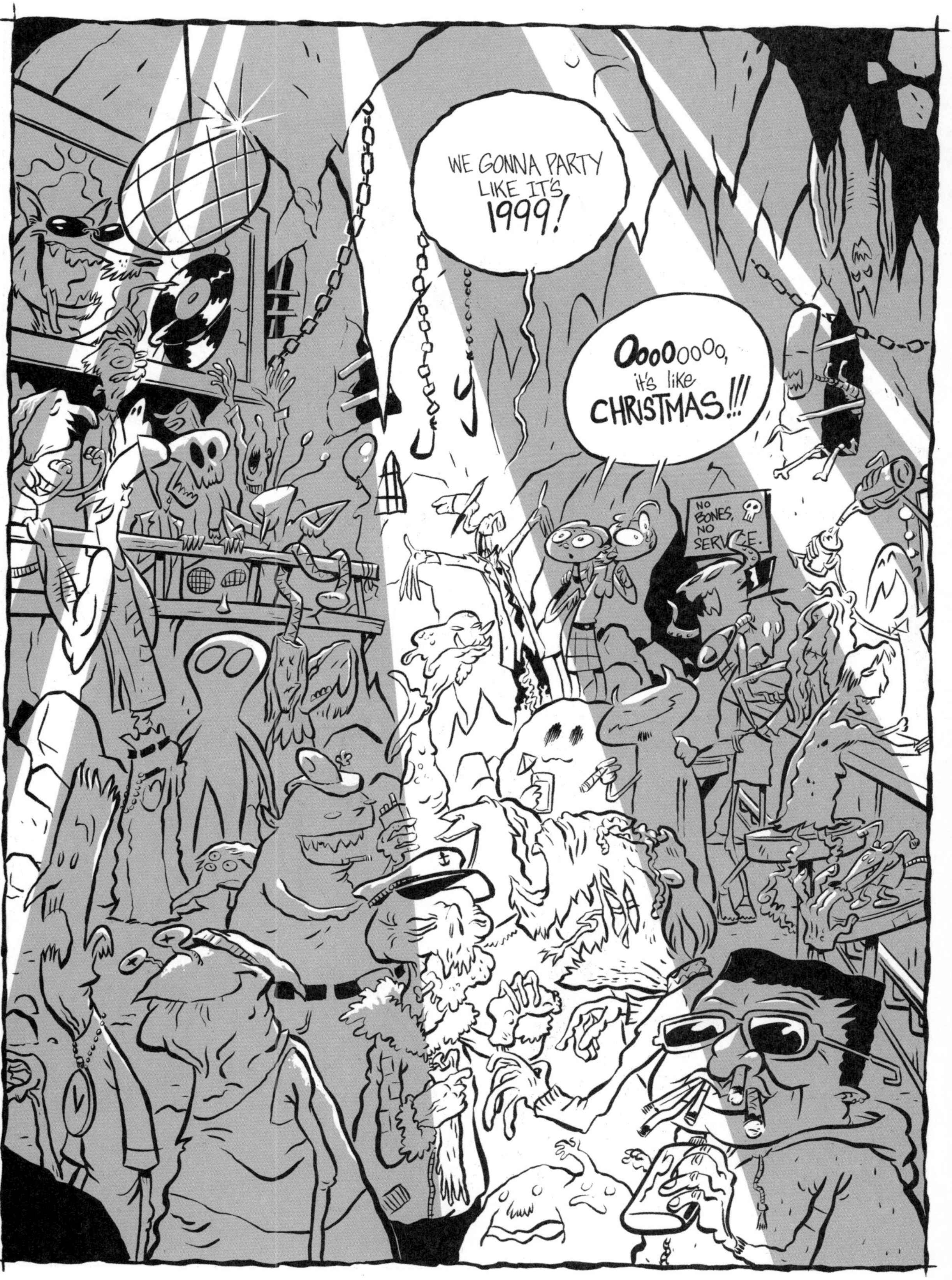
WE GONNA PARTY LIKE IT'S 1999!
Ooooooo, it's like CHRISTMAS!!!
NO BONES, NO SERVICE.

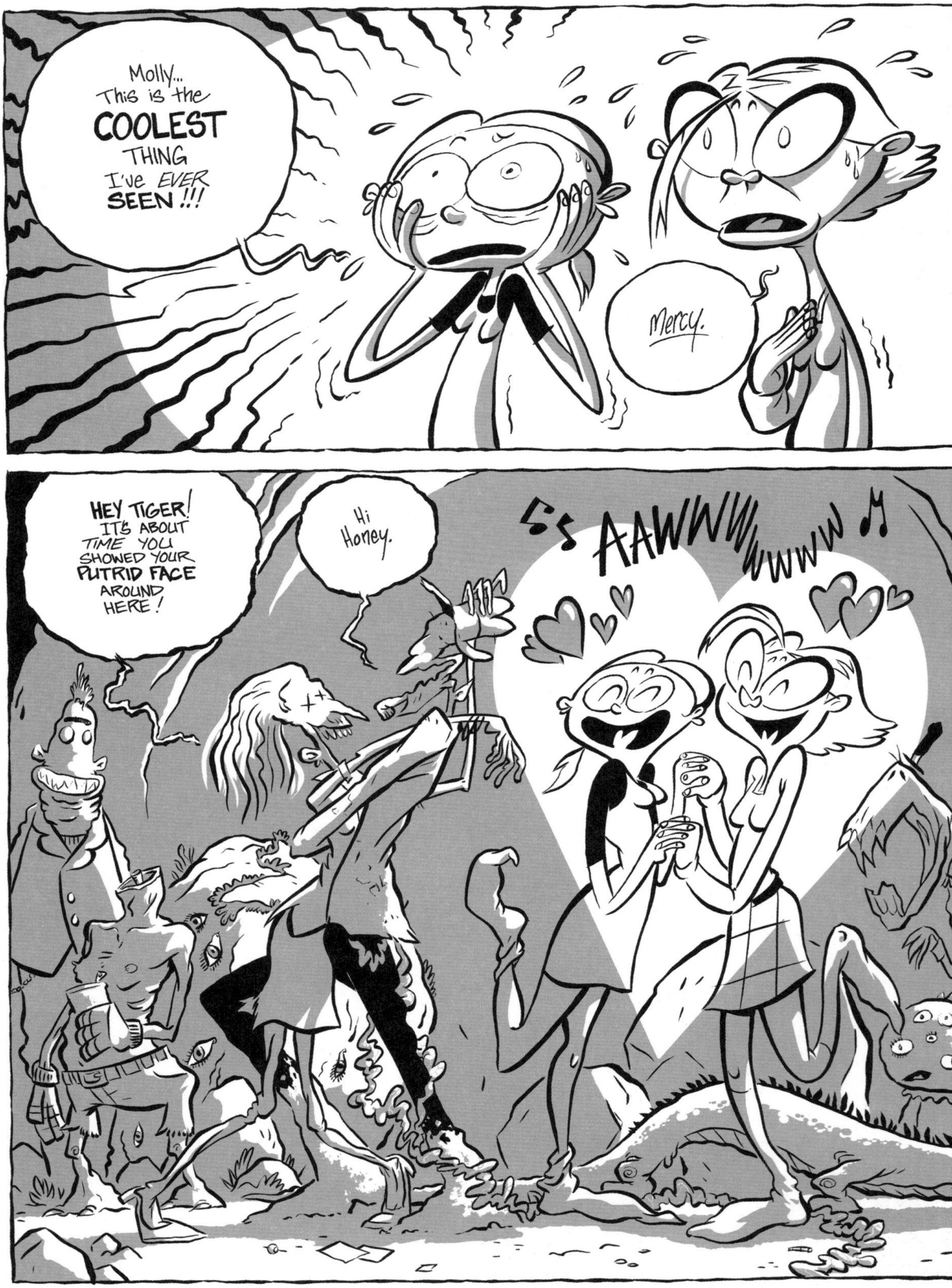

Molly... This is the COOLEST THING I've EVER SEEN!!!
Mercy.
HEY TIGER! IT'S ABOUT TIME YOU SHOWED YOUR PUTRID FACE AROUND HERE!
Hi Honey.
AAWWWWWWWW

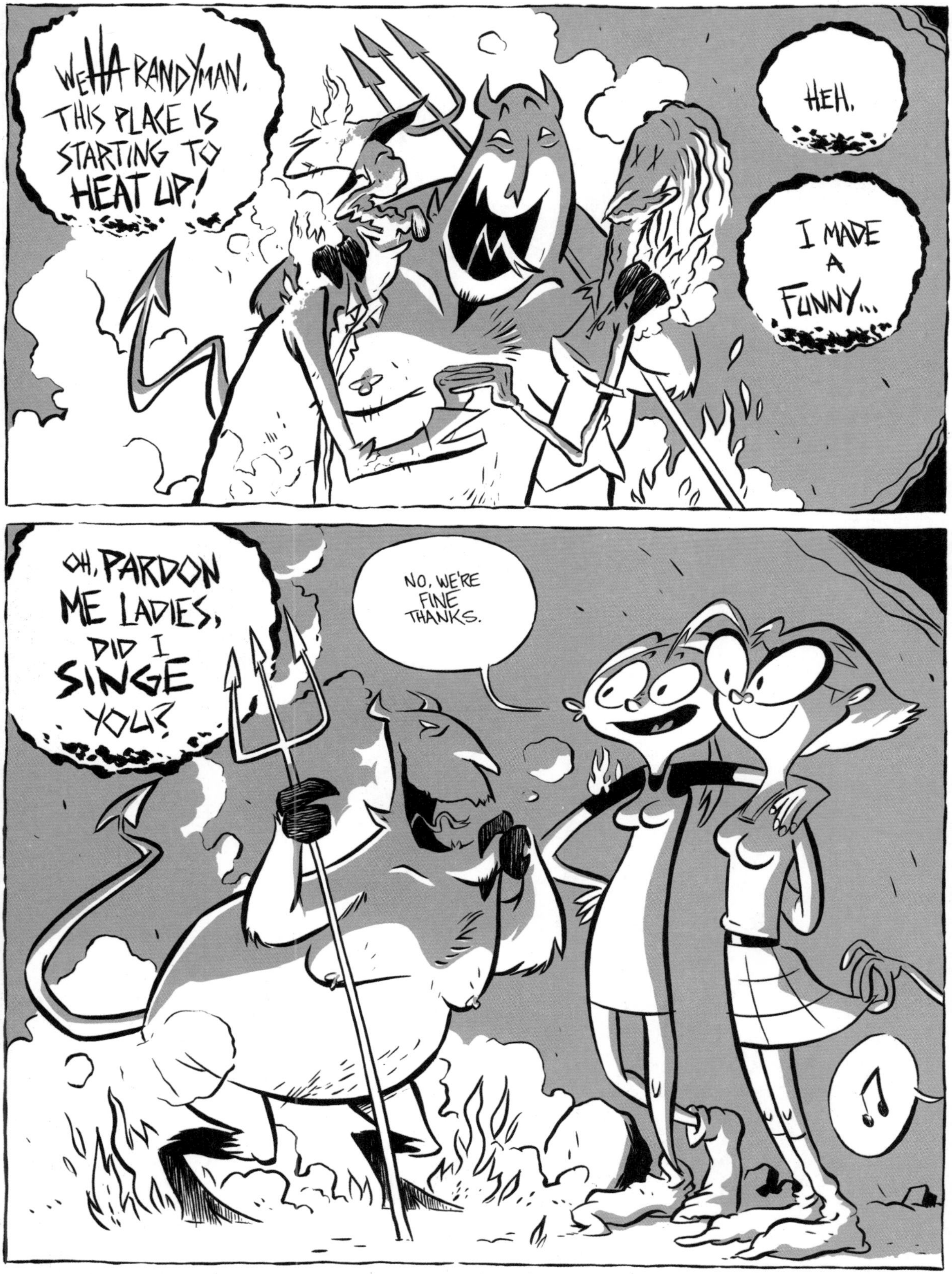
WeHA RANDYMAN. THIS PLACE IS STARTING TO HEAT UP!
HEH.
I MADE A FUNNY...
OH, PARDON ME LADIES, DID I SINGE YOU?
NO, WE'RE FINE THANKS.
♪

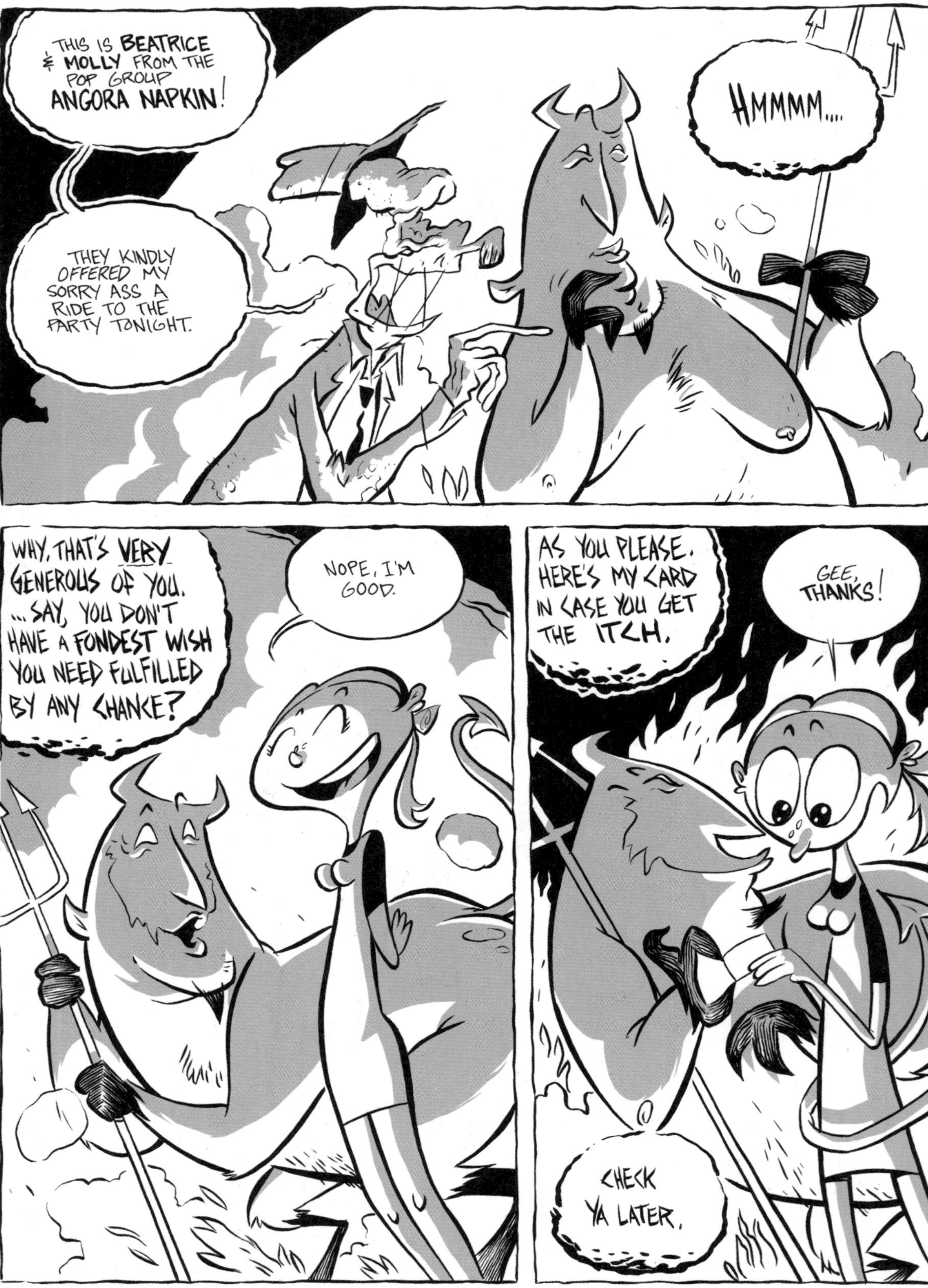
THIS IS BEATRICE & MOLLY FROM THE POP GROUP ANGORA NAPKIN!
THEY KINDLY OFFERED MY SORRY ASS A RIDE TO THE PARTY TONIGHT.
HMMMM...
WHY, THAT'S VERY GENEROUS OF YOU. ...SAY, YOU DON'T HAVE A FONDEST WISH YOU NEED FULFILLED BY ANY CHANCE?
NOPE, I'M GOOD.
AS YOU PLEASE. HERE'S MY CARD IN CASE YOU GET THE ITCH.
GEE, THANKS!
CHECK YA LATER.

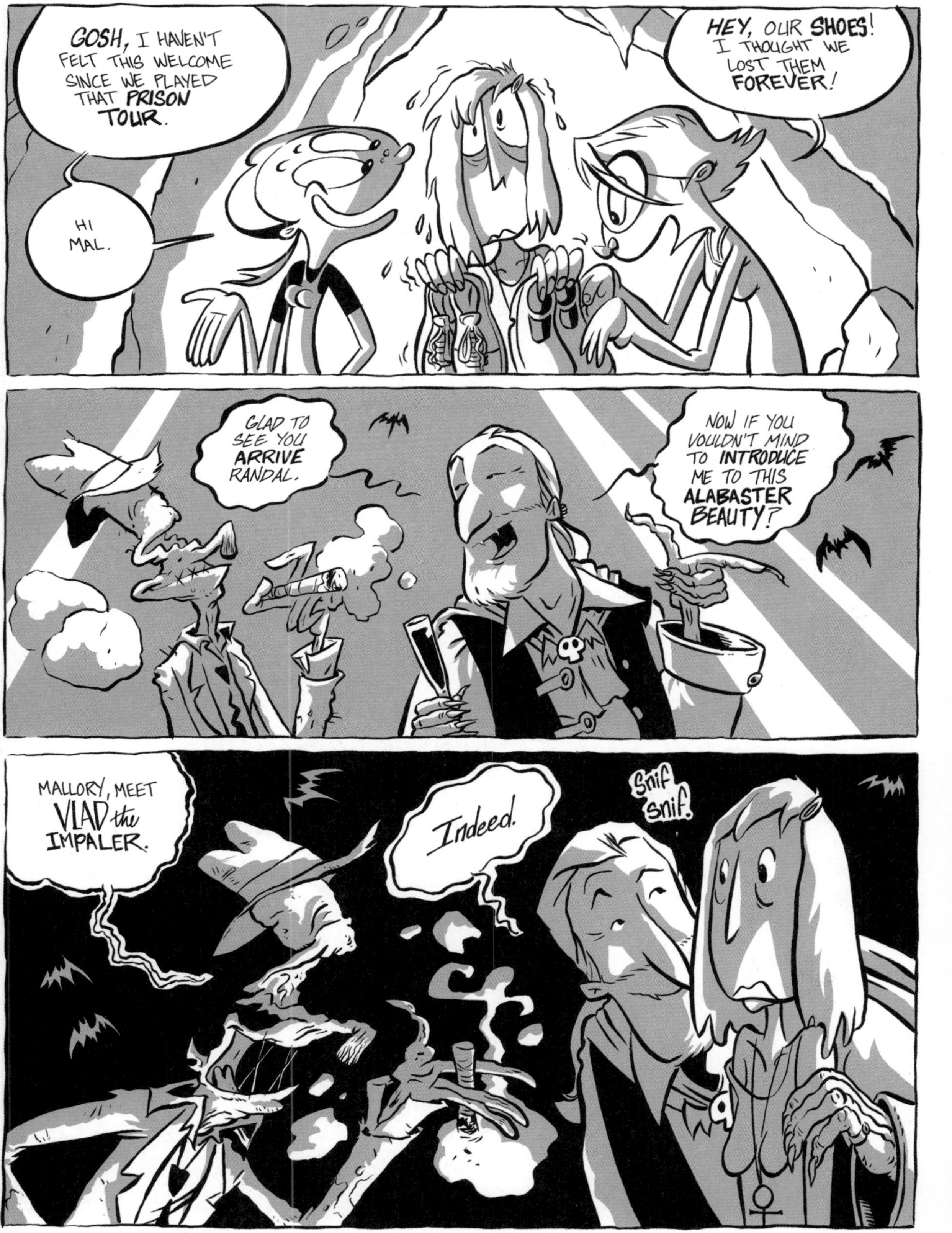
GOSH, I HAVEN'T FELT THIS WELCOME SINCE WE PLAYED THAT PRISON TOUR.
HI MAL.
HEY, OUR SHOES! I THOUGHT WE LOST THEM FOREVER!
GLAD TO SEE YOU ARRIVE RANDAL.
NOW IF YOU WOULDN'T MIND TO INTRODUCE ME TO THIS ALABASTER BEAUTY?
MALLORY, MEET VLAD the IMPALER.
Indeed.
Snif snif.

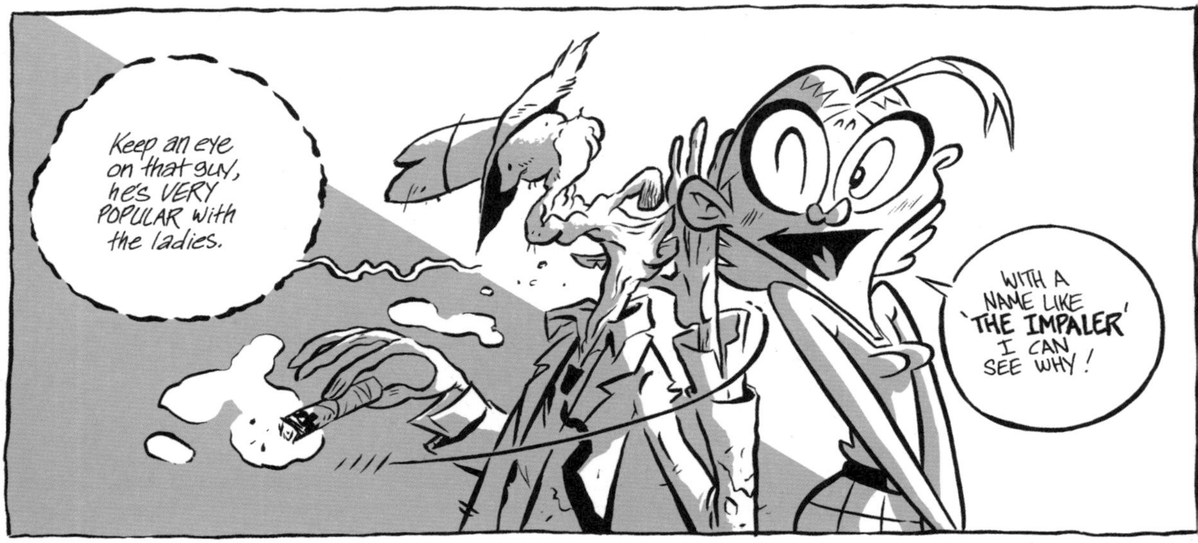
Keep an eye on that guy, he's VERY POPULAR with the ladies.
WITH A NAME LIKE 'THE IMPALER' I CAN SEE WHY!

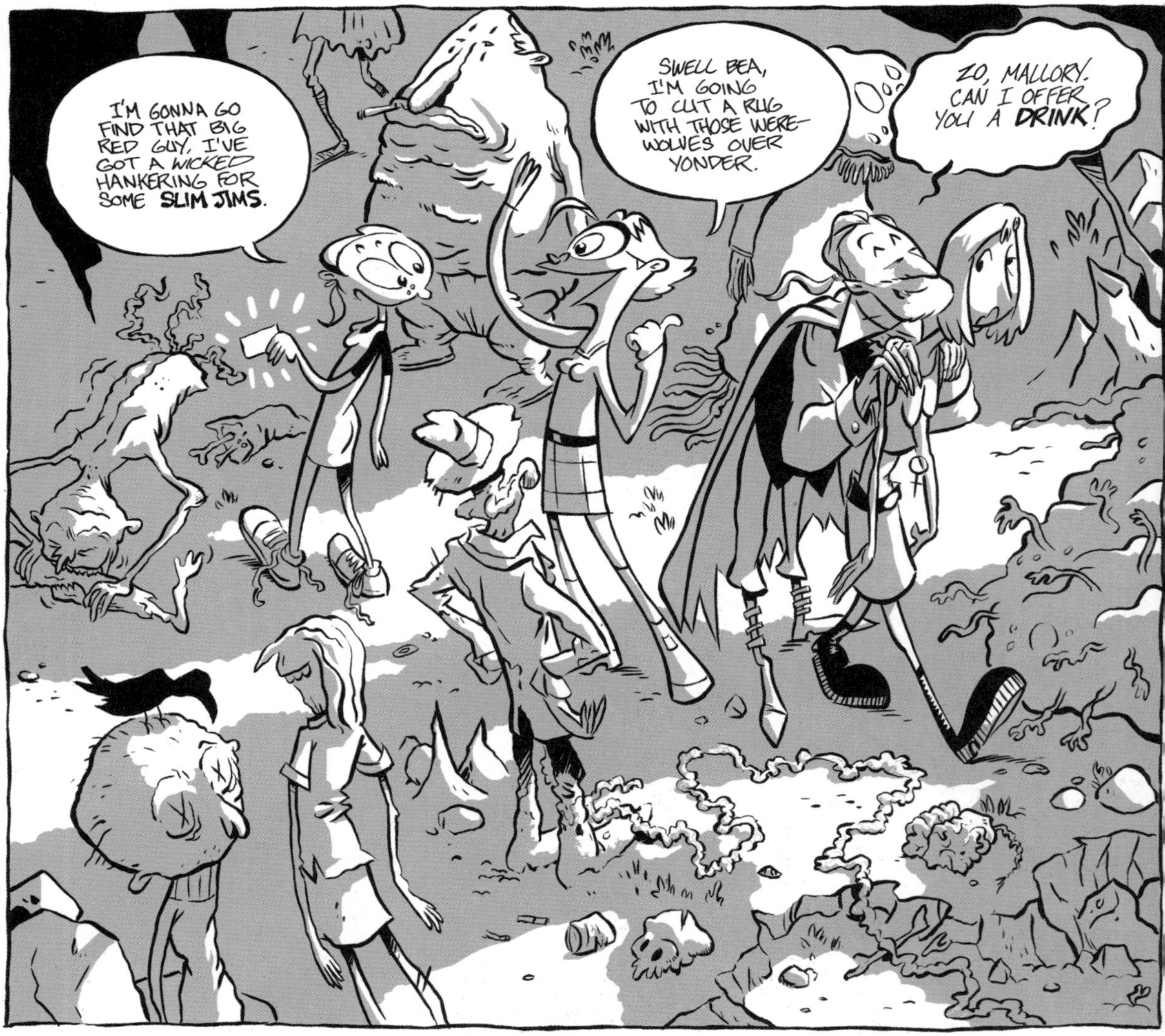
I'M GONNA GO FIND THAT BIG RED GUY, I'VE GOT A WICKED HANKERING FOR SOME SLIM JIMS.
SWELL BEA, I'M GOING TO CUT A RUG WITH THOSE WERE-WOLVES OVER YONDER.
ZO, MALLORY. CAN I OFFER YOU A DRINK?

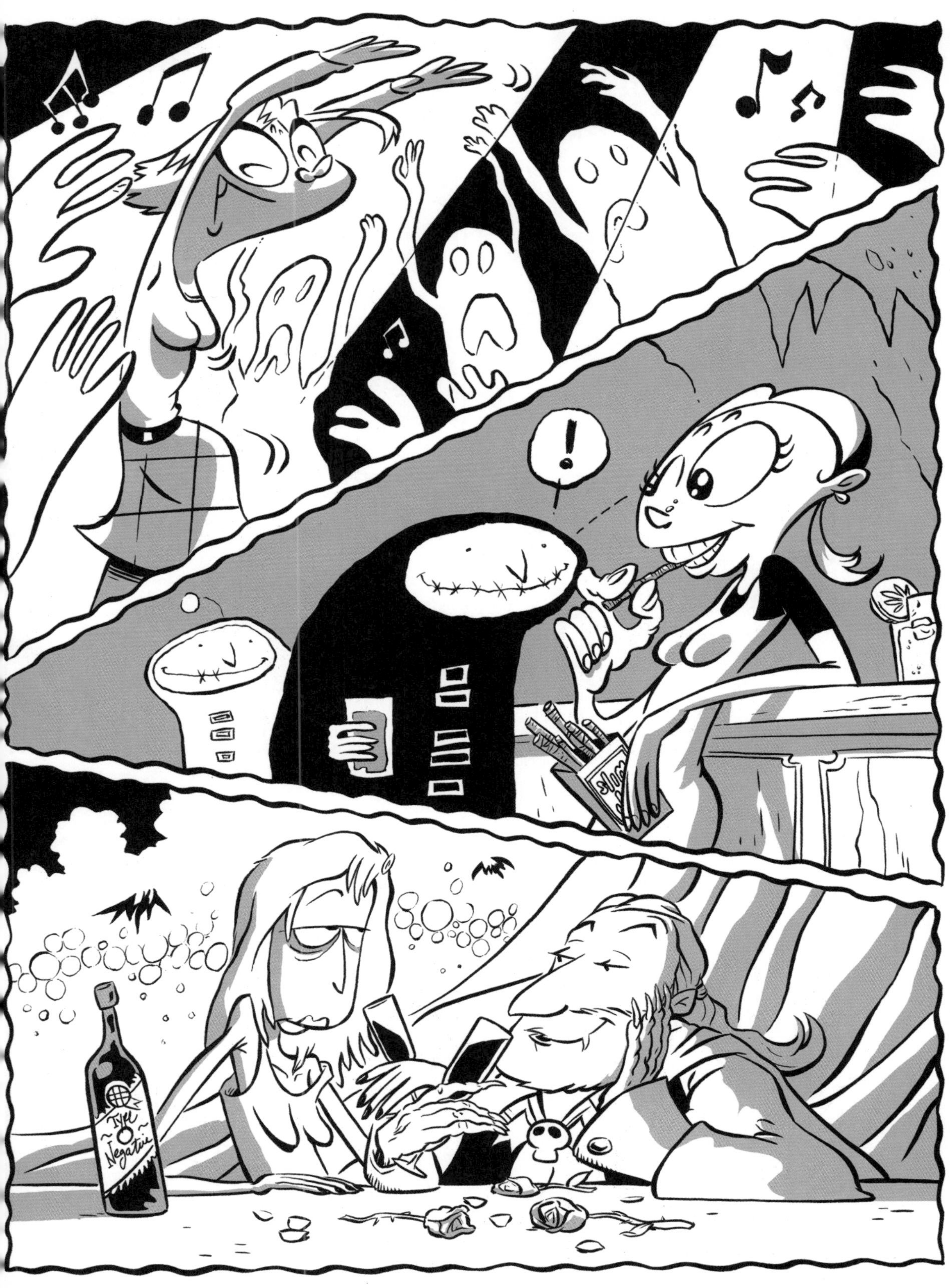
!
Slum
Type
O
Negative

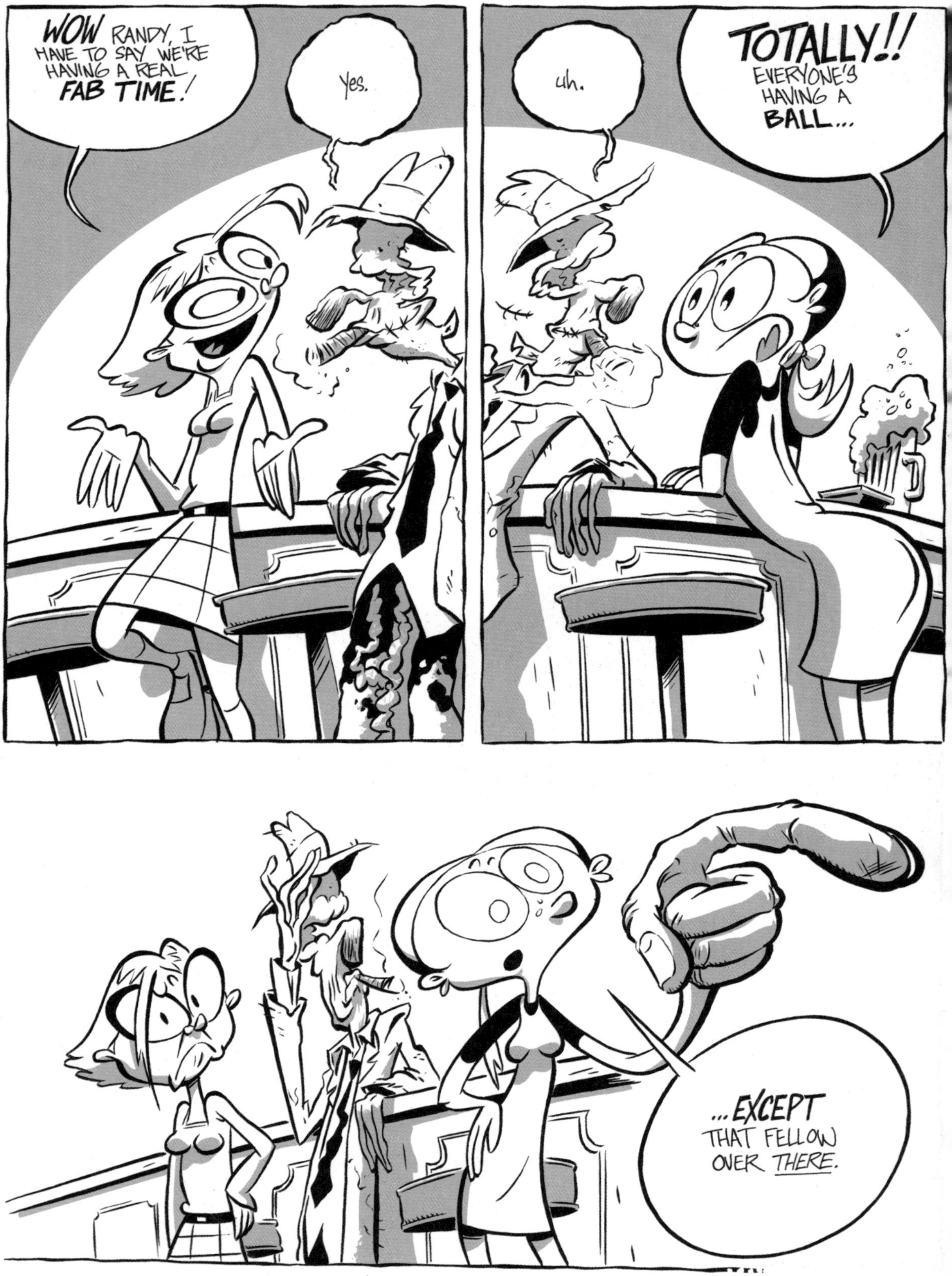
WOW RANDY, I HAVE TO SAY WE'RE HAVING A REAL FAB TIME!
Yes.
uh.
TOTALLY!! EVERYONE'S HAVING A BALL...
...EXCEPT THAT FELLOW OVER THERE.

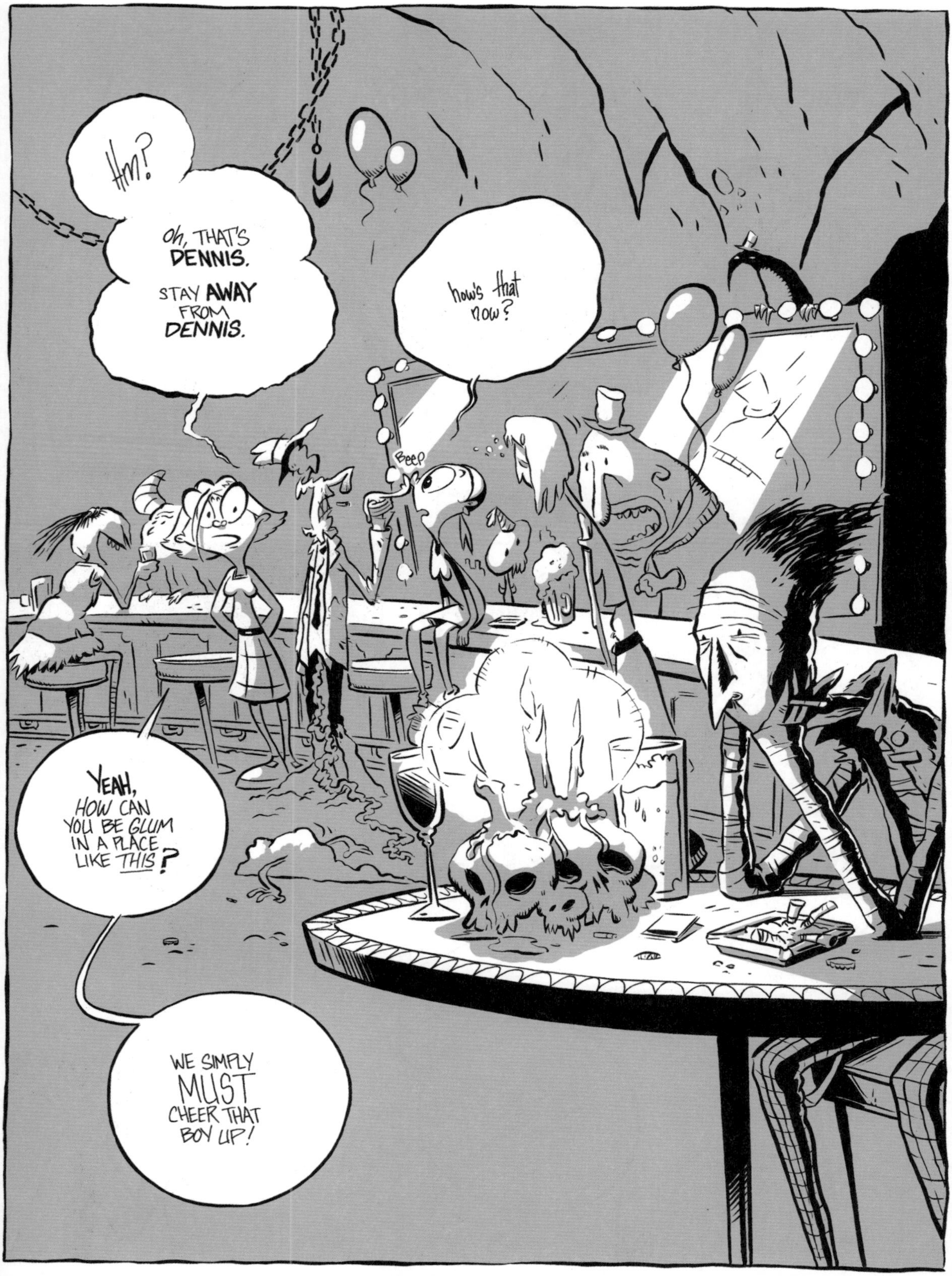
Hm?
Oh, THAT'S DENNIS. STAY AWAY FROM DENNIS.
how's that now?
Beep
YEAH, HOW CAN YOU BE GLUM IN A PLACE LIKE THIS?
WE SIMPLY MUST CHEER THAT BOY UP!

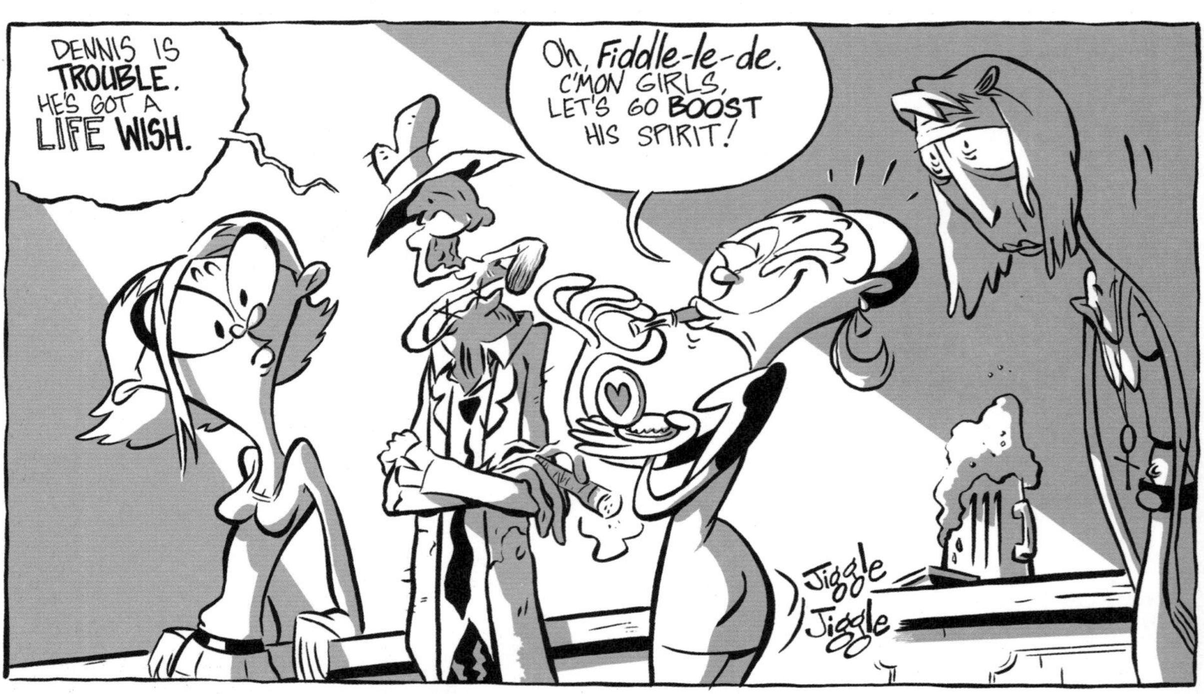
DENNIS IS TROUBLE. HE'S GOT A LIFE WISH.
Oh, Fiddle-le-de. C'MON GIRLS, LET'S GO BOOST HIS SPIRIT!
Jiggle Jiggle

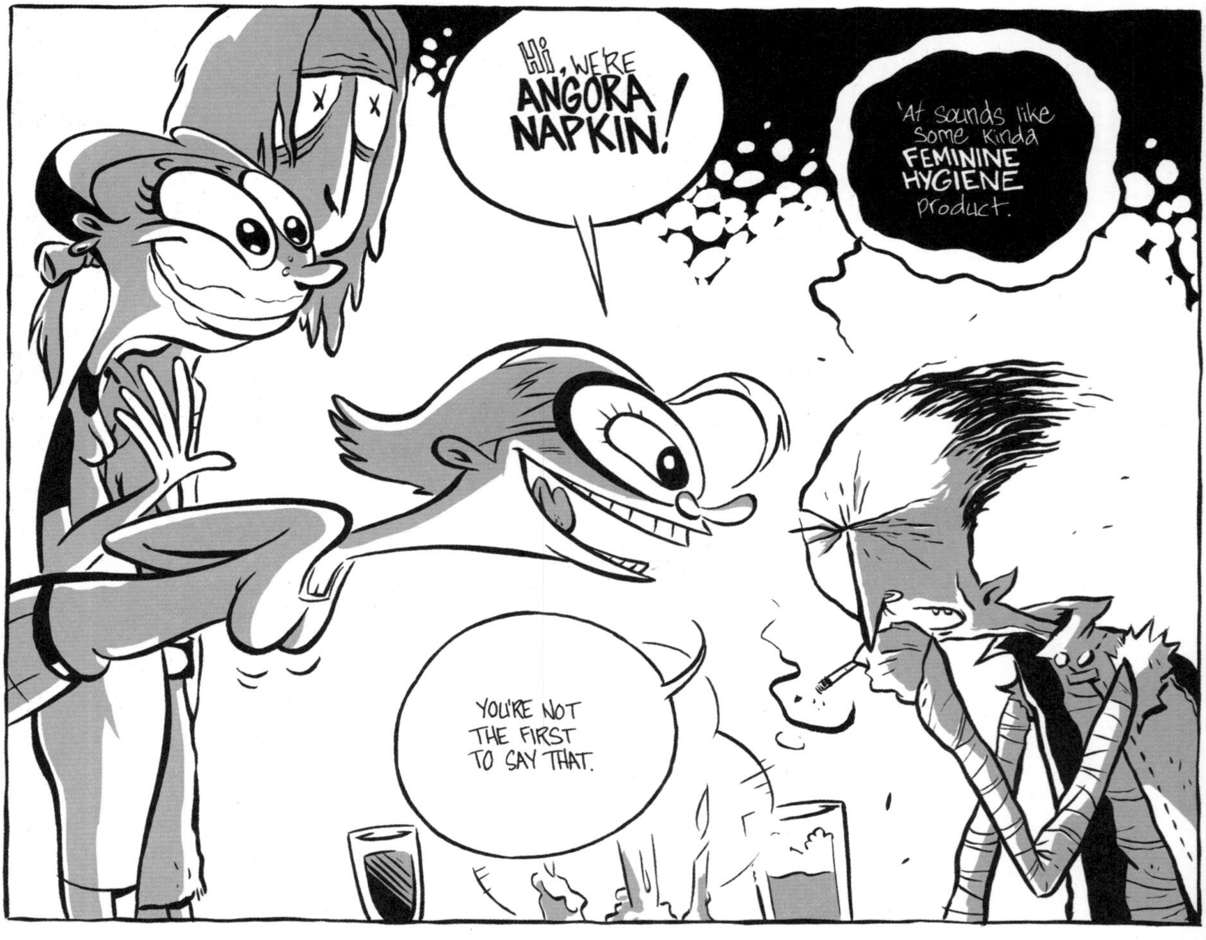
Hi, WE'RE ANGORA NAPKIN!
'At sounds like some kinda FEMININE HYGIENE product.
YOU'RE NOT THE FIRST TO SAY THAT.

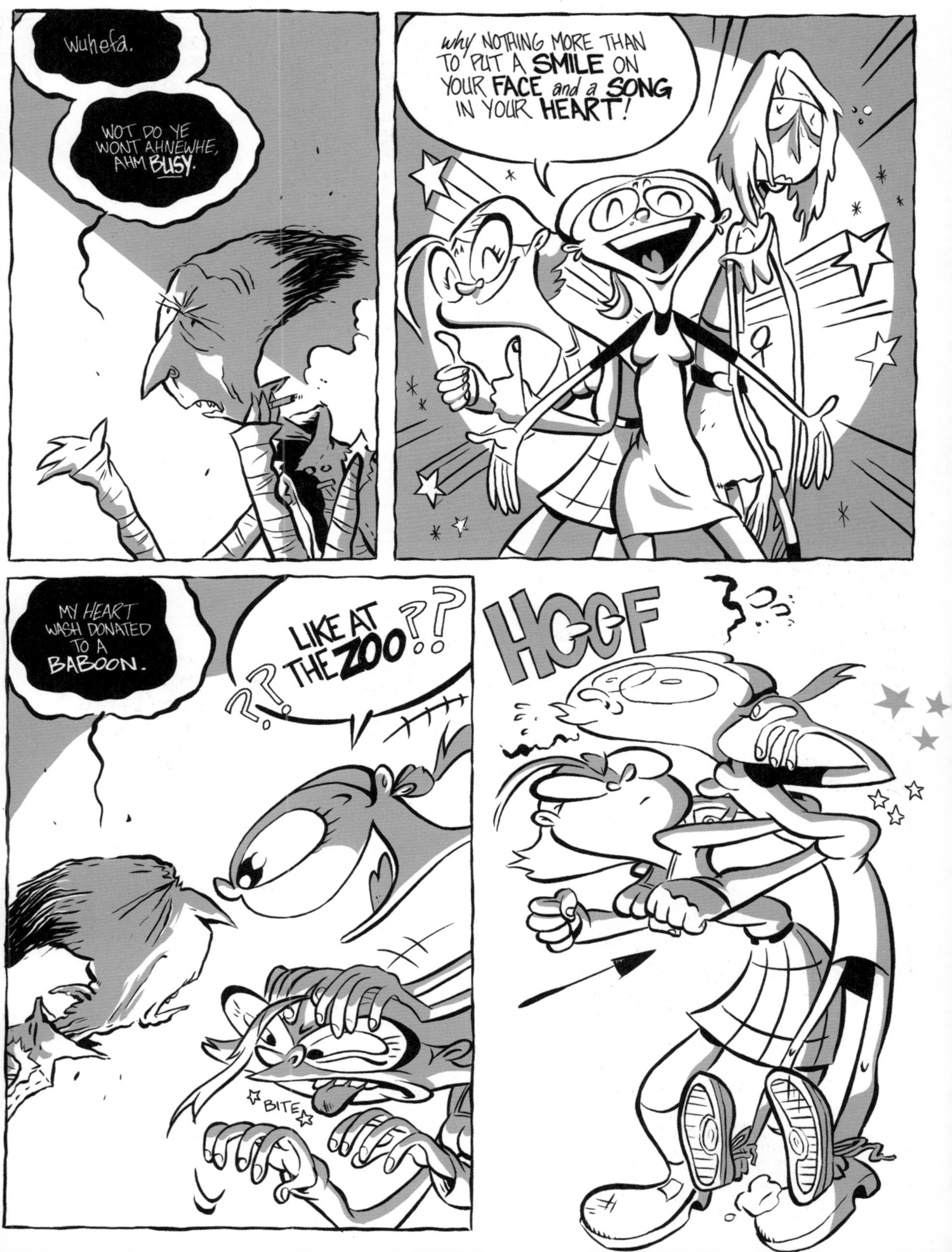
wuhefa.
WOT DO YE WONT AHNEWHE, AHM BUSY.
why NOTHING MORE THAN TO PUT A SMILE ON YOUR FACE and a SONG IN YOUR HEART!
MY HEART WASH DONATED TO A BABOON.
LIKE AT THE ZOO??
BITE
HOOF

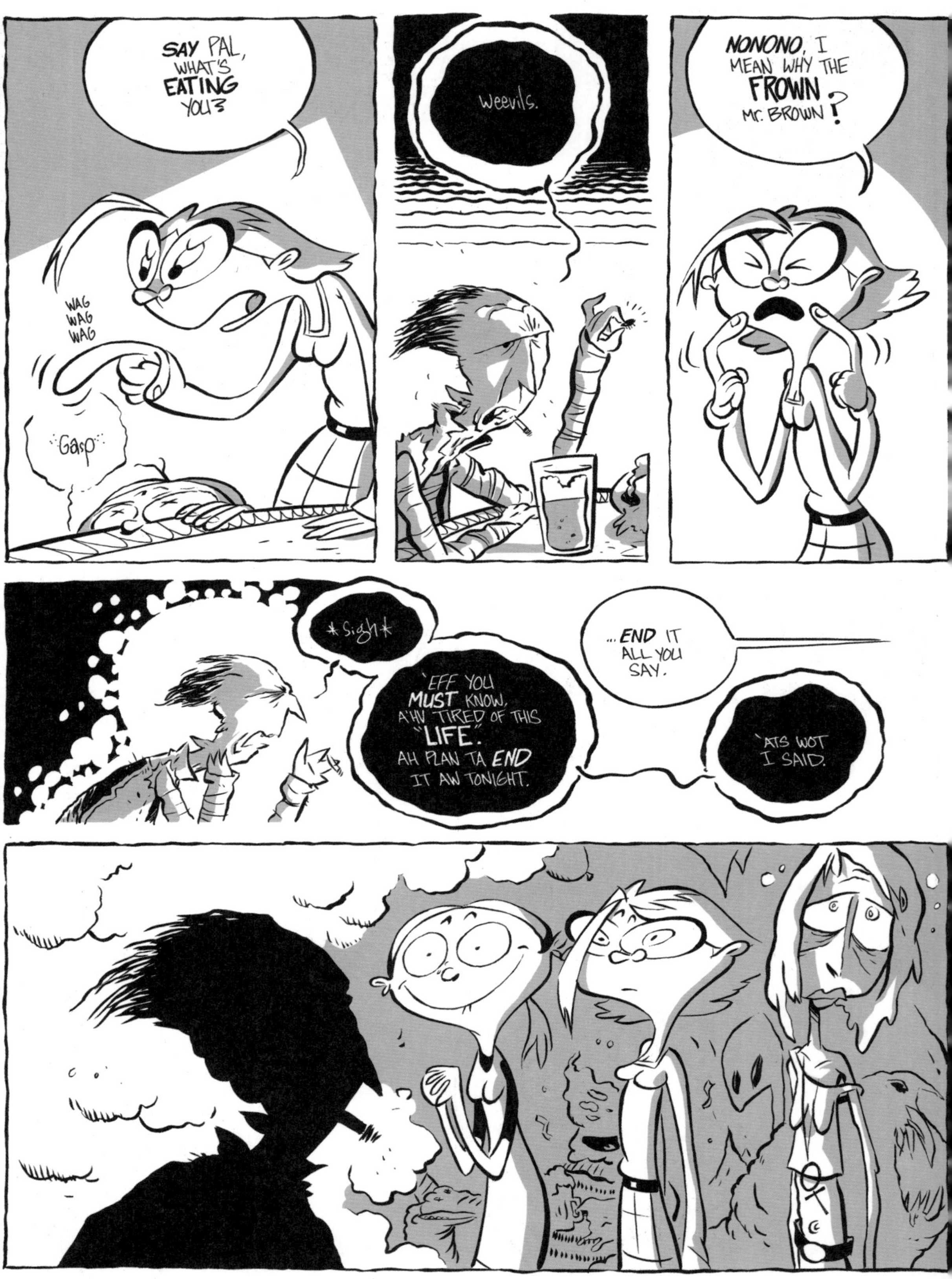
SAY PAL, WHAT'S EATING YOU?
WAG WAG WAG
Gasp
weevils.
NONONO, I MEAN WHY THE FROWN MR. BROWN?
Sigh
`EFF YOU MUST KNOW, A'HV TIRED OF THIS "LIFE". AH PLAN TA END IT AW TONIGHT.
...END IT ALL YOU SAY.
`ATS WOT I SAID.

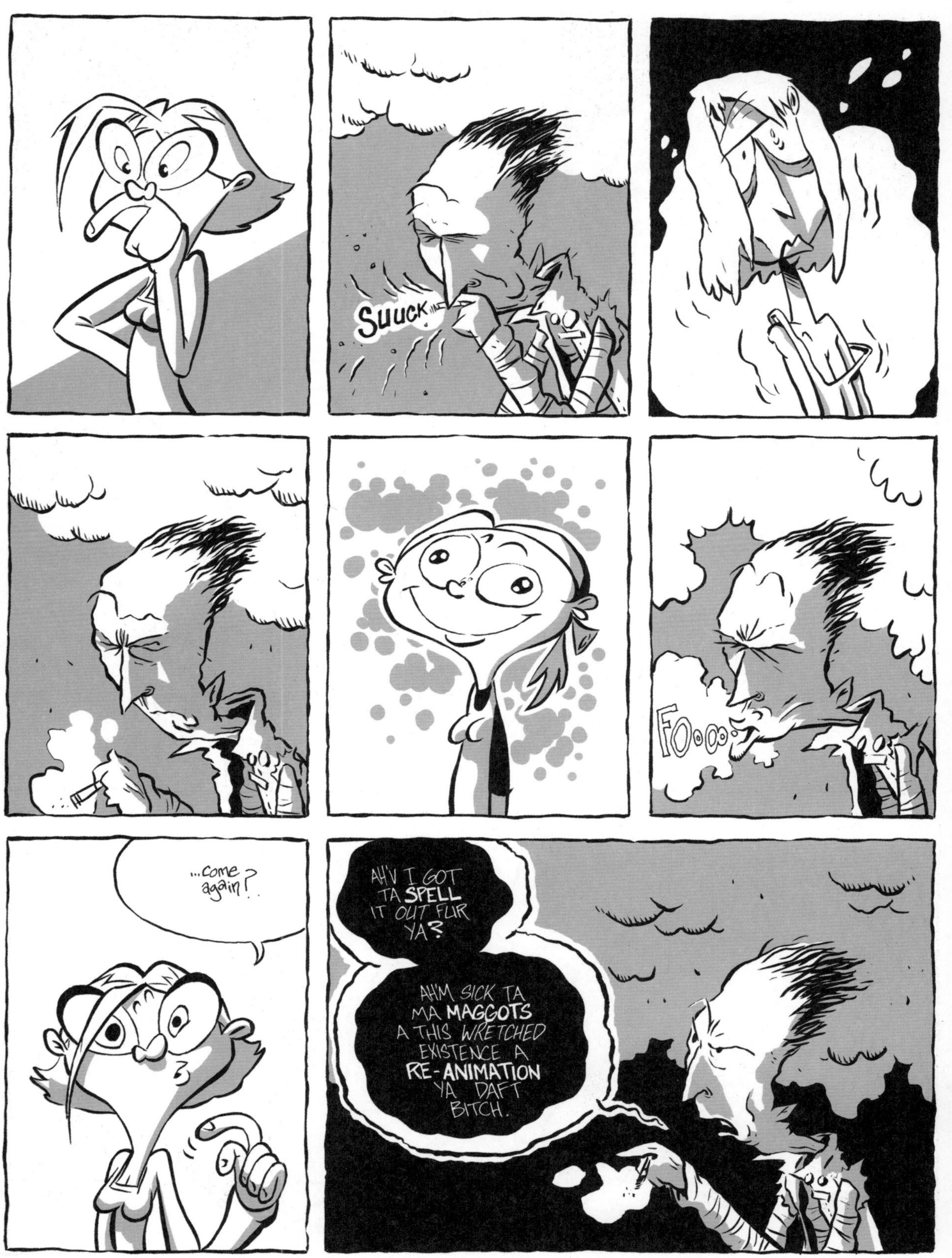
SUUCK
FO∘∘∘
...come again?
AH'V I GOT TA SPELL IT OUT FUR YA?
AH'M SICK TA MA MAGGOTS A THIS WRETCHED EXISTENCE A RE-ANIMATION YA DAFT BITCH.

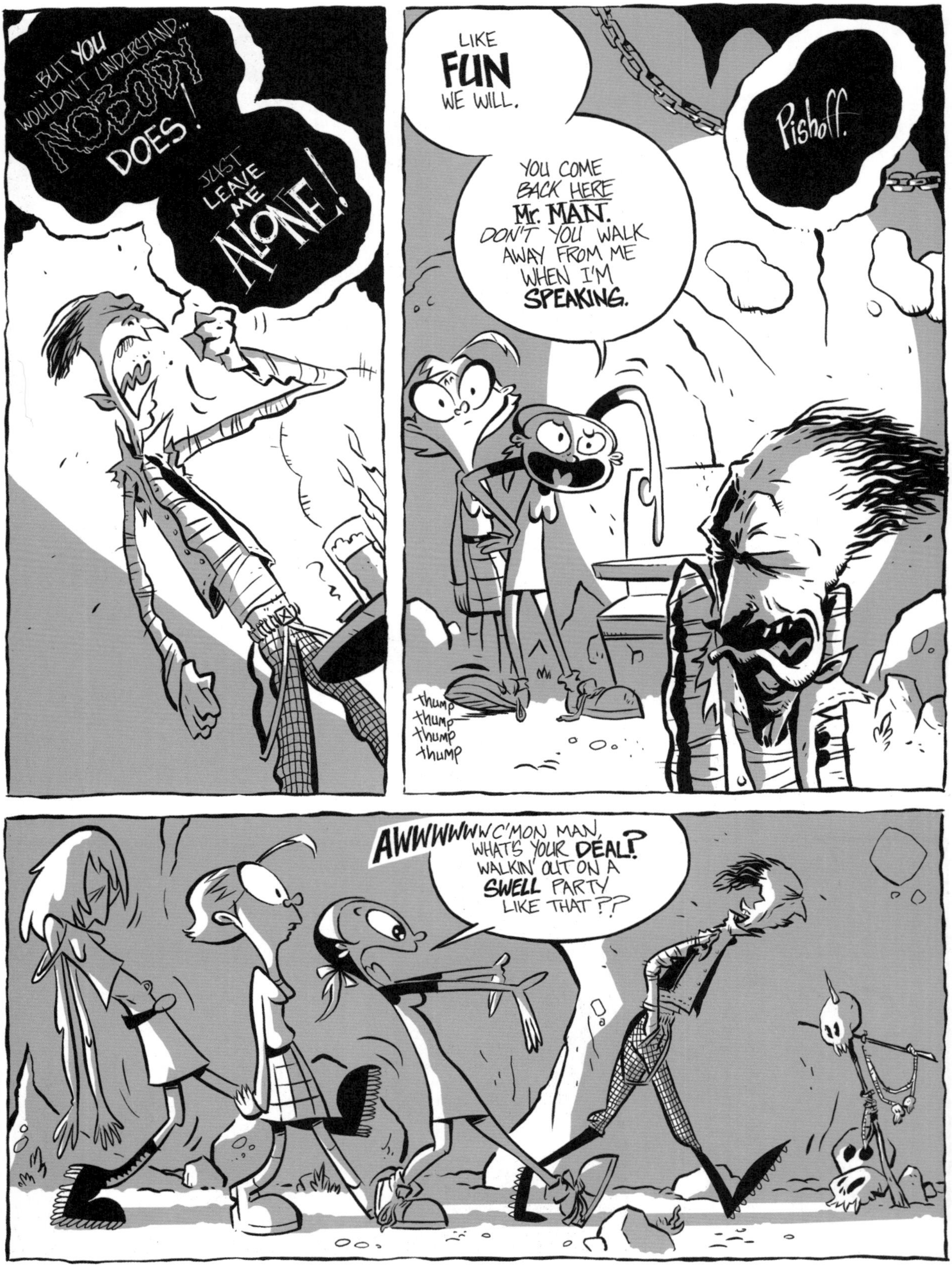

...BUT YOU WOULDN'T UNDERSTAND... NOBODY DOES!
JUST LEAVE ME ALONE!
LIKE FUN WE WILL.
YOU COME BACK HERE Mr. MAN. DON'T YOU WALK AWAY FROM ME WHEN I'M SPEAKING.
Pishoff.
thump thump thump thump
AWWWWWW C'MON MAN, WHAT'S YOUR DEAL!? WALKIN' OUT ON A SWELL PARTY LIKE THAT ??

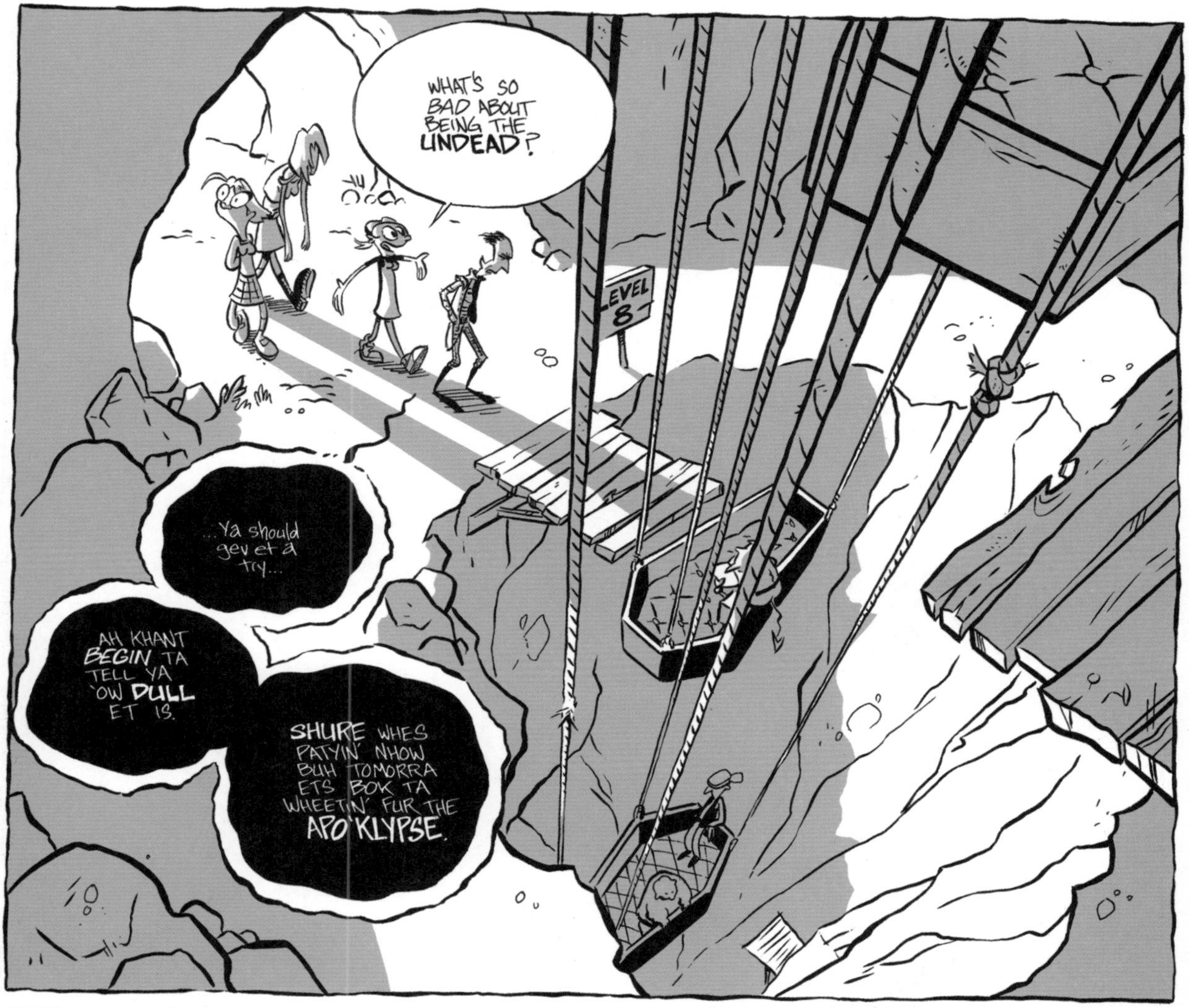
WHAT'S SO BAD ABOUT BEING THE UNDEAD?
LEVEL 8
...Ya should gev et a try...
AH KHANT BEGIN TA TELL YA 'OW DULL ET IS.
SHURE WHES PATYIN' NHOW BUH TOMORRA ETS BOK TA WHEETIN' FUR THE APO'KLYPSE.
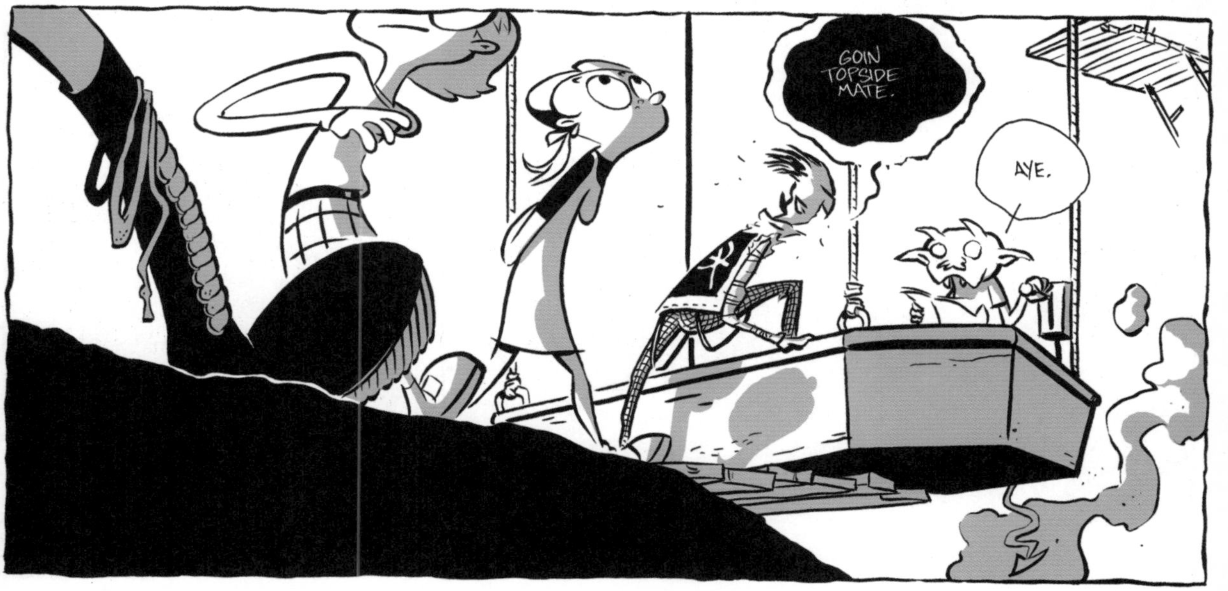
GOIN TOPSIDE MATE.
AYE.

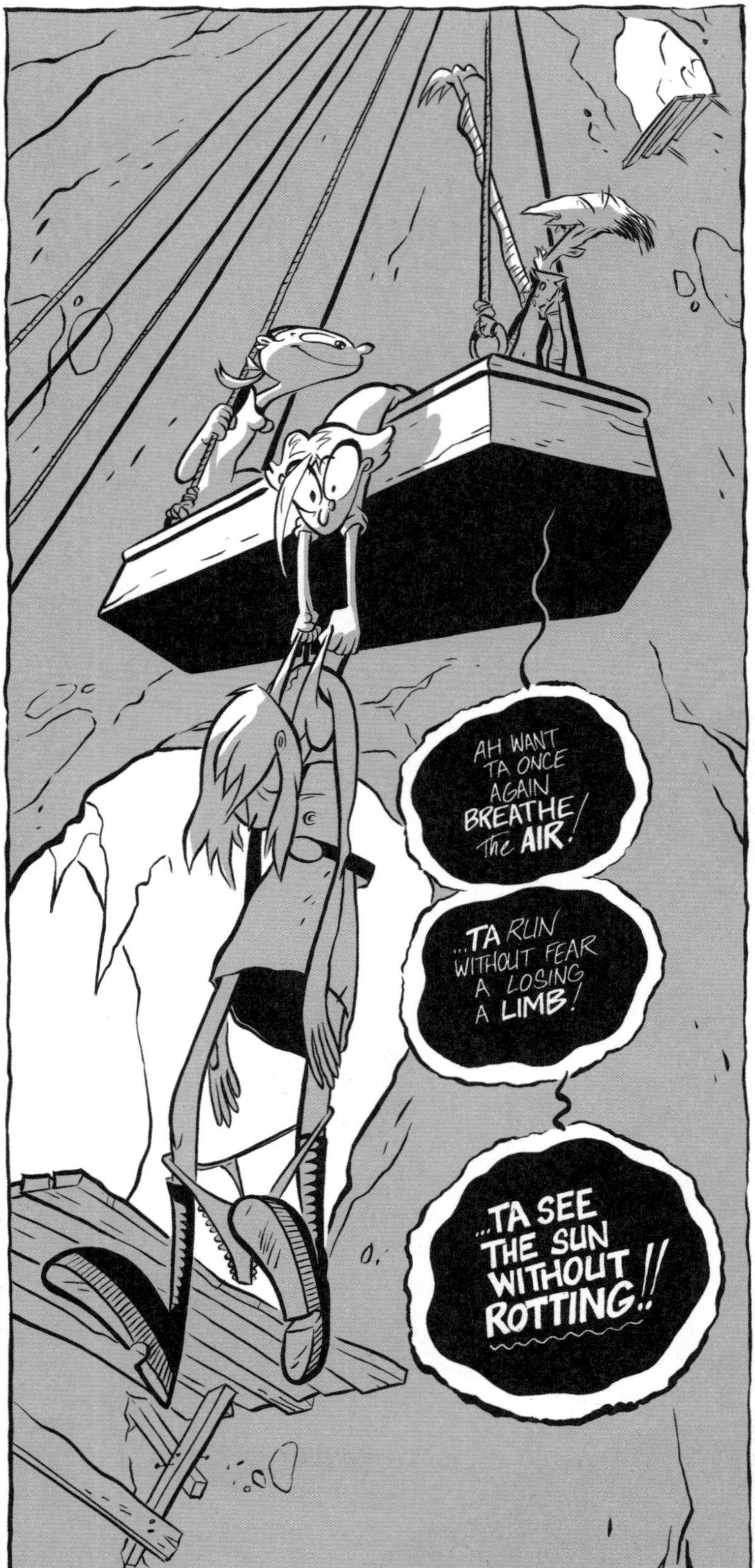
AH WANT TA ONCE AGAIN BREATHE THE AIR!
...TA RUN WITHOUT FEAR A LOSING A LIMB!
...TA SEE THE SUN WITHOUT ROTTING!!

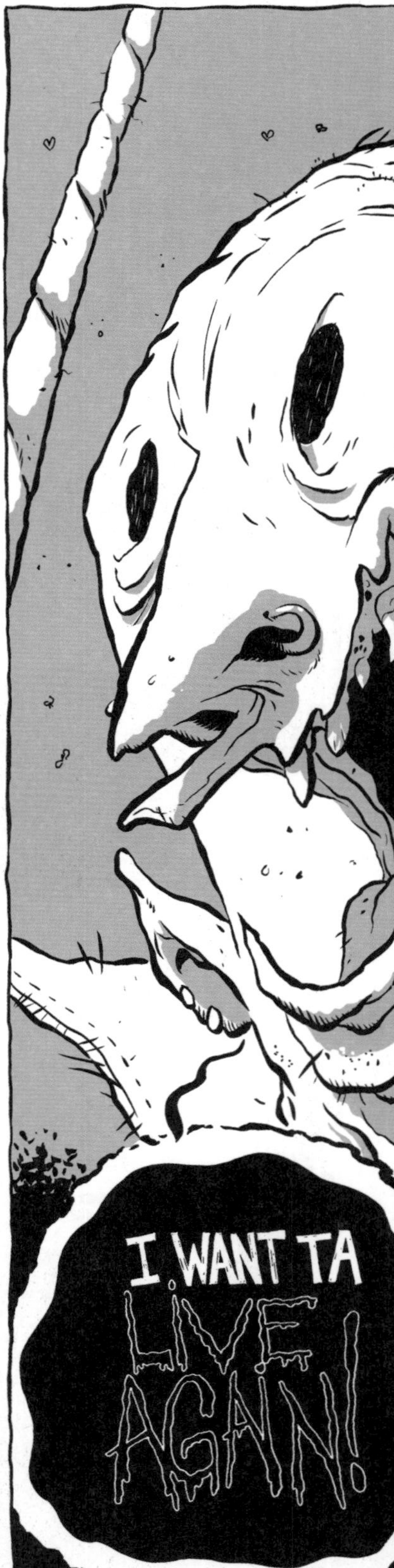
I WANT TA LIVE AGAIN!

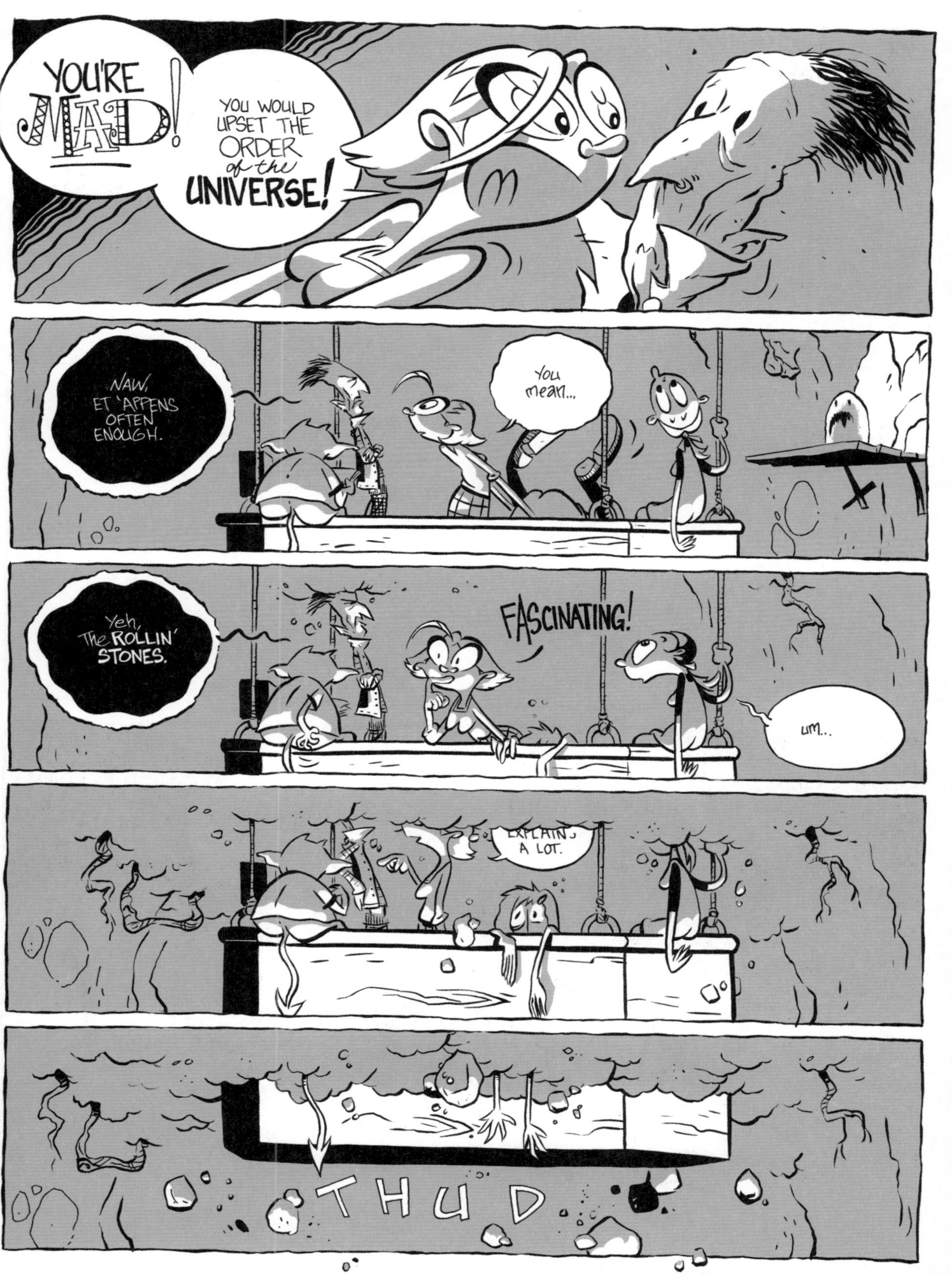

YOU'RE MAD!
YOU WOULD UPSET THE ORDER of the UNIVERSE!
NAW, ET 'APPENS OFTEN ENOUGH.
You mean...
Yeh, The ROLLIN' STONES.
FASCINATING!
um...
A LOT.
THUD

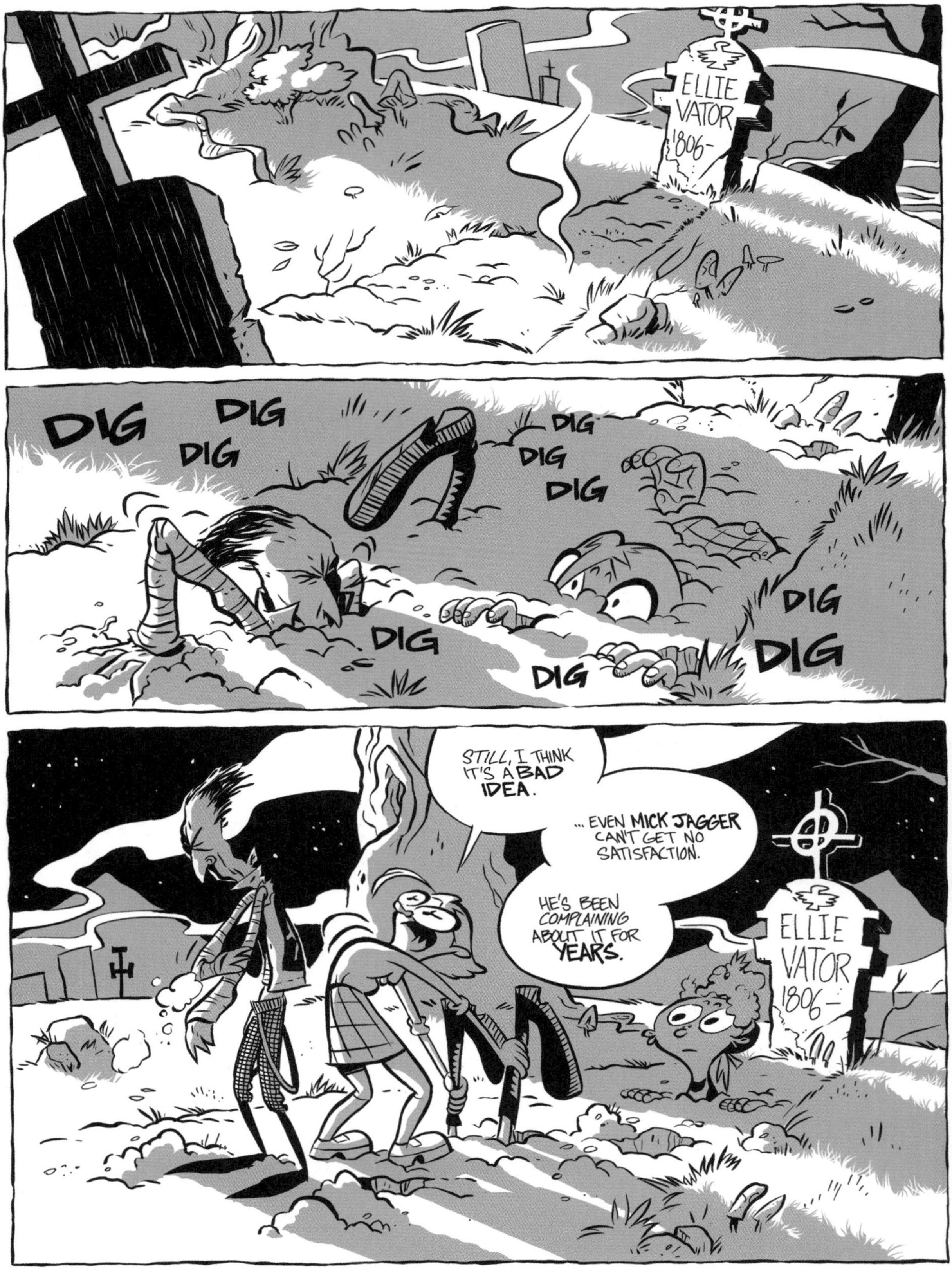
ELLIE VATOR 1806–
DIG DIG DIG
DIG DIG DIG
DIG DIG DIG DIG
STILL, I THINK IT'S A BAD IDEA.
... EVEN MICK JAGGER CAN'T GET NO SATISFACTION.
HE'S BEEN COMPLAINING ABOUT IT FOR YEARS.
ELLIE VATOR 1806–

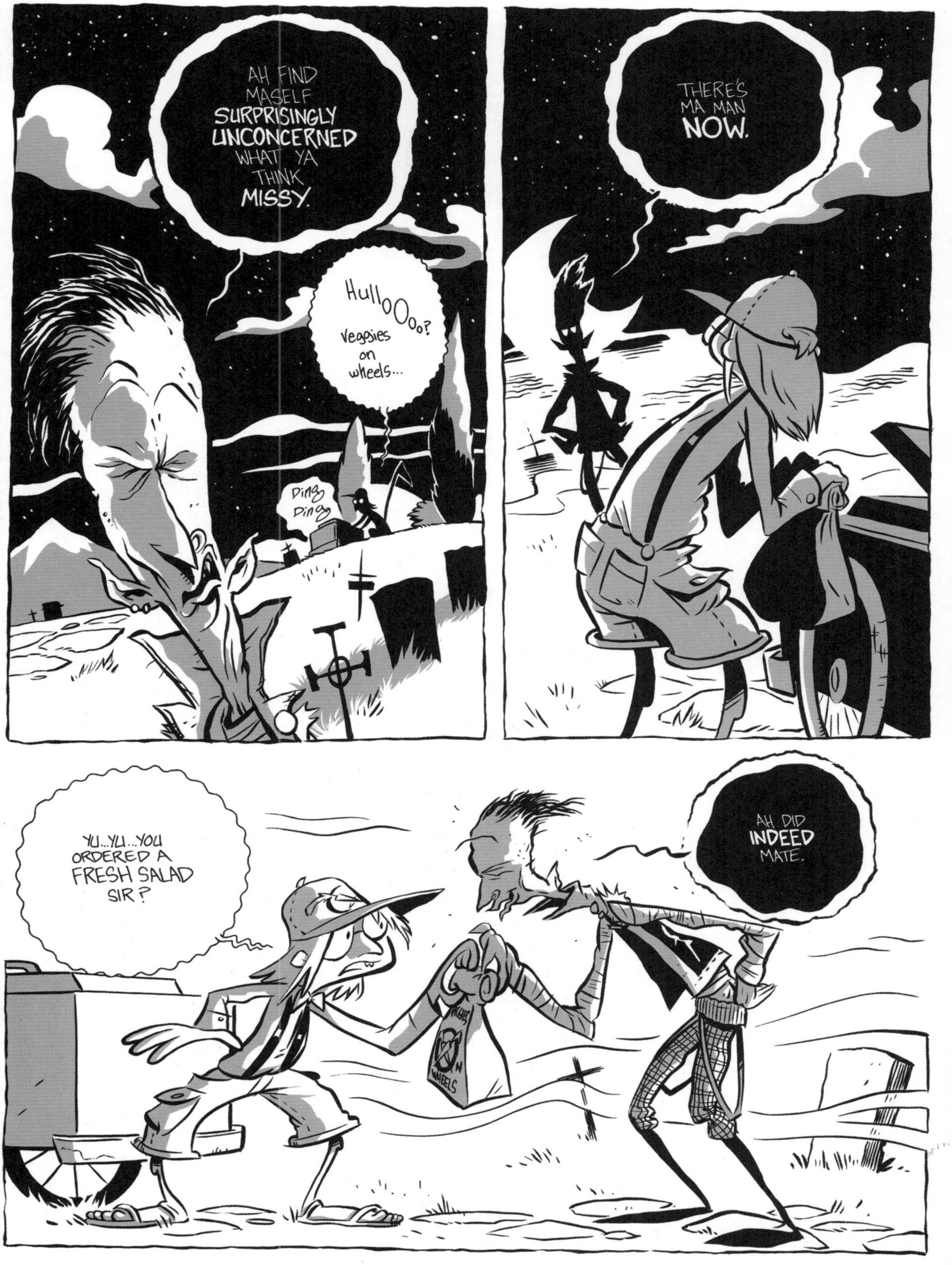
AH FIND MASELF SURPRISINGLY UNCONCERNED WHAT YA THINK MISSY.
HulloOoo? Veggies on wheels...
Ding Ding
THERE'S MA MAN NOW.
YU...YU...YOU ORDERED A FRESH SALAD SIR?
AH DID INDEED MATE.

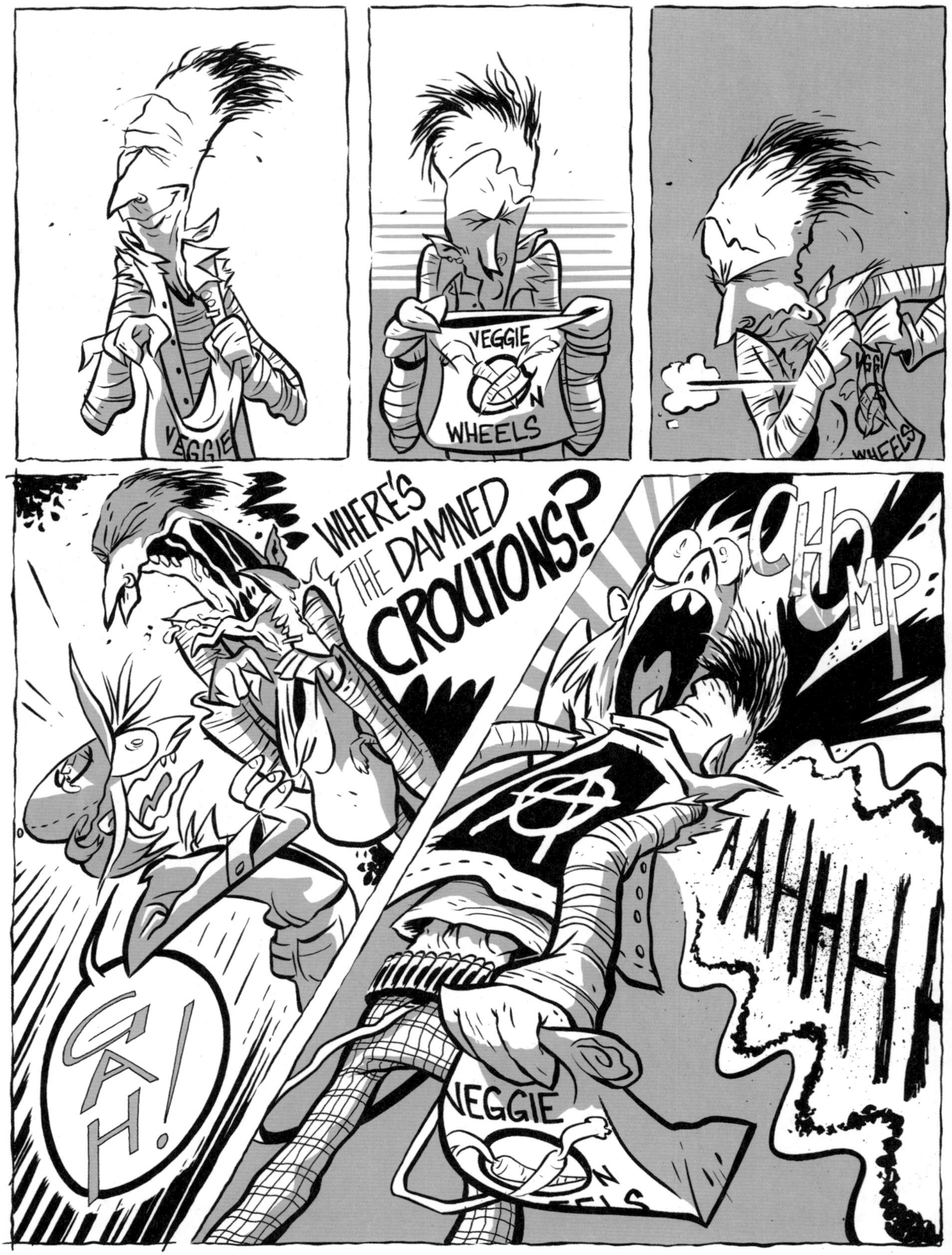

VEGGIE
VEGGIE N WHEELS
VEGGI WHEELS
WHERE'S THE DAMNED CROUTONS?
CHOMP
GAH!
AAHHHH
VEGGIE

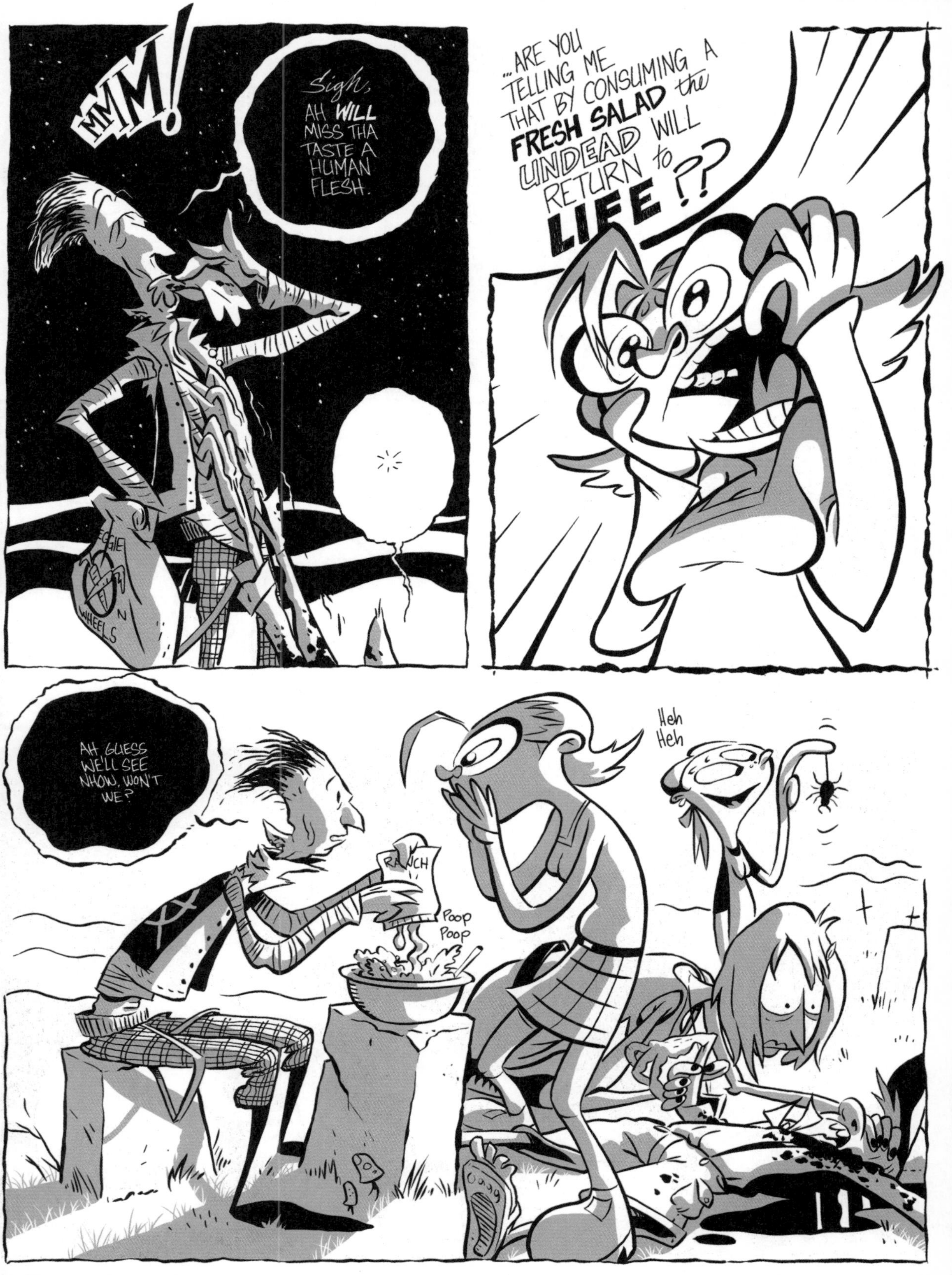
MMM!
Sigh, AH WILL MISS THA TASTE A HUMAN FLESH.
...ARE YOU TELLING ME THAT BY CONSUMING A FRESH SALAD the UNDEAD WILL RETURN to LIFE ??
AH GUESS WE'LL SEE NHOW, WON'T WE?
Heh Heh
RANCH
Poop Poop

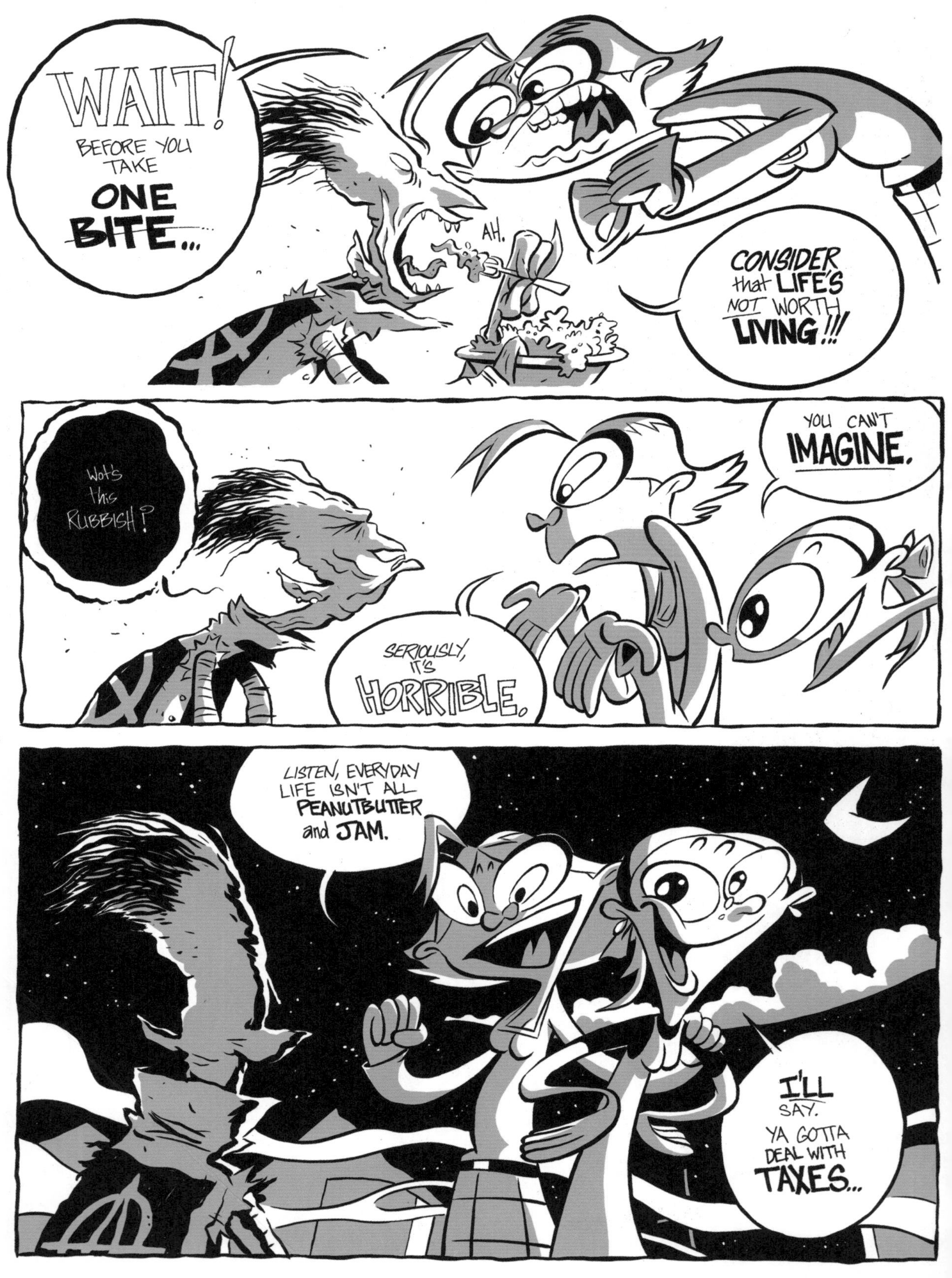
WAIT! BEFORE YOU TAKE ONE BITE...
AH.
CONSIDER that LIFE'S NOT WORTH LIVING!!!
Wot's this RUBBISH?
YOU CAN'T IMAGINE.
SERIOUSLY, IT'S HORRIBLE.
LISTEN, EVERYDAY LIFE ISN'T ALL PEANUTBUTTER and JAM.
I'LL SAY. YA GOTTA DEAL WITH TAXES...

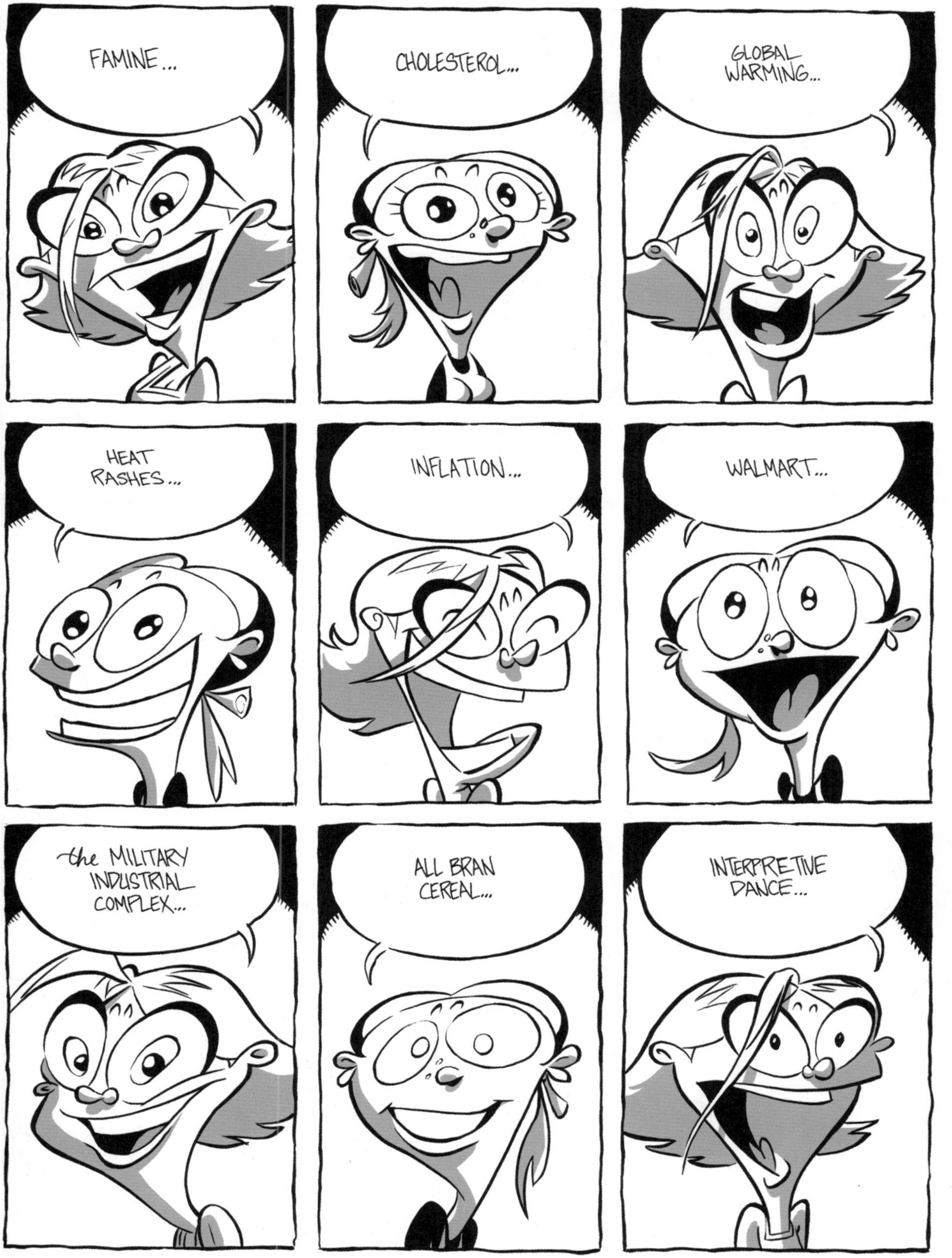
FAMINE...
CHOLESTEROL...
GLOBAL WARMING...
HEAT RASHES...
INFLATION...
WALMART...
the MILITARY INDUSTRIAL COMPLEX...
ALL BRAN CEREAL...
INTERPRETIVE DANCE...

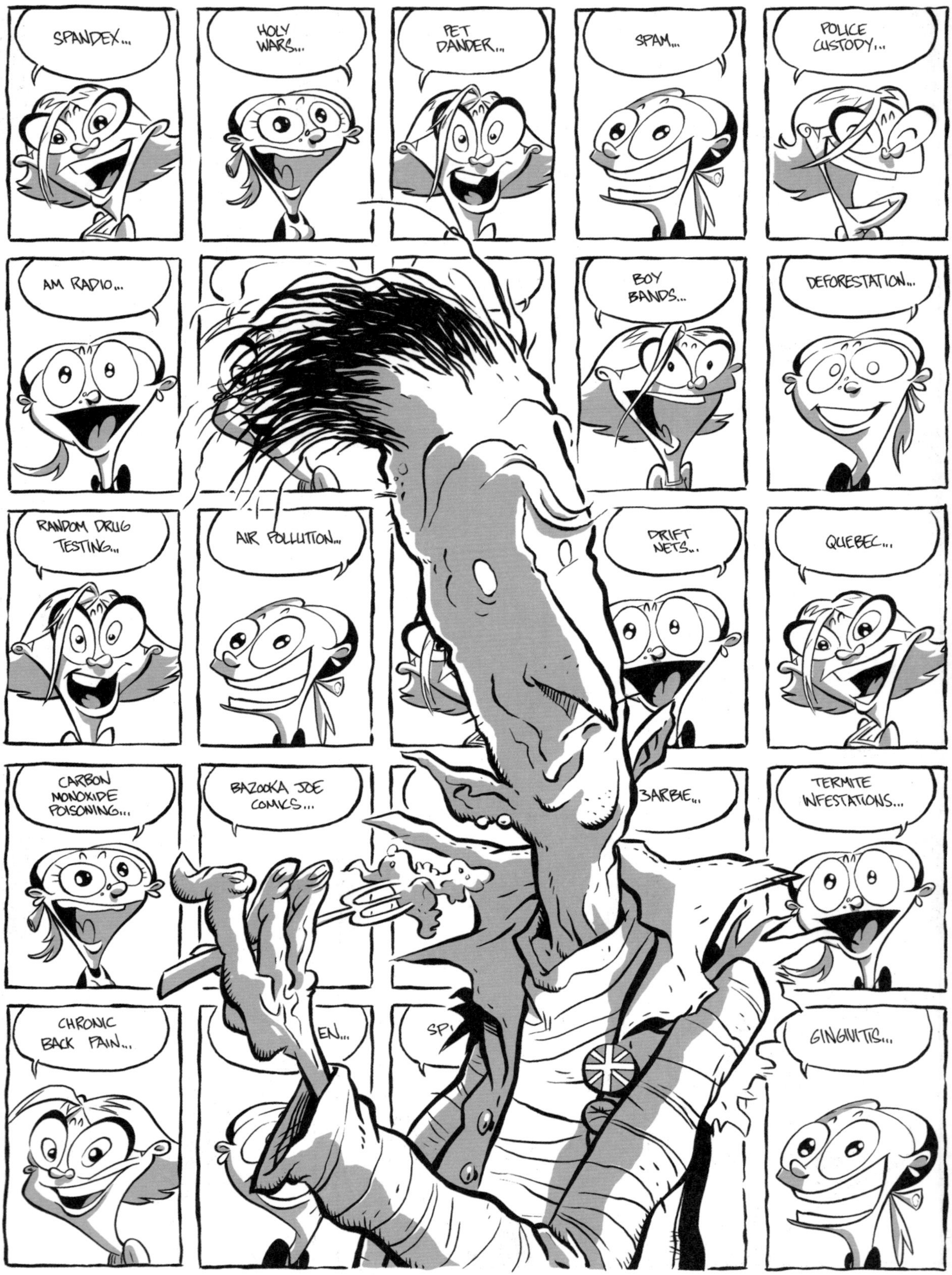
SPANDEX...
HOLY WARS...
PET DANDER...
SPAM...
POLICE CUSTODY...
AM RADIO...
BOY BANDS...
DEFORESTATION...
RANDOM DRUG TESTING...
AIR POLLUTION...
DRIFT NETS...
QUEBEC...
CARBON MONOXIDE POISONING...
BAZOOKA JOE COMICS...
BARBIE...
TERMITE INFESTATIONS...
CHRONIC BACK PAIN...
GINGIVITIS...

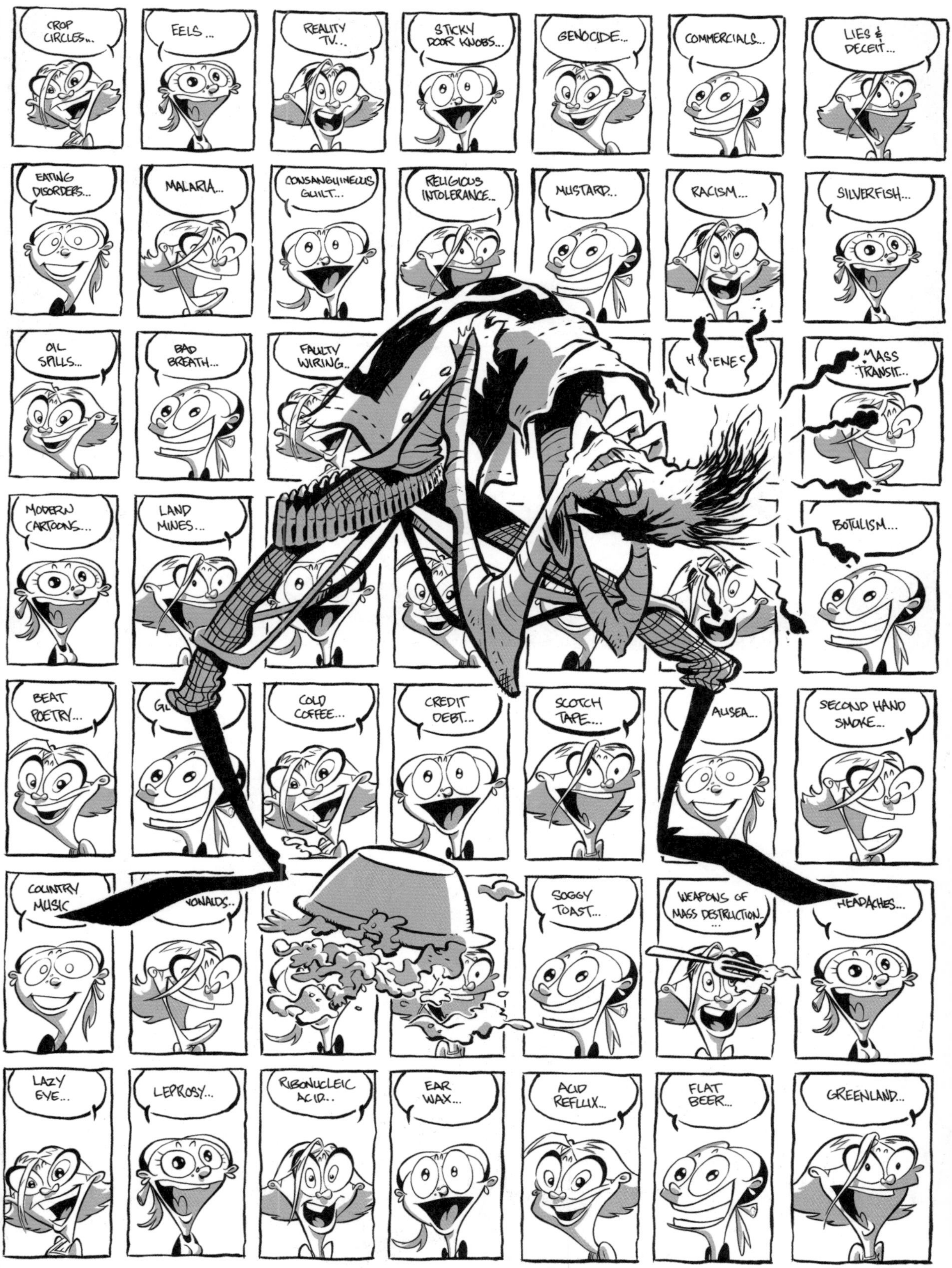
CROP CIRCLES...
EELS...
REALITY TV...
STICKY DOOR KNOBS...
GENOCIDE...
COMMERCIALS...
LIES & DECEIT...
EATING DISORDERS...
MALARIA...
CONSANGUINEOUS GUILT...
RELIGIOUS INTOLERANCE...
MUSTARD...
RACISM...
SILVERFISH...
OIL SPILLS...
BAD BREATH...
FAULTY WIRING...
MASS TRANSIT...
MODERN CARTOONS...
LAND MINES...
BOTULISM...
BEAT POETRY...
COLD COFFEE...
CREDIT DEBT...
SCOTCH TAPE...
SECOND HAND SMOKE...
COUNTRY MUSIC
SOGGY TOAST...
WEAPONS OF MASS DESTRUCTION...
HEADACHES...
LAZY EYE...
LEPROSY...
RIBONUCLEIC ACID...
EAR WAX...
ACID REFLUX...
FLAT BEER...
GREENLAND...

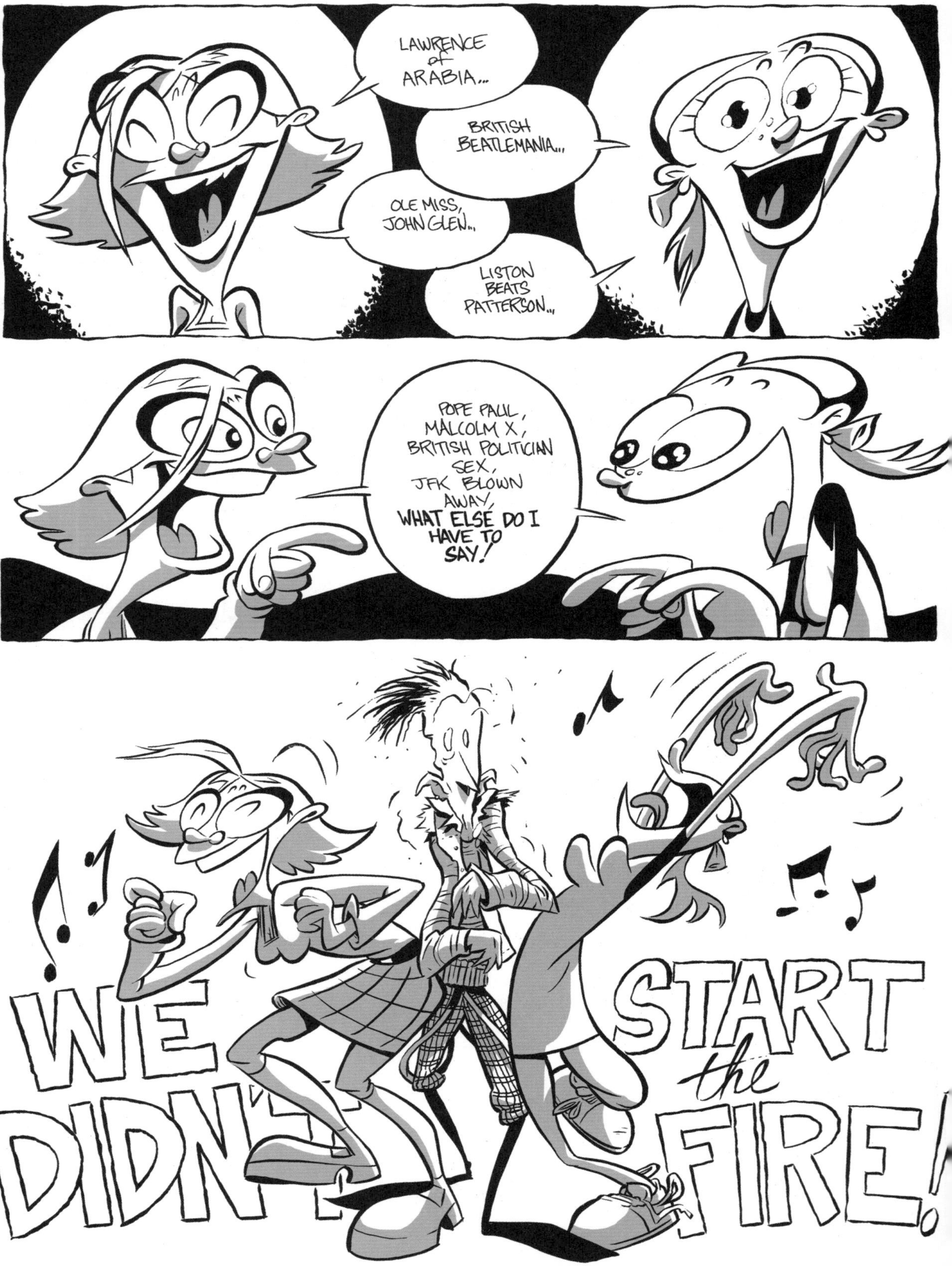
LAWRENCE of ARABIA...
BRITISH BEATLEMANIA...
OLE MISS, JOHN GLEN...
LISTON BEATS PATTERSON...
POPE PAUL, MALCOLM X, BRITISH POLITICIAN SEX, JFK BLOWN AWAY, WHAT ELSE DO I HAVE TO SAY!
WE DIDN'T START the FIRE!

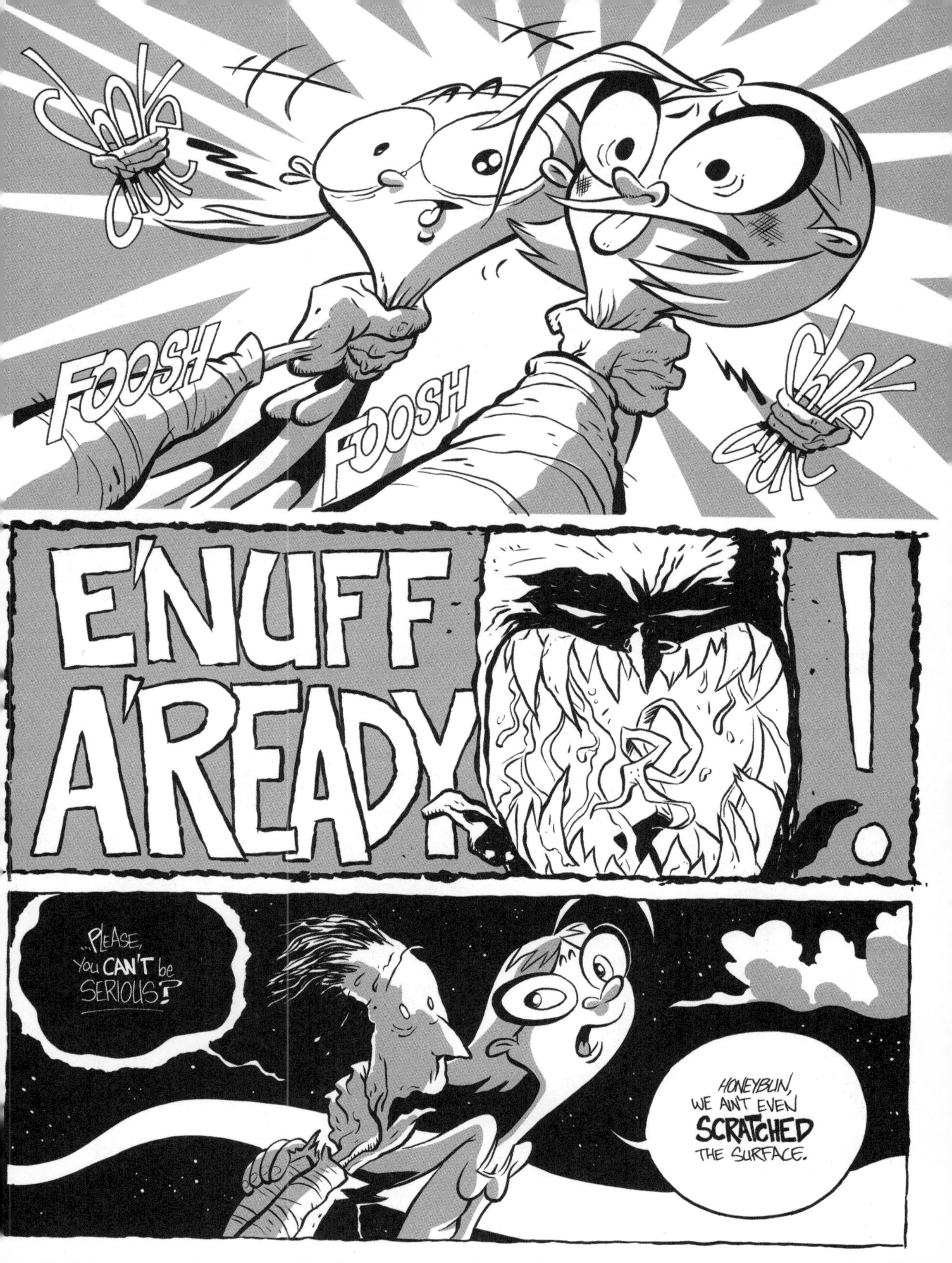
FOOSH
FOOSH
E'NUFF A'READY!
...PLEASE, YOU CAN'T BE SERIOUS?
HONEYBUN, WE AIN'T EVEN SCRATCHED THE SURFACE.

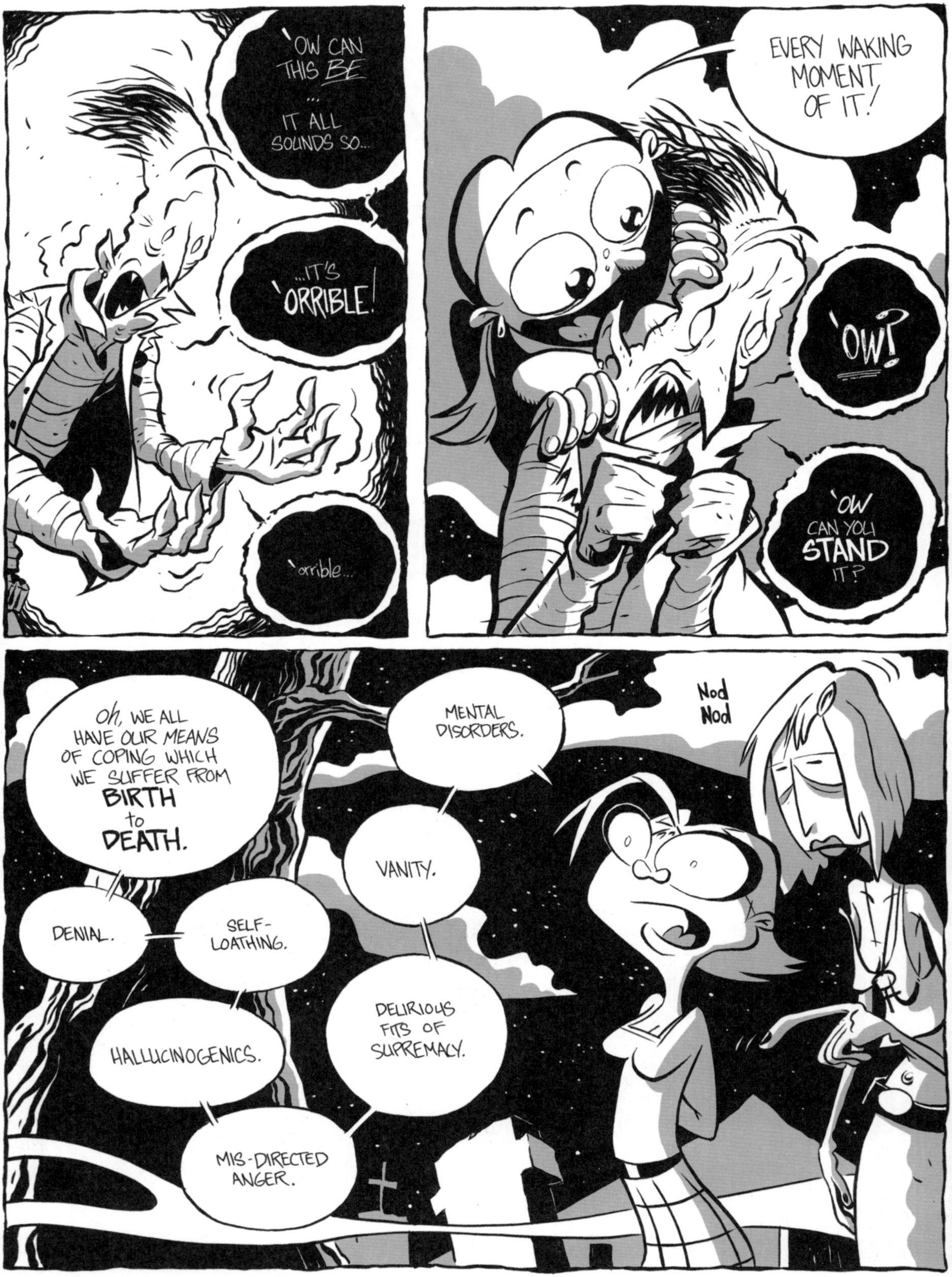
'OW CAN THIS BE ... IT ALL SOUNDS SO...
...IT'S 'ORRIBLE!
'orrible...
EVERY WAKING MOMENT OF IT!
'OW?
'OW CAN YOU STAND IT?
Nod Nod
Oh, WE ALL HAVE OUR MEANS OF COPING WHICH WE SUFFER FROM BIRTH to DEATH.
DENIAL.
SELF-LOATHING.
HALLUCINOGENICS.
MIS-DIRECTED ANGER.
DELIRIOUS FITS OF SUPREMACY.
VANITY.
MENTAL DISORDERS.

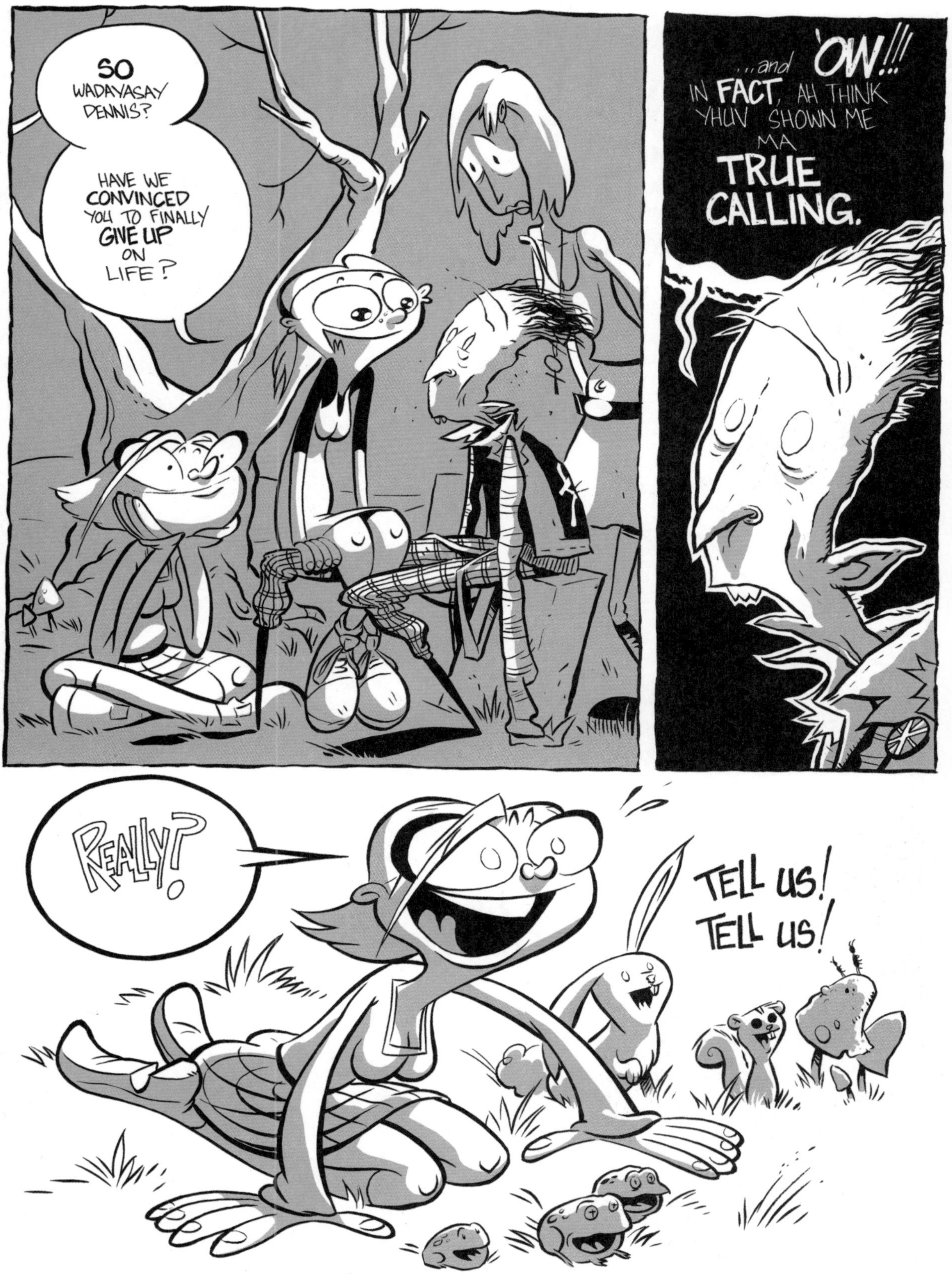
SO WADAYASAY DENNIS?
HAVE WE CONVINCED YOU TO FINALLY GIVE UP ON LIFE?
...and 'OW!!!
IN FACT, AH THINK YHUV SHOWN ME MA TRUE CALLING.
REALLY?
TELL US! TELL US!

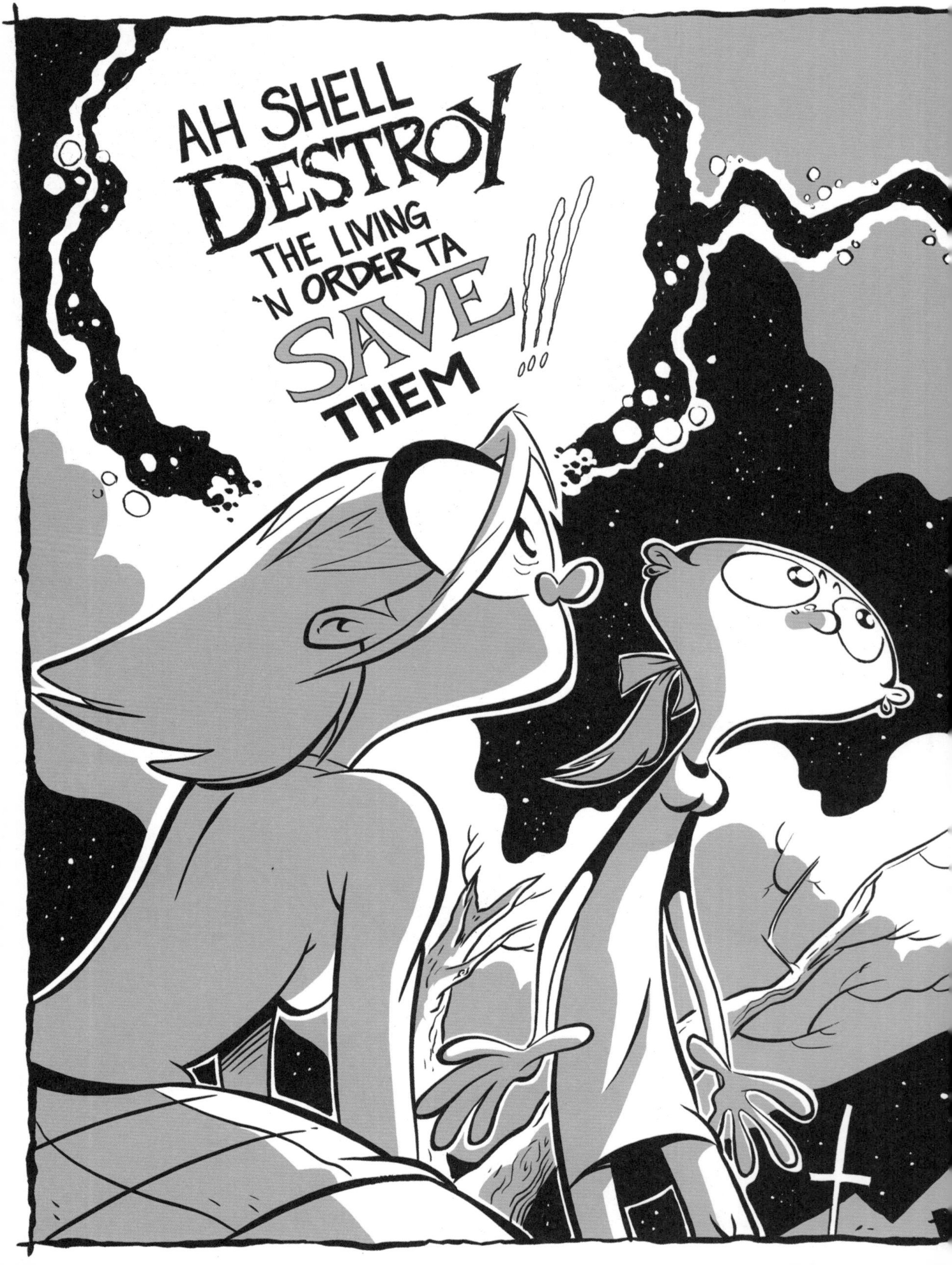
AH SHELL DESTROY THE LIVING 'N ORDER TA SAVE THEM!!!

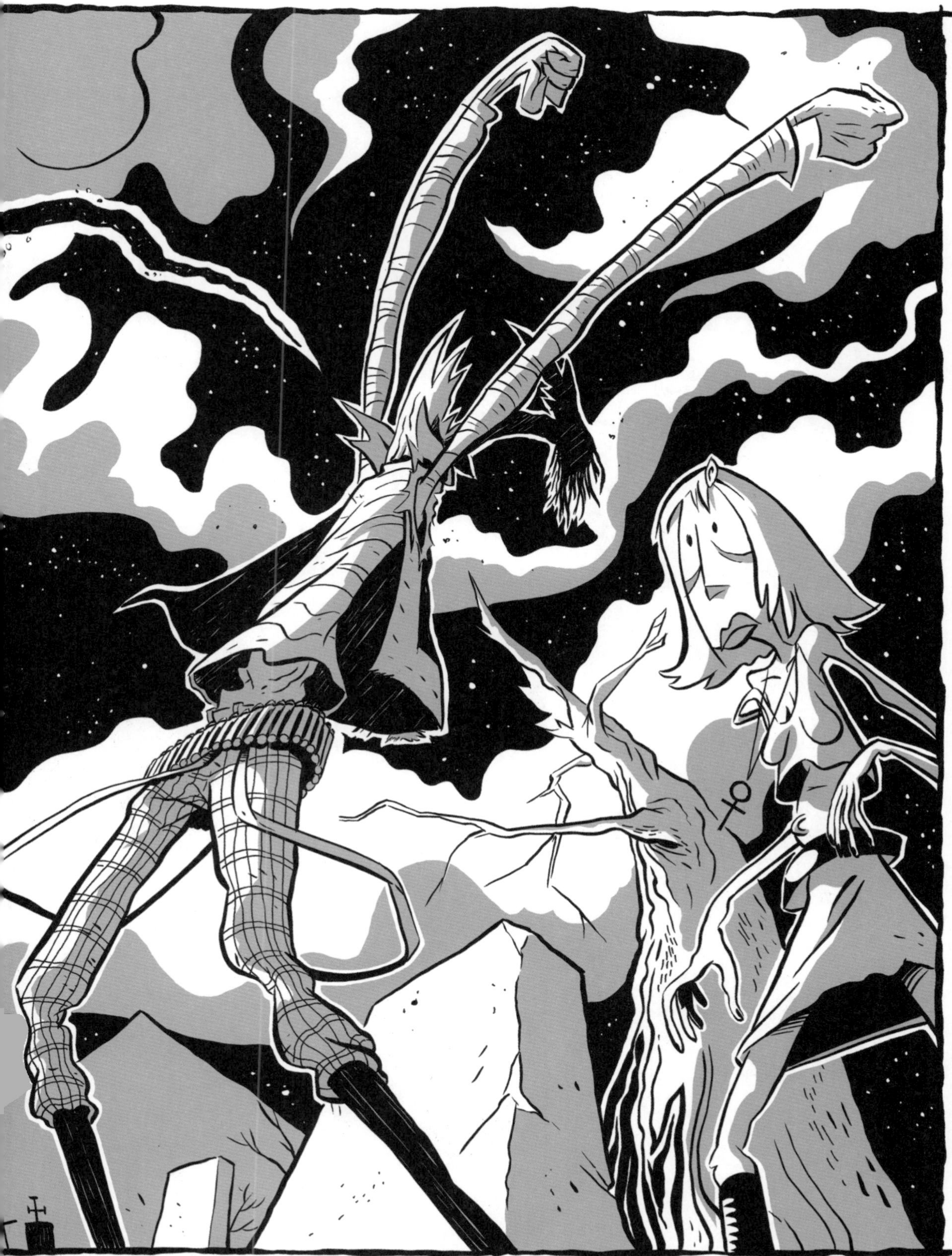

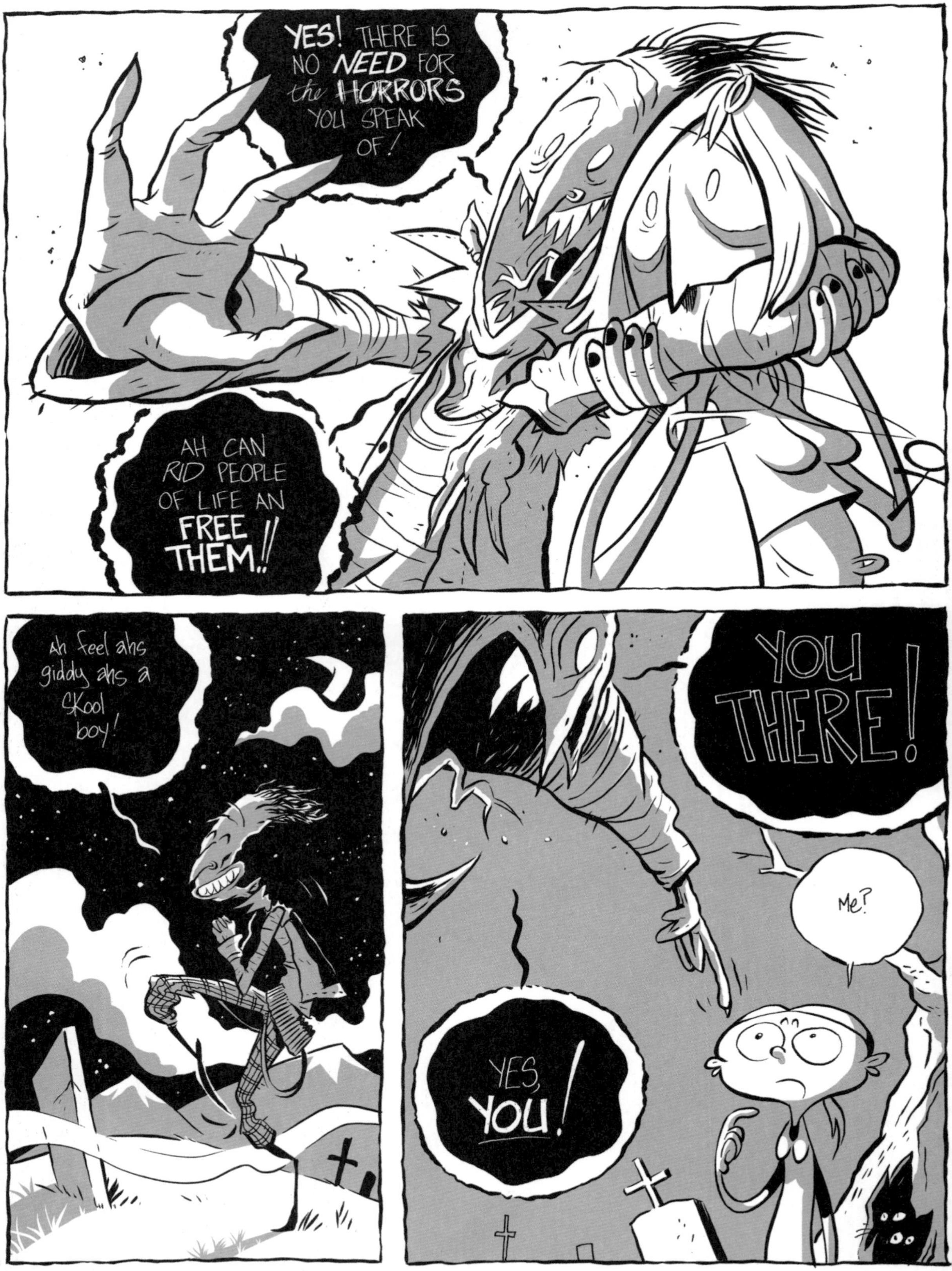
YES! THERE IS NO NEED FOR the HORRORS YOU SPEAK OF!
AH CAN RID PEOPLE OF LIFE AN FREE THEM!!
ah feel ahs giddy ahs a skool boy!
YOU THERE!
Me?
YES, YOU!

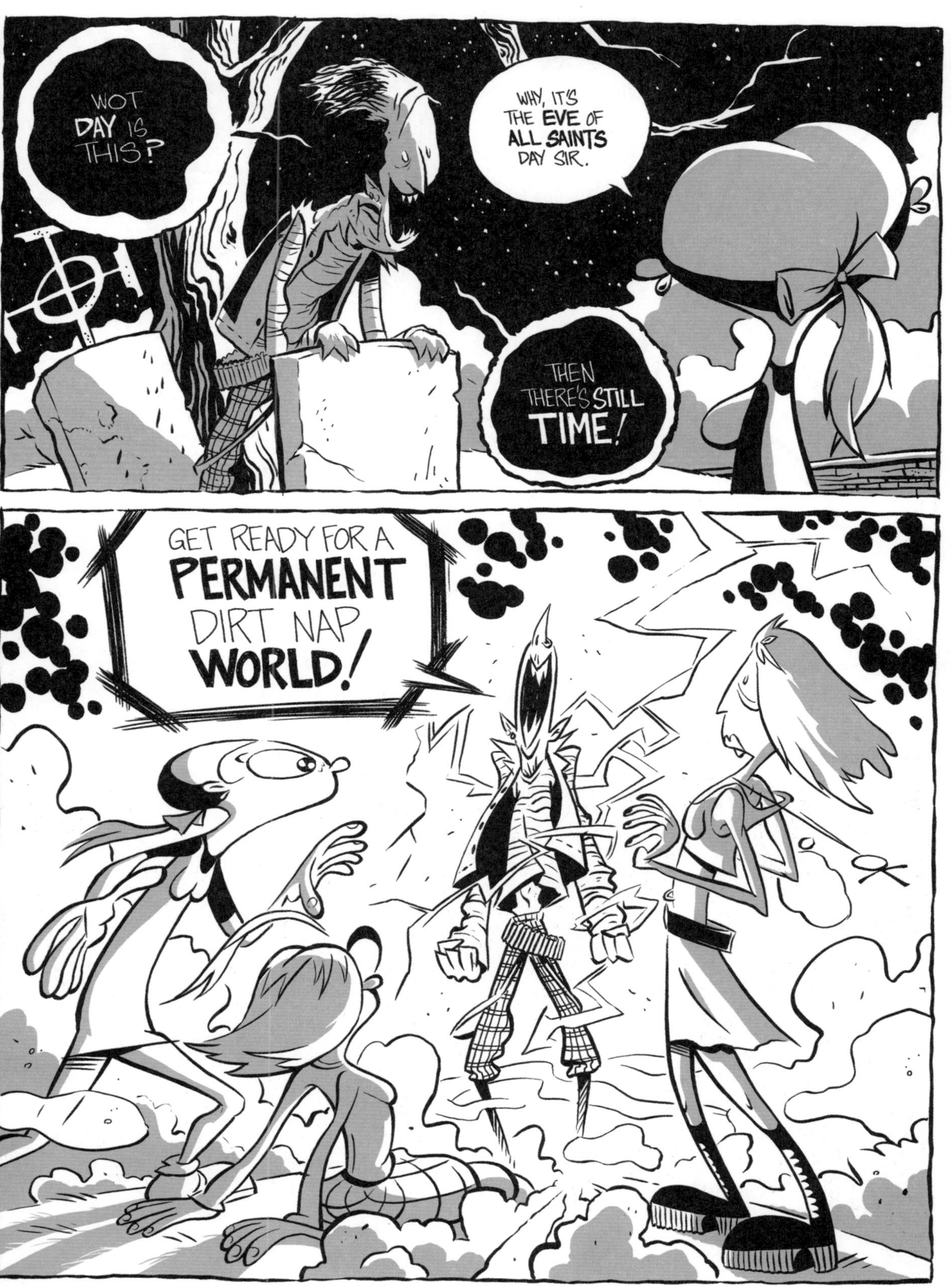
WOT DAY IS THIS?
WHY, IT'S THE EVE OF ALL SAINTS DAY SIR.
THEN THERE'S STILL TIME!
GET READY FOR A PERMANENT DIRT NAP WORLD!

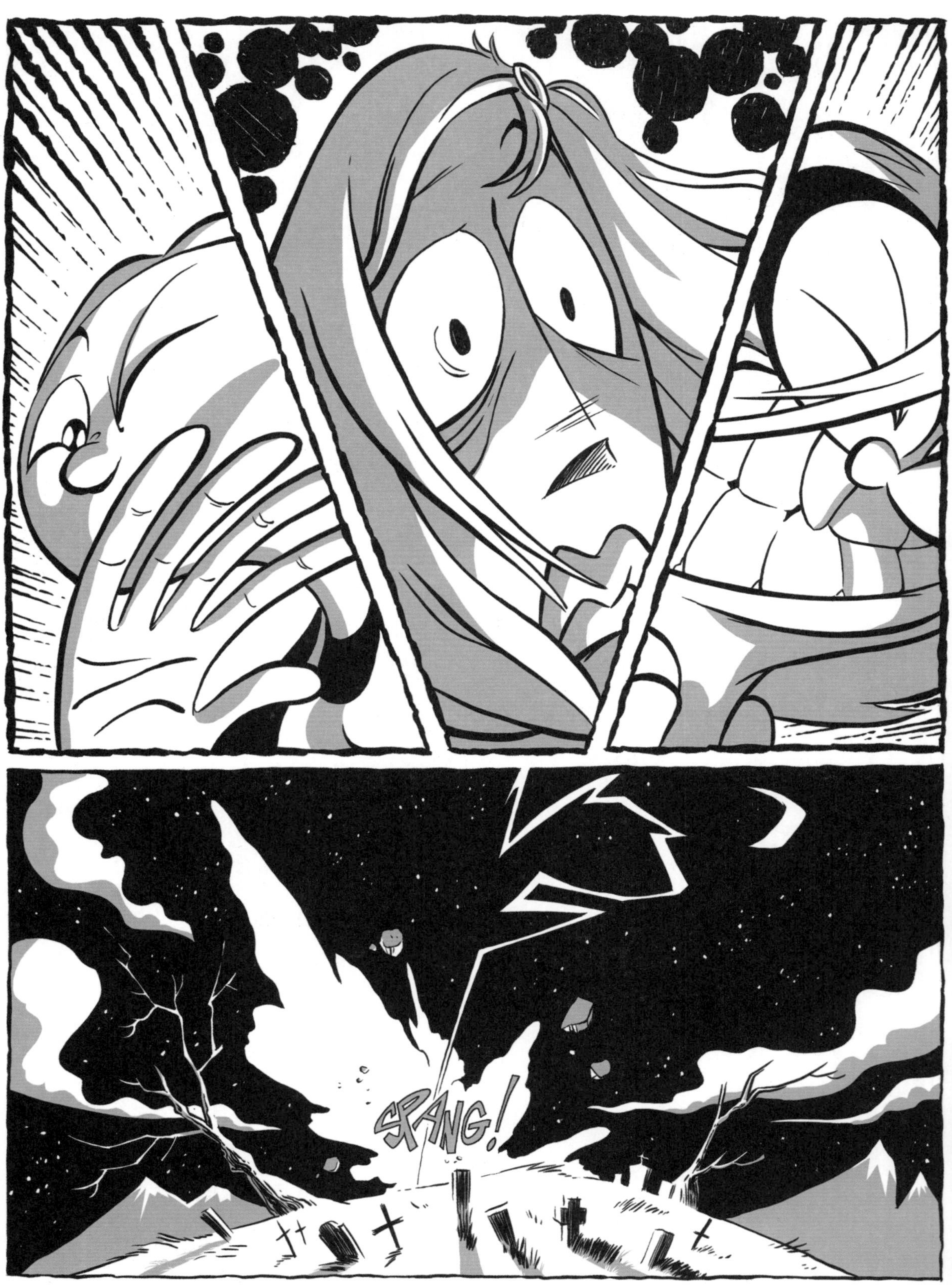
SPANG!

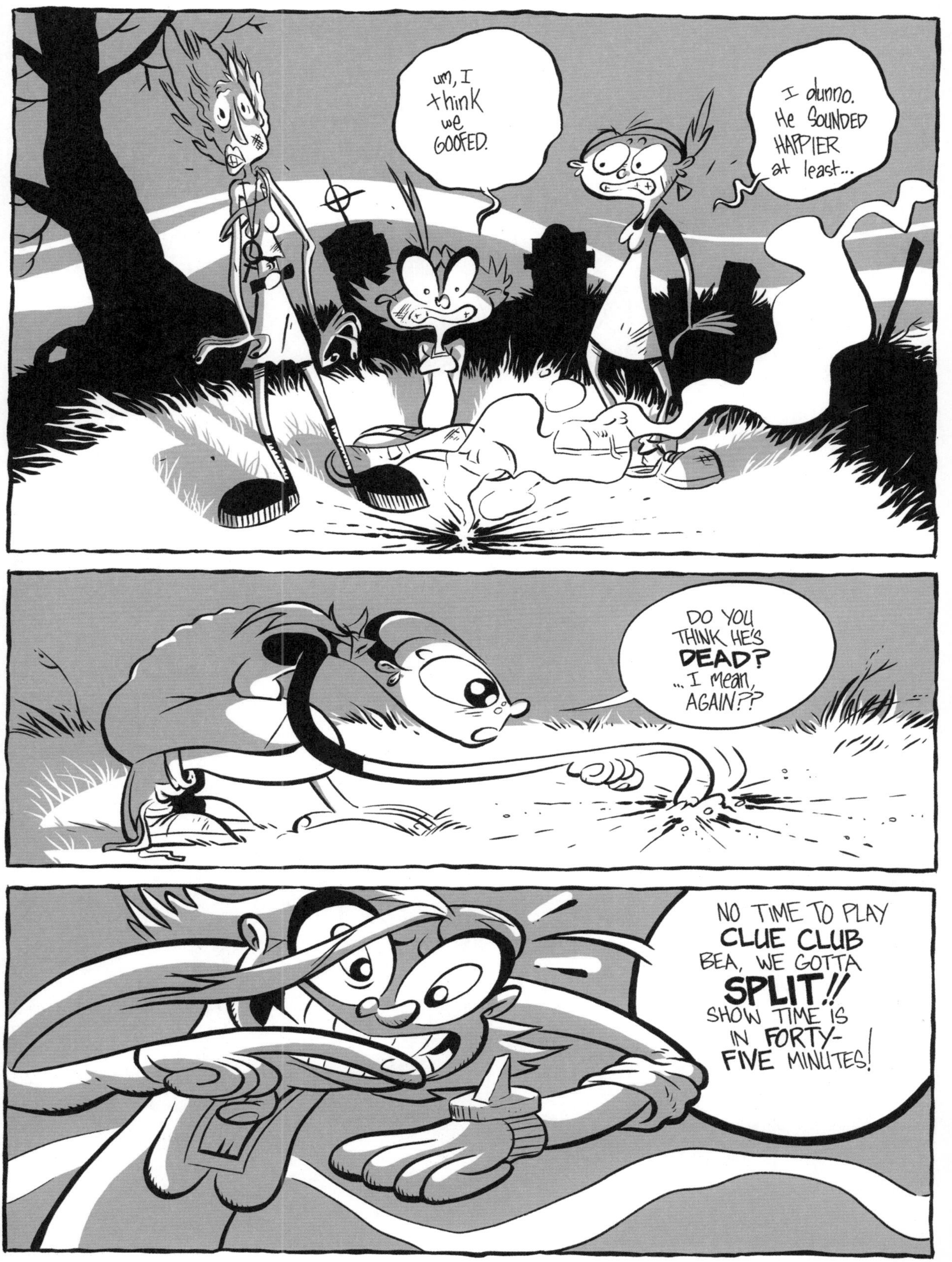
um, I think we GOOFED.
I dunno. He SOUNDED HAPPIER at least...
DO YOU THINK HE'S DEAD? ... I mean, AGAIN??
NO TIME TO PLAY CLUE CLUB BEA, WE GOTTA SPLIT!! SHOW TIME IS IN FORTY-FIVE MINUTES!

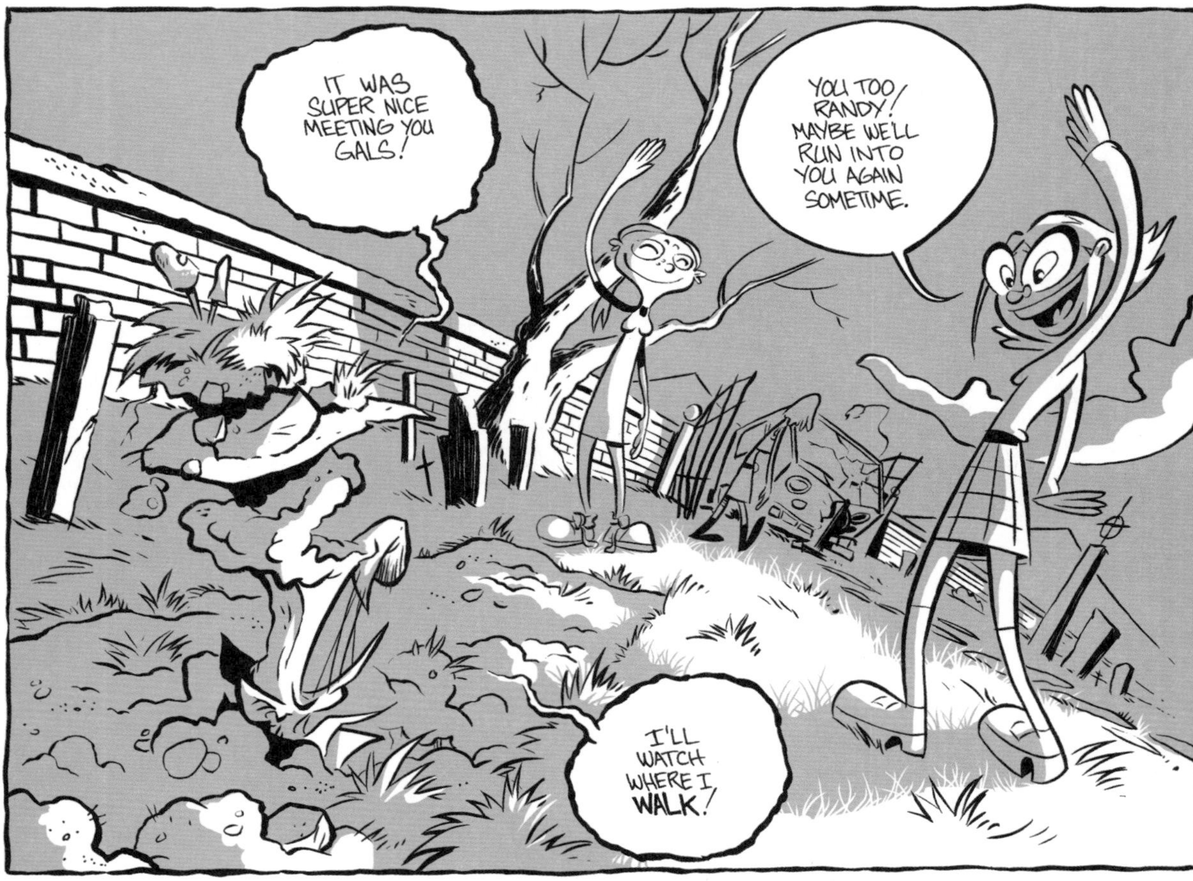
IT WAS SUPER NICE MEETING YOU GALS!
YOU TOO! RANDY! MAYBE WE'LL RUN INTO YOU AGAIN SOMETIME.
I'LL WATCH WHERE I WALK!

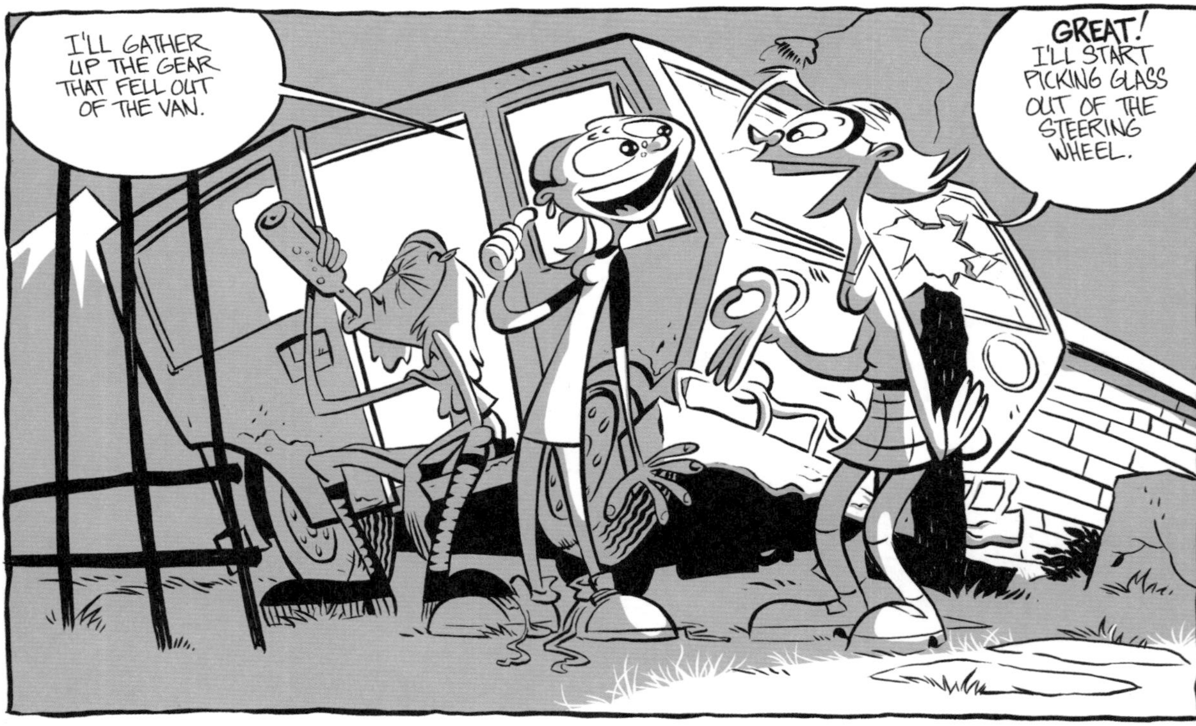
I'LL GATHER UP THE GEAR THAT FELL OUT OF THE VAN.
GREAT! I'LL START PICKING GLASS OUT OF THE STEERING WHEEL.

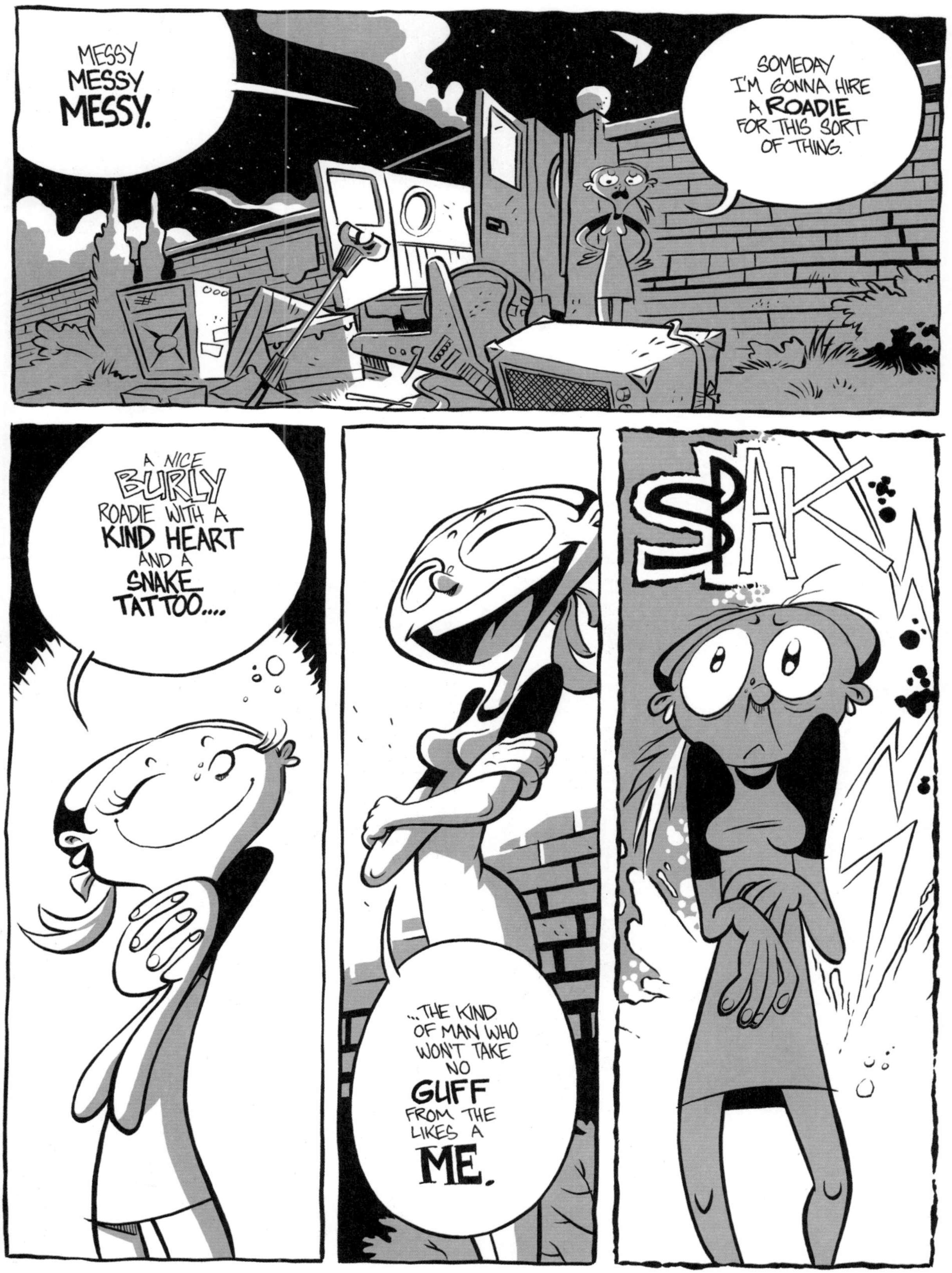
MESSY MESSY MESSY.
SOMEDAY I'M GONNA HIRE A ROADIE FOR THIS SORT OF THING.
A NICE BURLY ROADIE WITH A KIND HEART AND A SNAKE TATTOO....
...THE KIND OF MAN WHO WON'T TAKE NO GUFF FROM THE LIKES A ME.
SPAK

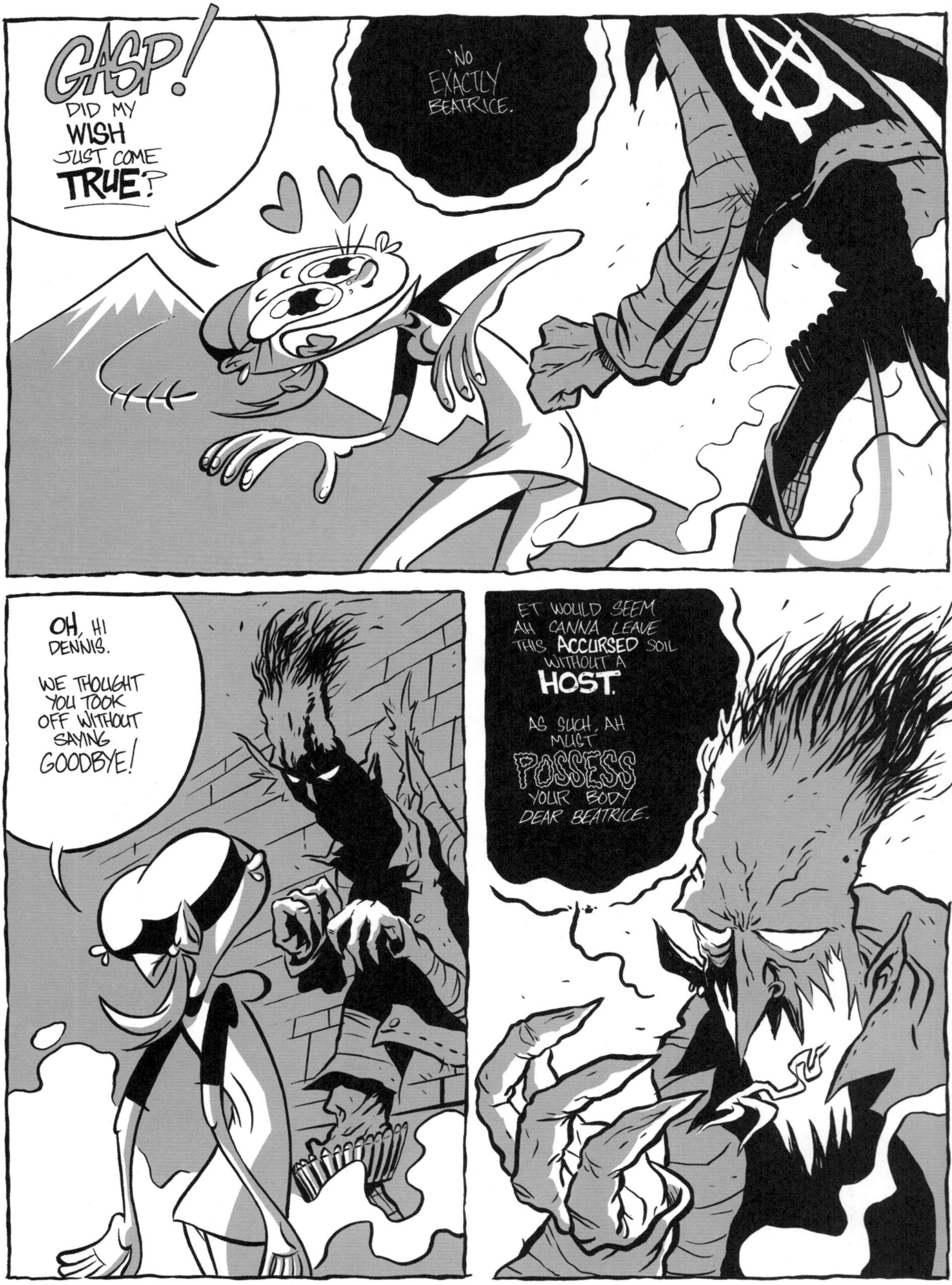
GASP! DID MY WISH JUST COME TRUE?
`NO EXACTLY BEATRICE.
OH, HI DENNIS.
WE THOUGHT YOU TOOK OFF WITHOUT SAYING GOODBYE!
ET WOULD SEEM AH CANNA LEAVE THIS ACCURSED SOIL WITHOUT A HOST.
AS SUCH, AH MUST POSSESS YOUR BODY DEAR BEATRICE.

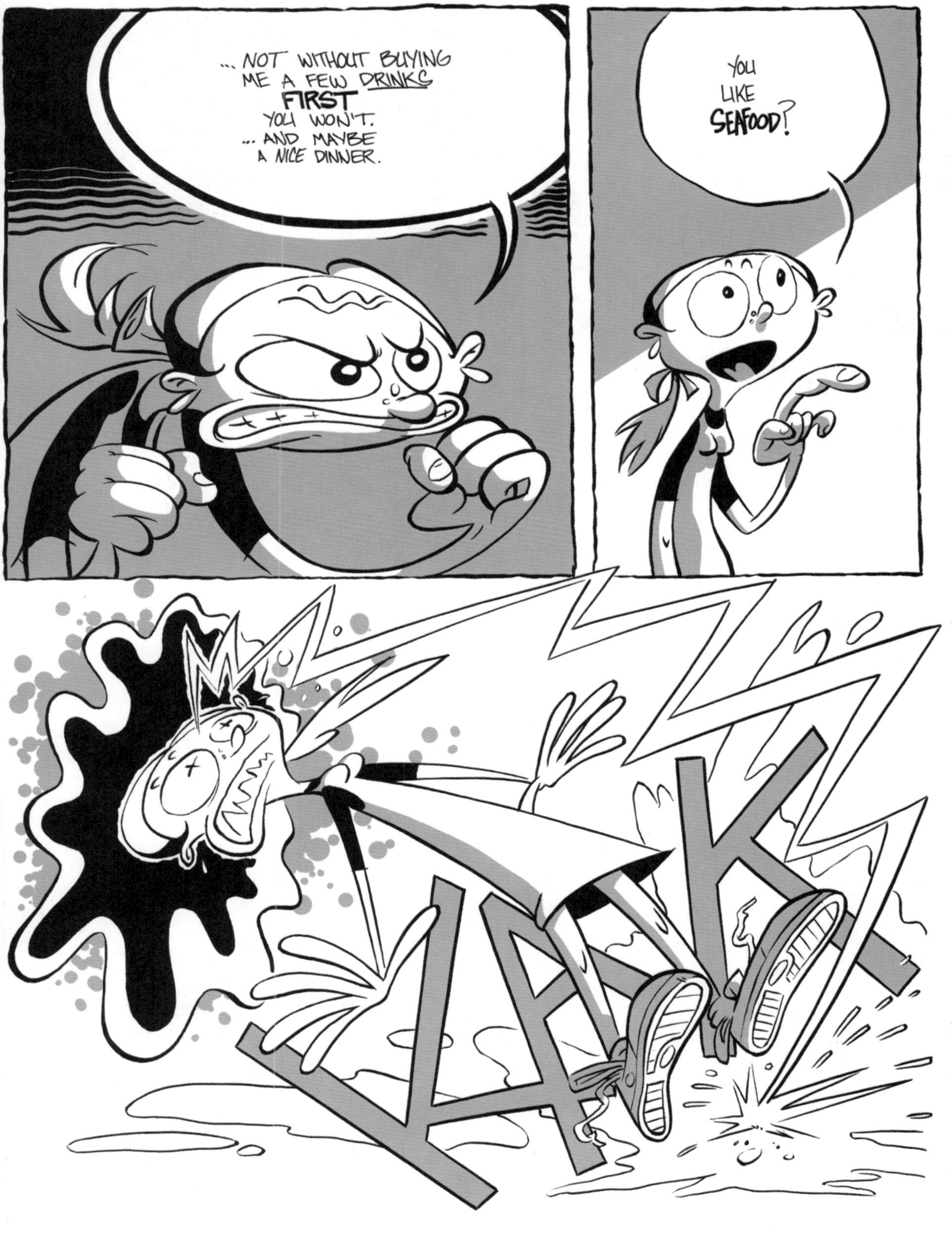
... NOT WITHOUT BUYING ME A FEW DRINKS FIRST YOU WON'T. ... AND MAYBE A NICE DINNER.
YOU LIKE SEAFOOD?

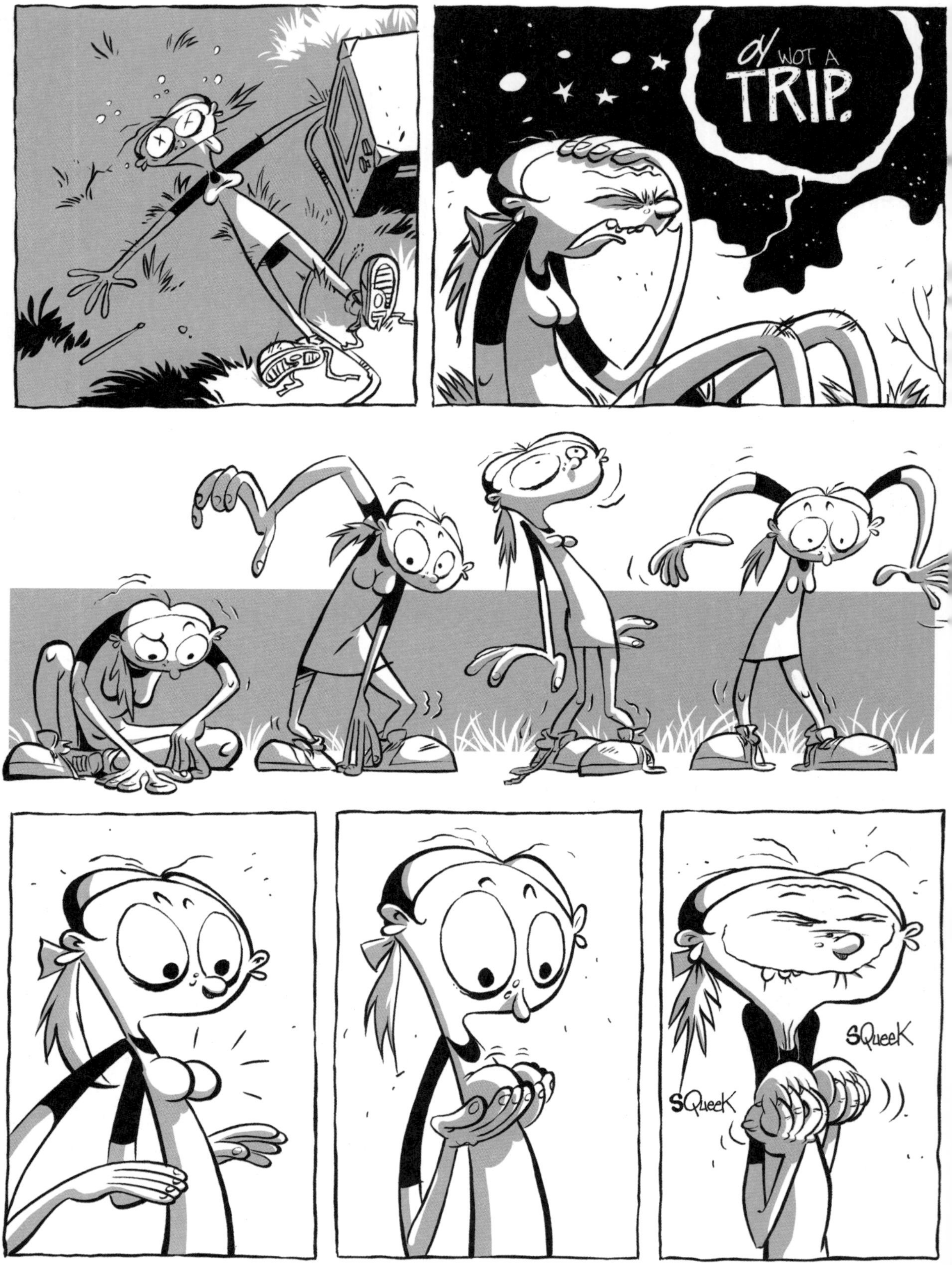

oy WOT A TRIP.
SQueeK
SQueeK

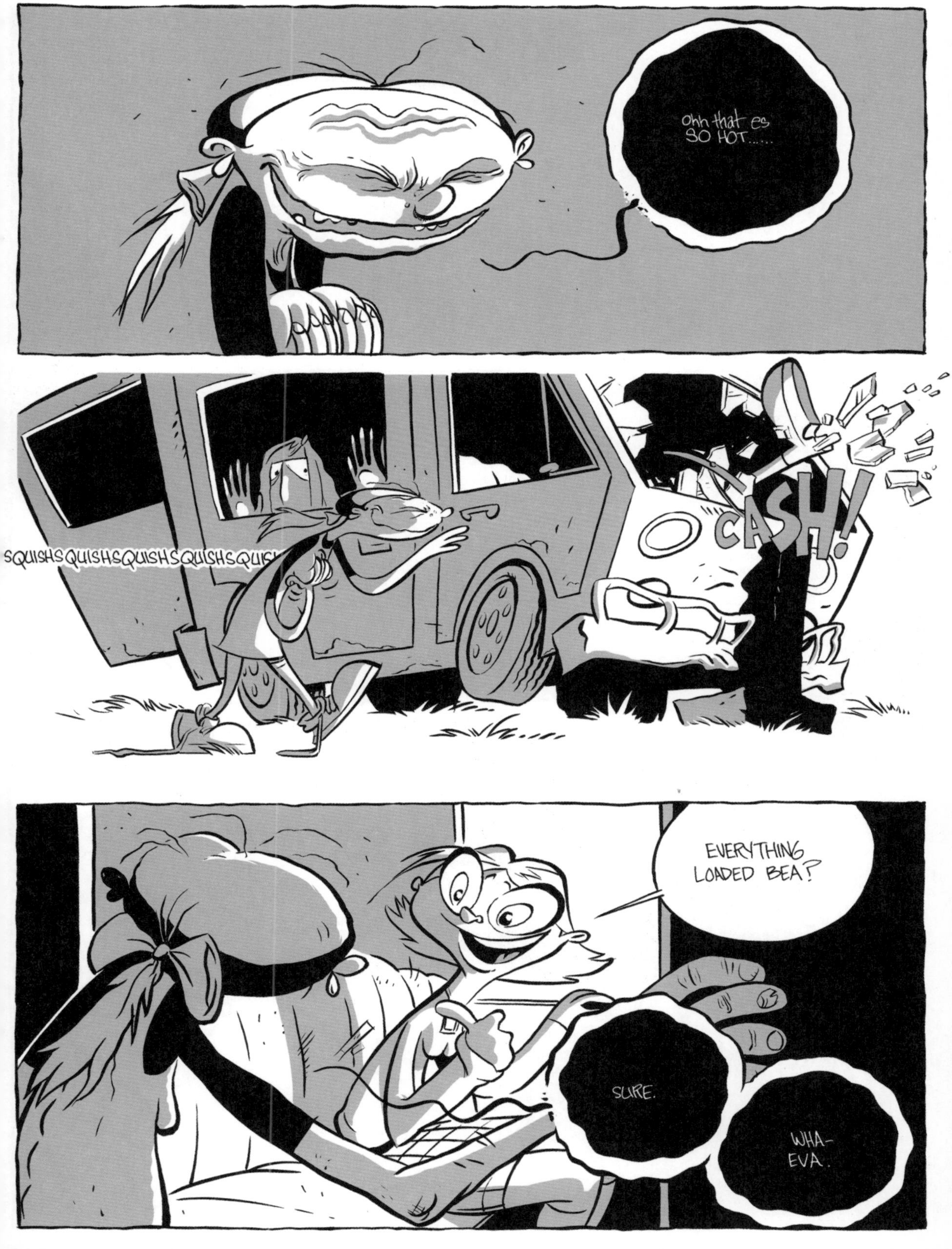

ohh that es SO HOT......
SQUISHSQUISHSQUISHSQUISHSQUISH
CASH!
EVERYTHING LOADED BEA?
SURE.
WHA-EVA.

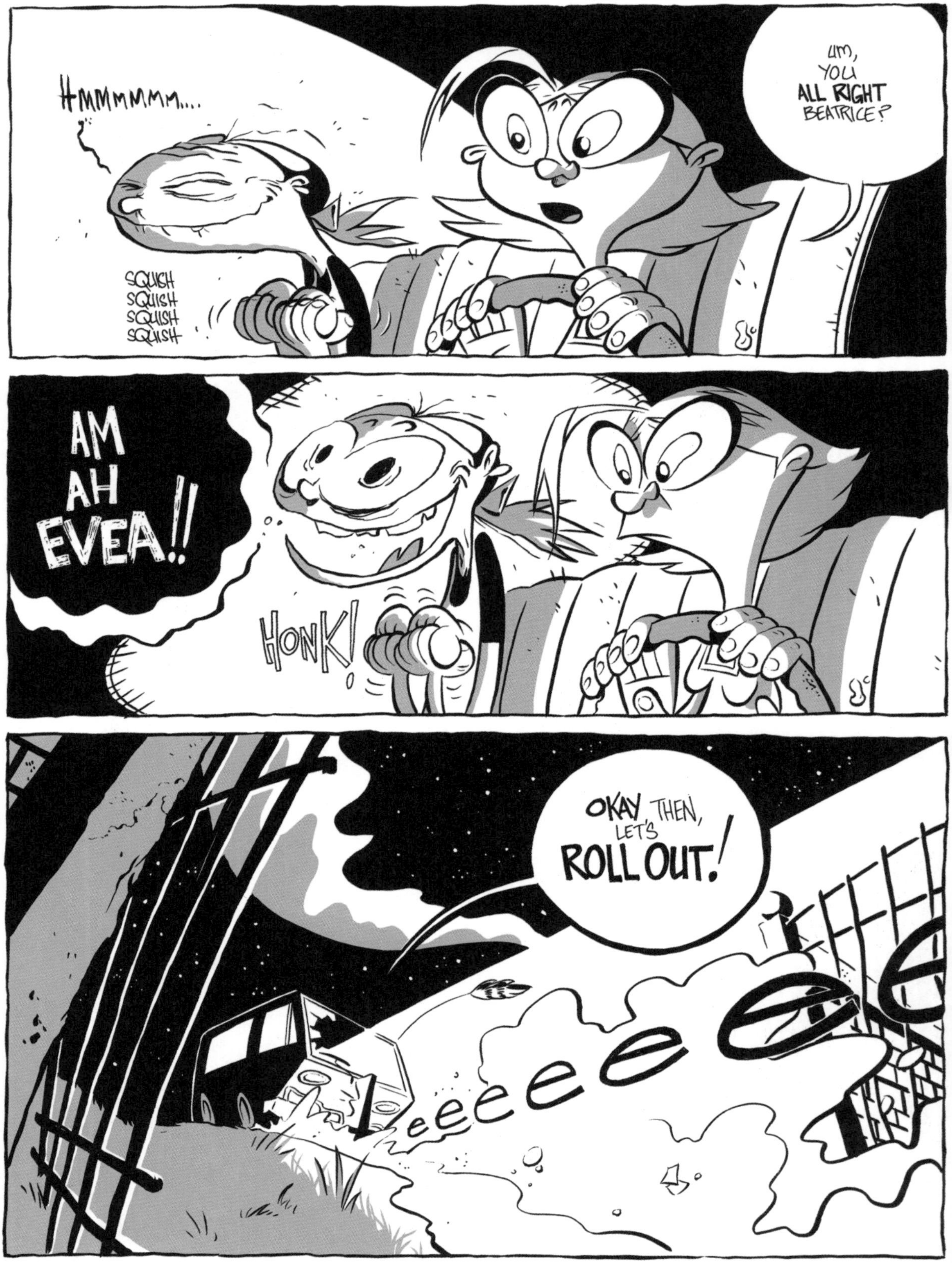

HMMMMMM....
SQUISH SQUISH SQUISH SQUISH
UM, YOU ALL RIGHT BEATRICE?
AM AH EVEA!!
HONK!
OKAY THEN, LET'S ROLL OUT!
eeeeeeee

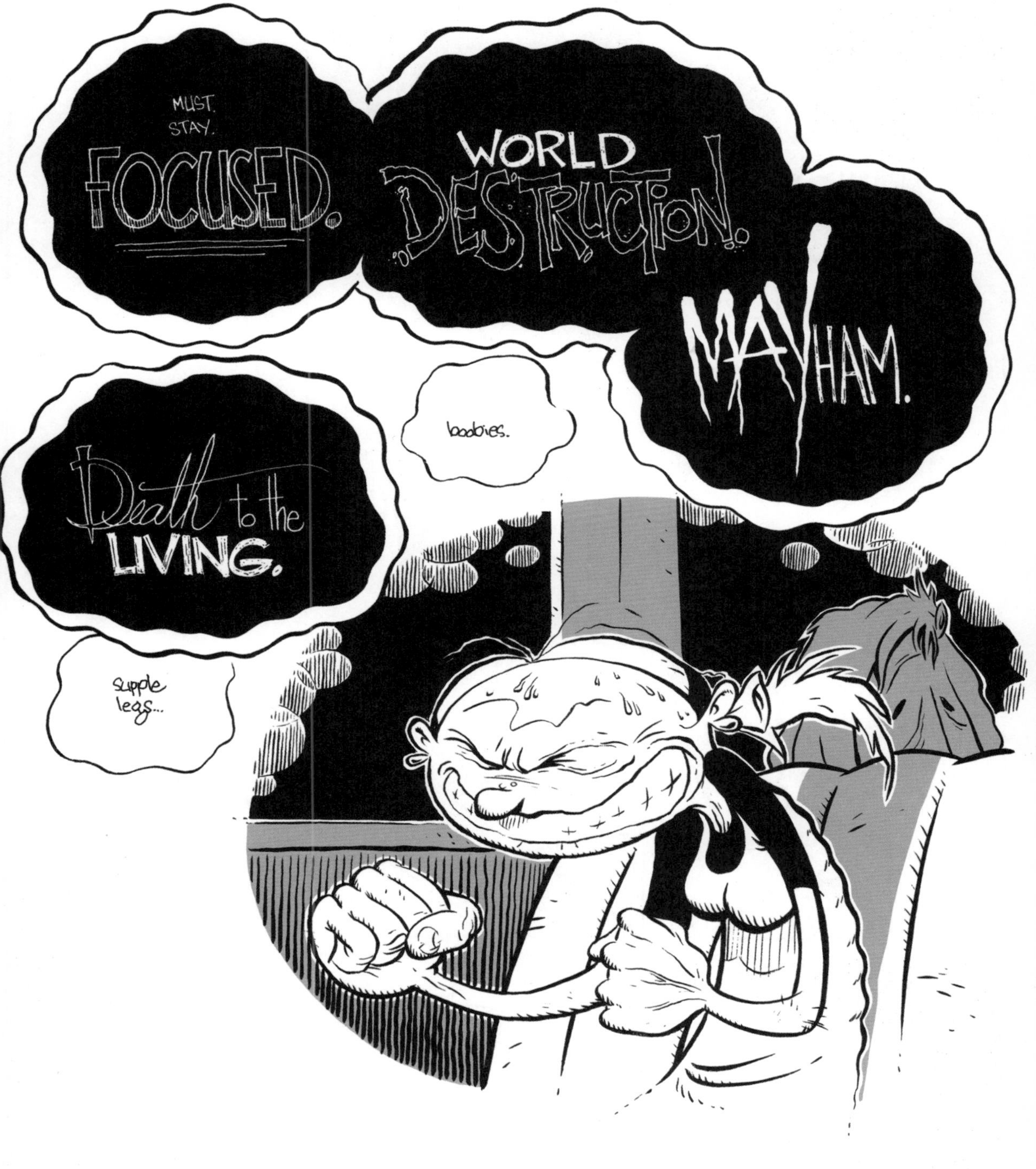

MUST. STAY. FOCUSED.
WORLD DESTRUCTION.
MAYHAM.
boobies.
Death to the LIVING.
supple legs...

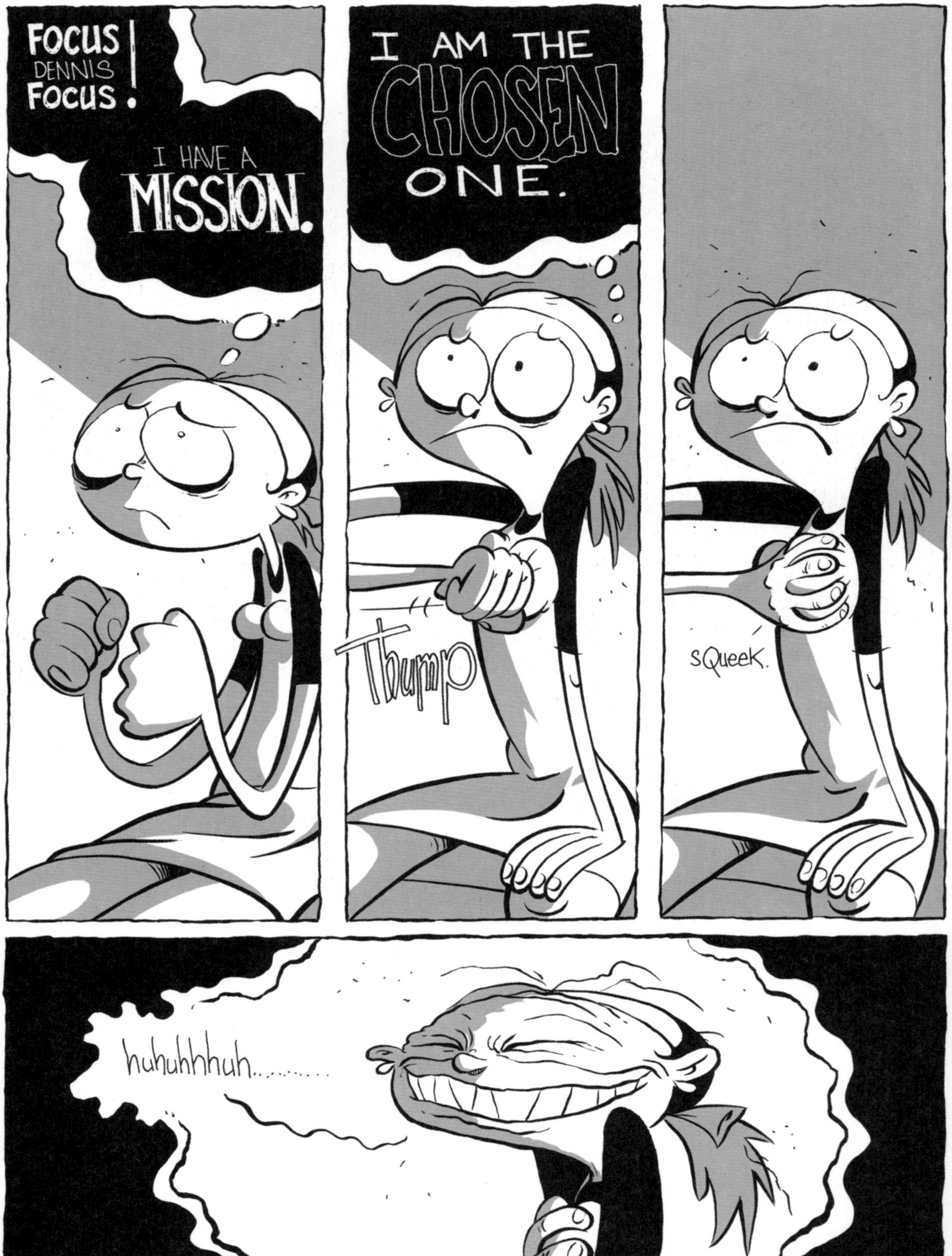
FOCUS DENNIS FOCUS!
I HAVE A MISSION.
I AM THE CHOSEN ONE.
Thump
sQueek.
huhuhhhuh..........

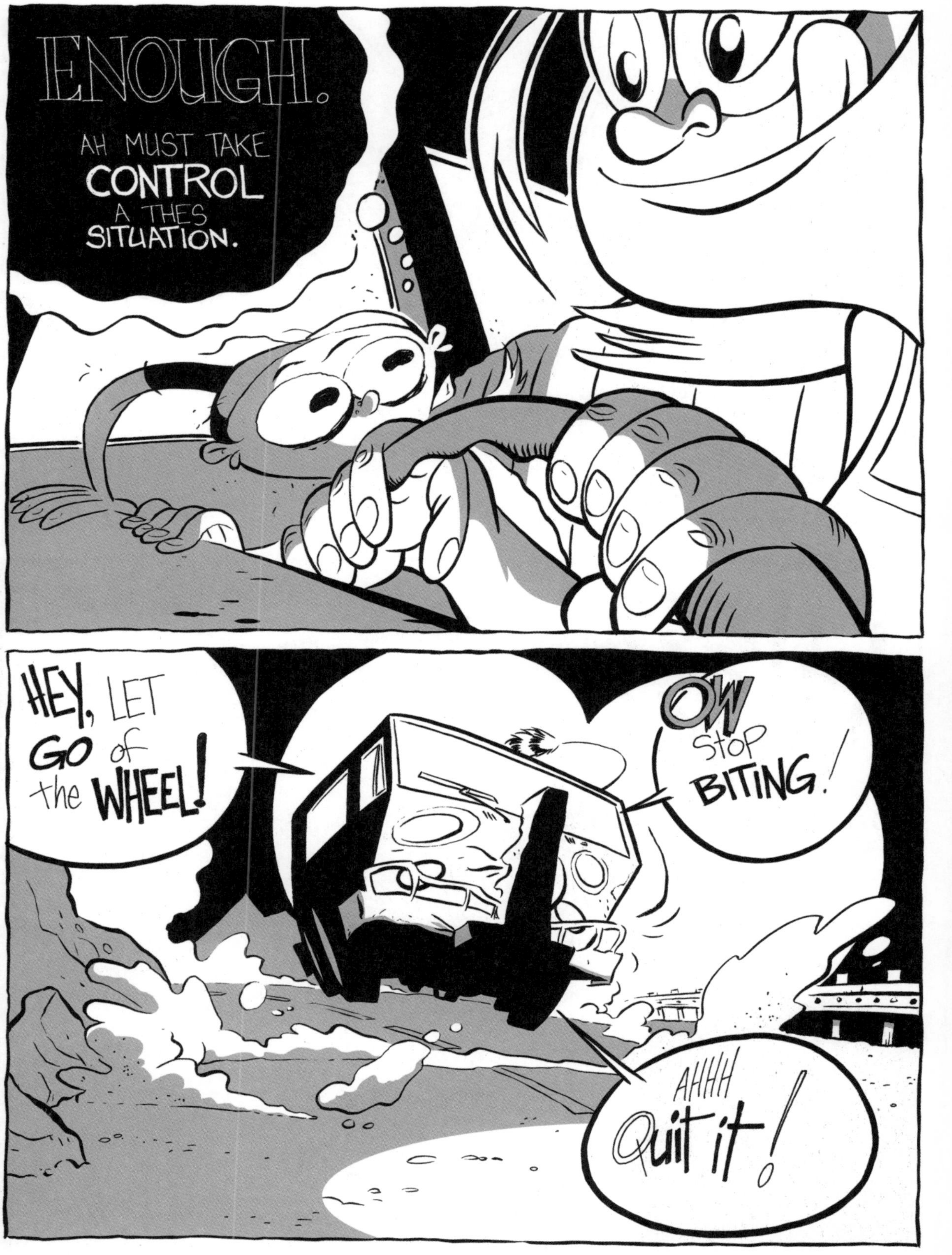
ENOUGH.
AH MUST TAKE CONTROL A THES SITUATION.
HEY, LET GO of the WHEEL!
OW Stop BITING!
AHHH Quit it!

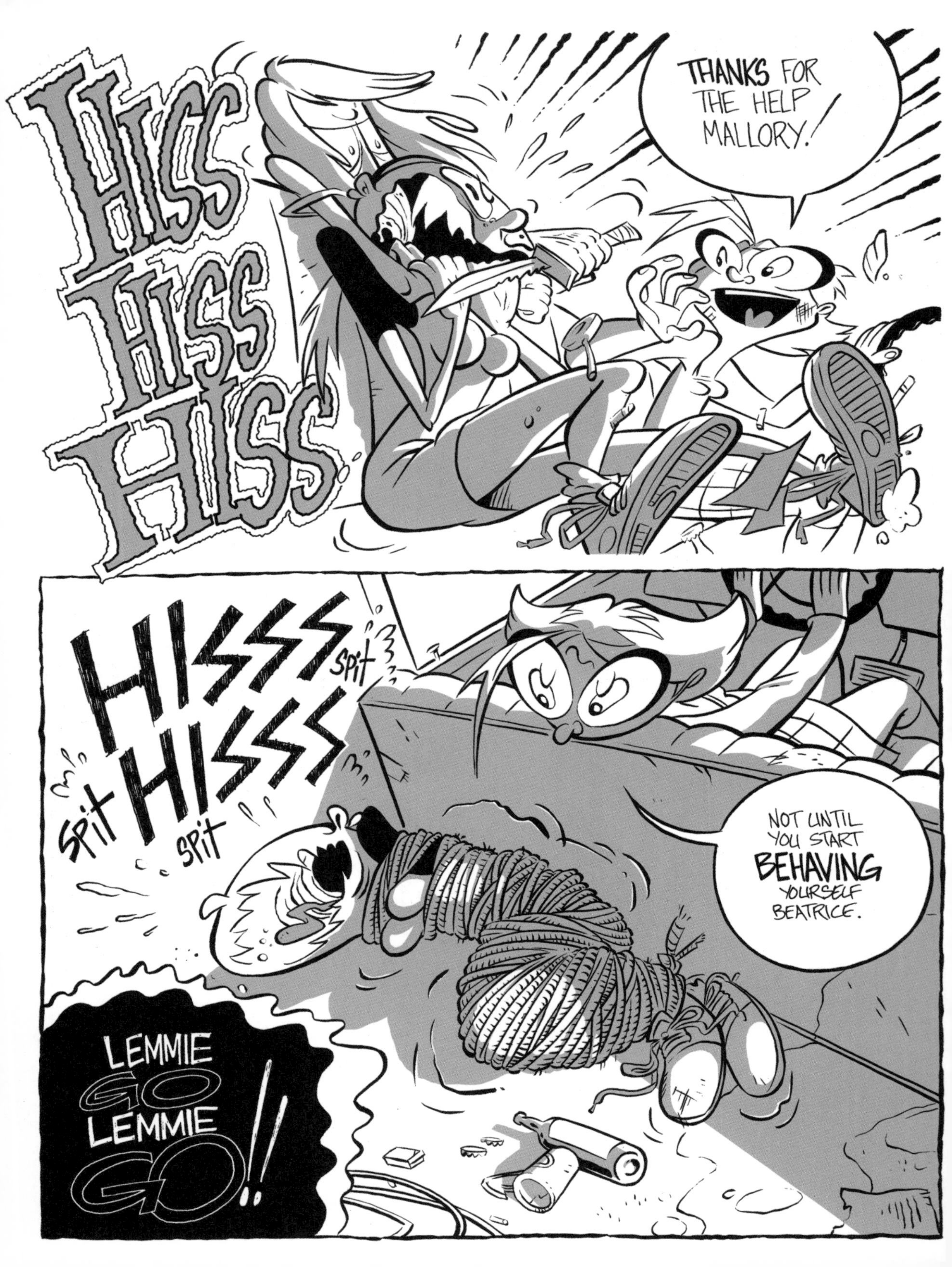
HISS HISS HISS
THANKS FOR THE HELP MALLORY!
HISSS spit HISSS spit spit spit
NOT UNTIL YOU START BEHAVING YOURSELF BEATRICE.
LEMMIE GO LEMMIE GO!!

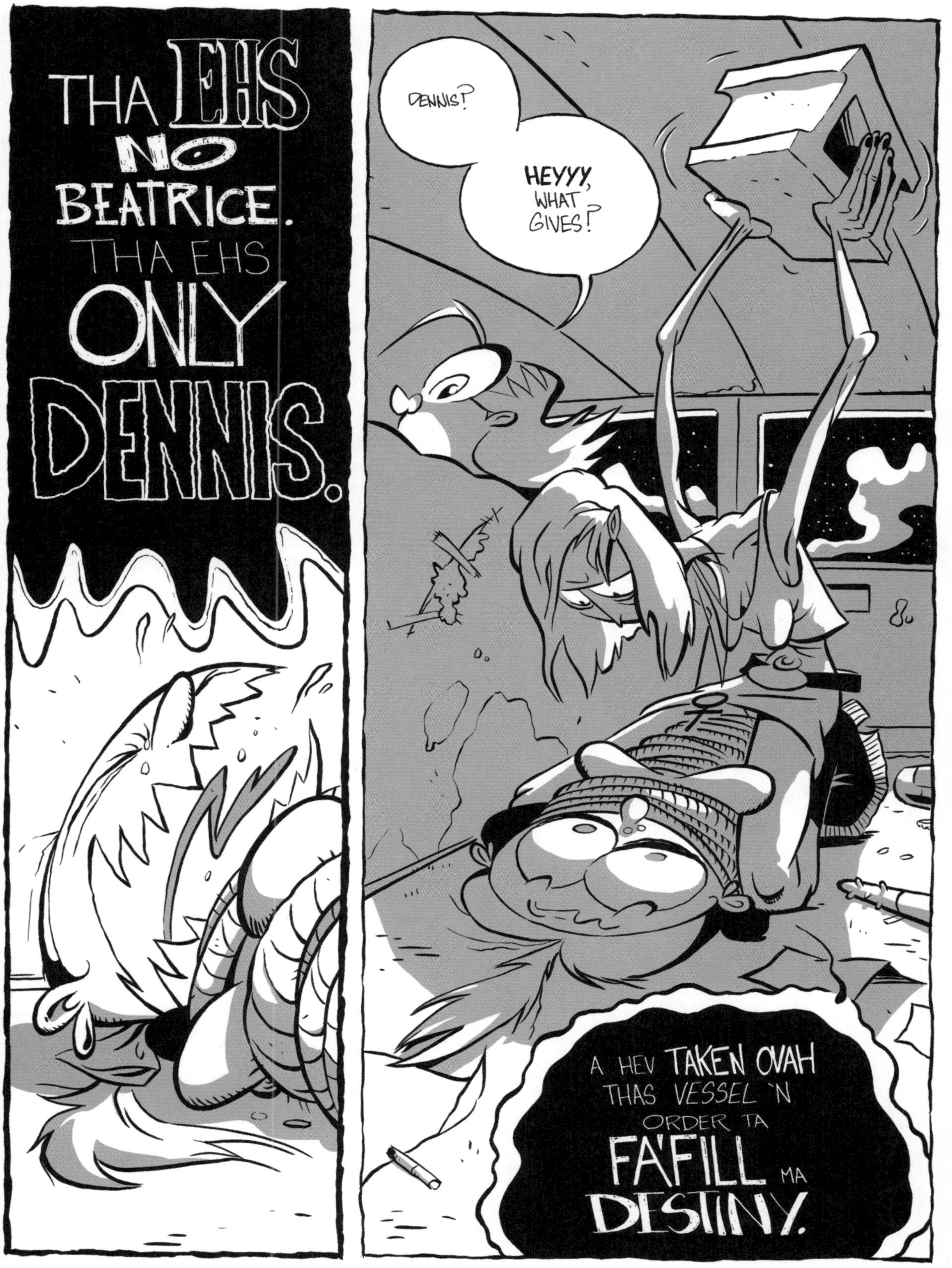
THA EHS NO BEATRICE.
THA EHS ONLY DENNIS.
DENNIS?
HEYYY, WHAT GIVES?
A HEV TAKEN OVAH THAS VESSEL 'N ORDER TA FA'FILL MA DESTINY.

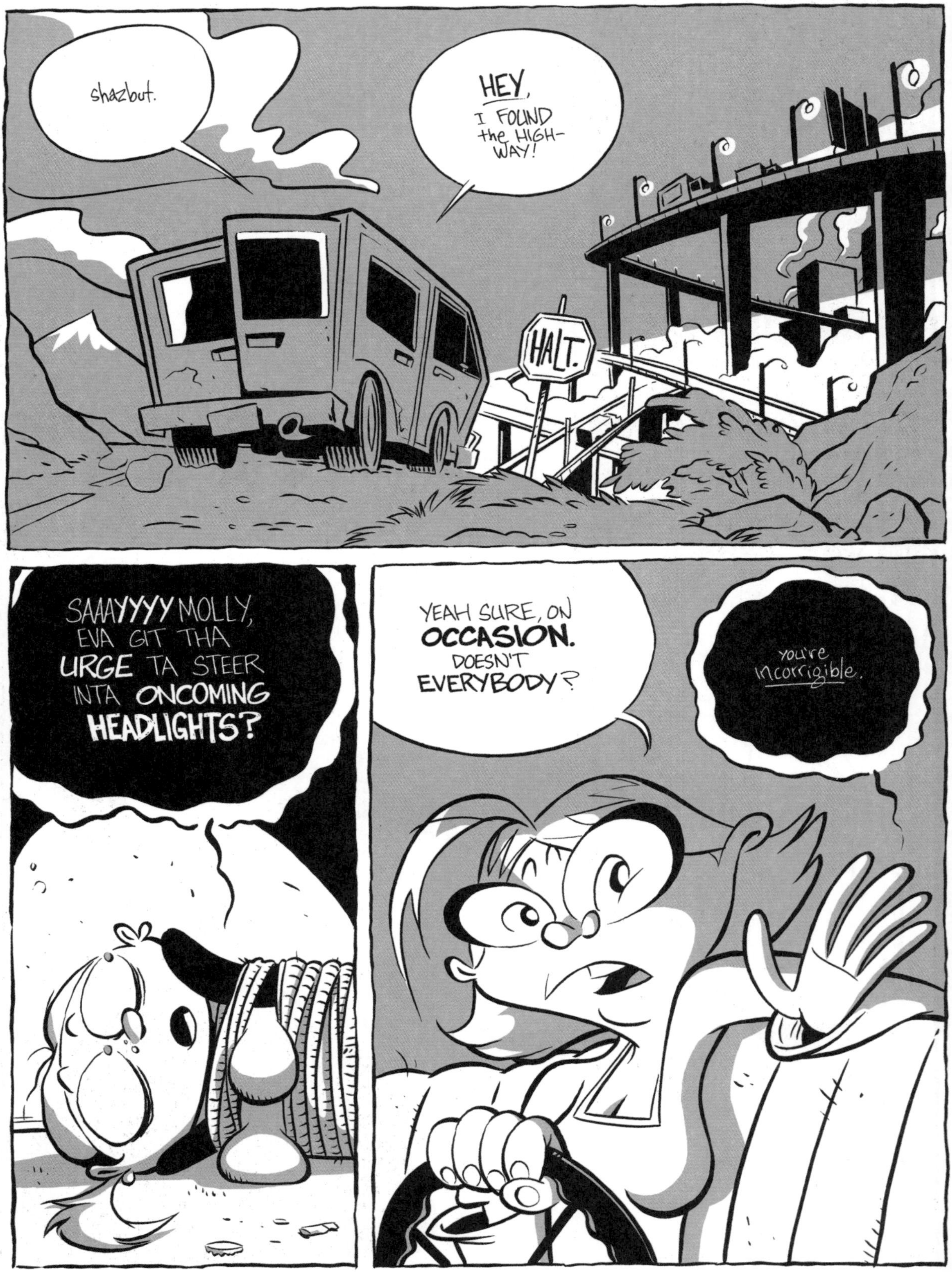
shazbut.
HEY, I FOUND the HIGH-WAY!
HALT.
SAAAYYYY MOLLY, EVA GIT THA URGE TA STEER INTA ONCOMING HEADLIGHTS?
YEAH SURE, ON OCCASION. DOESN'T EVERYBODY?
you're incorrigible.

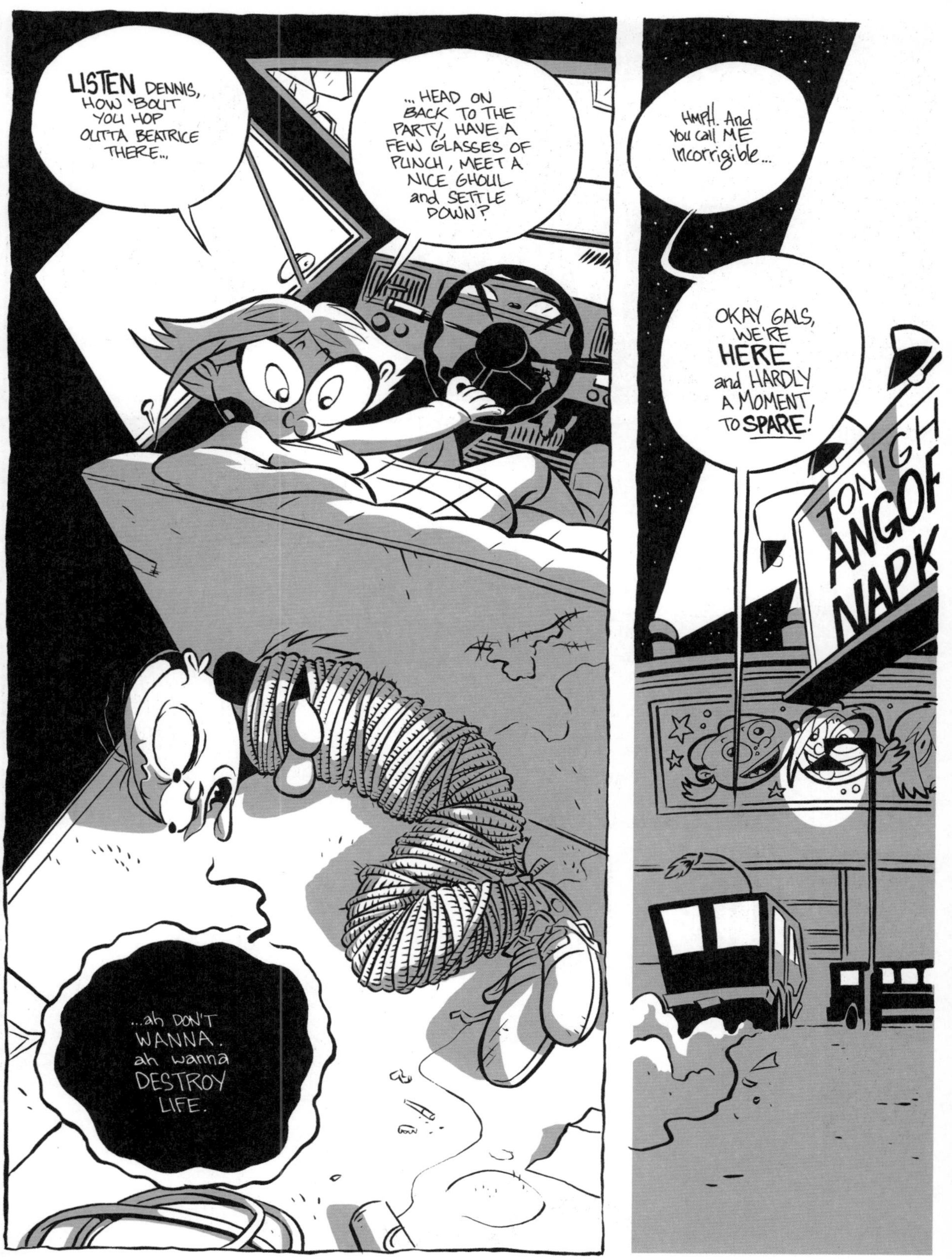
LISTEN DENNIS, HOW 'BOUT YOU HOP OUTTA BEATRICE THERE...
... HEAD ON BACK TO THE PARTY, HAVE A FEW GLASSES OF PUNCH, MEET A NICE GHOUL and SETTLE DOWN?
...ah DON'T WANNA. ah wanna DESTROY LIFE.
HMPH. And You call ME incorrigible...
OKAY GALS, WE'RE HERE and HARDLY A MOMENT TO SPARE!
TONIGH
ANGOR
NAPK

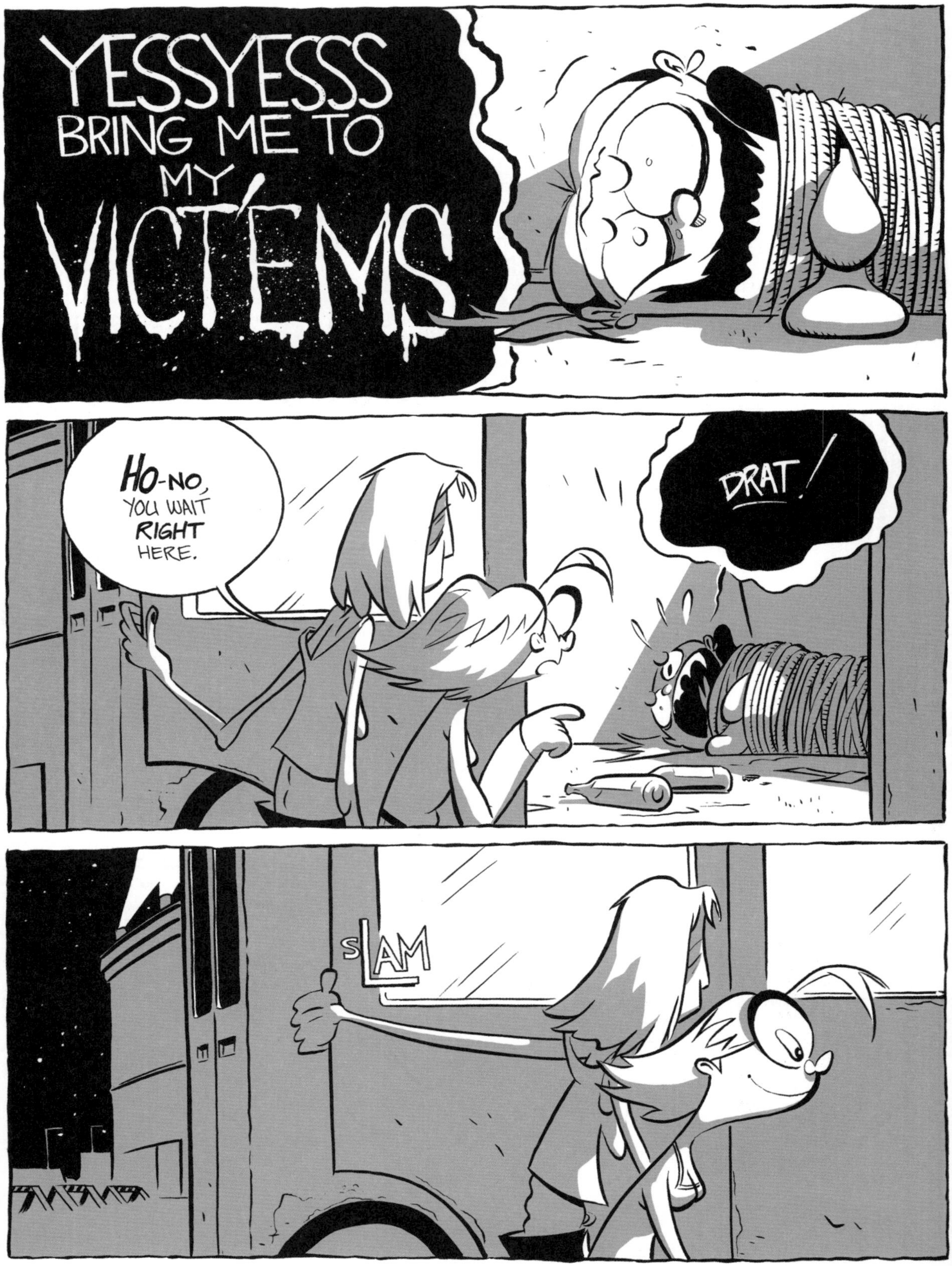
YESSYESSS BRING ME TO MY VICT'EMS
HO-NO, YOU WAIT RIGHT HERE.
DRAT!
SLAM

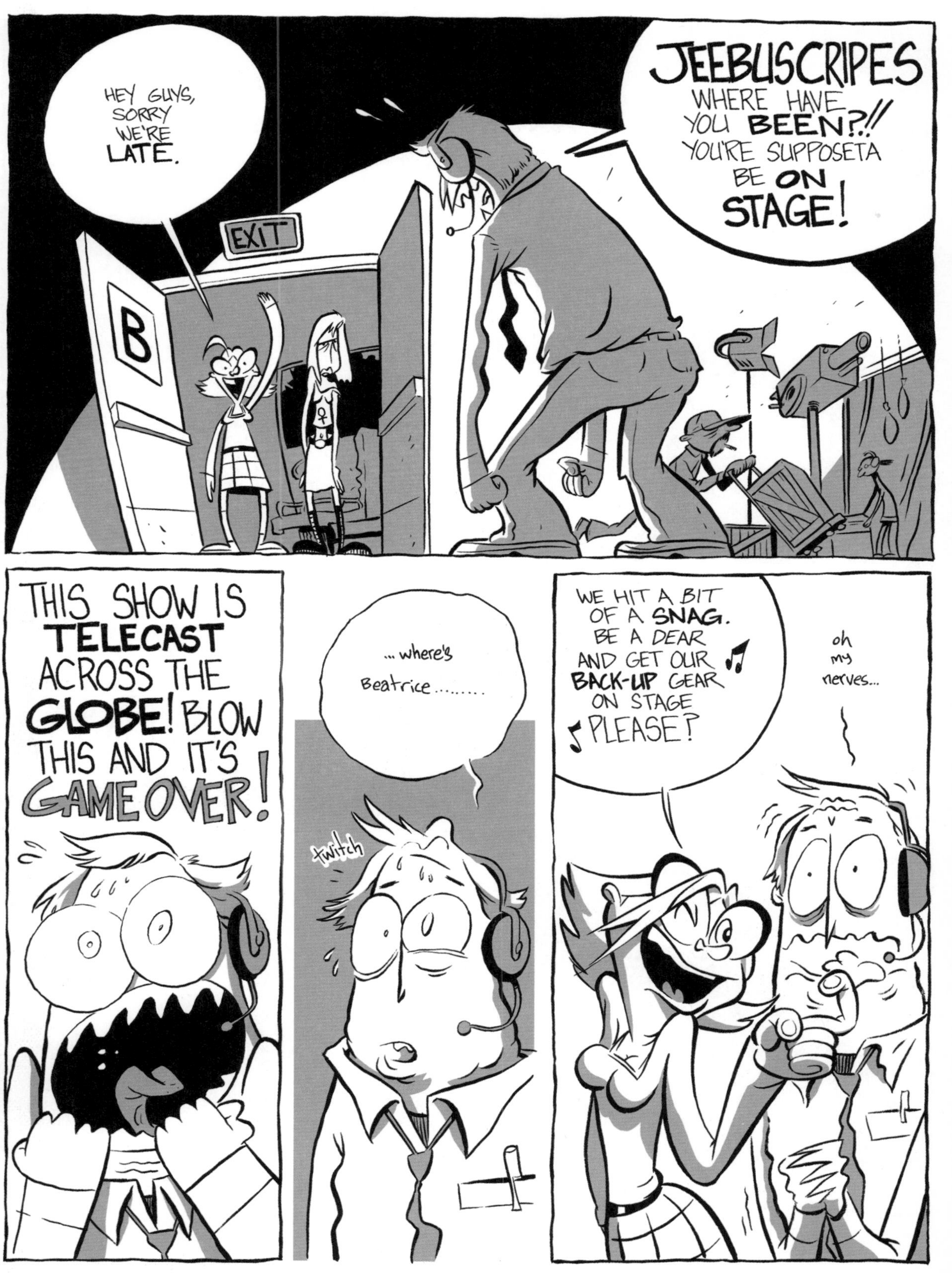
HEY GUYS, SORRY WE'RE LATE.
EXIT
B
JEEBUSCRIPES WHERE HAVE YOU BEEN?!! YOU'RE SUPPOSETA BE ON STAGE!
THIS SHOW IS TELECAST ACROSS THE GLOBE! BLOW THIS AND IT'S GAME OVER!
... where's Beatrice.........
twitch
WE HIT A BIT OF A SNAG. BE A DEAR AND GET OUR BACK-UP GEAR ON STAGE PLEASE?
oh my nerves...

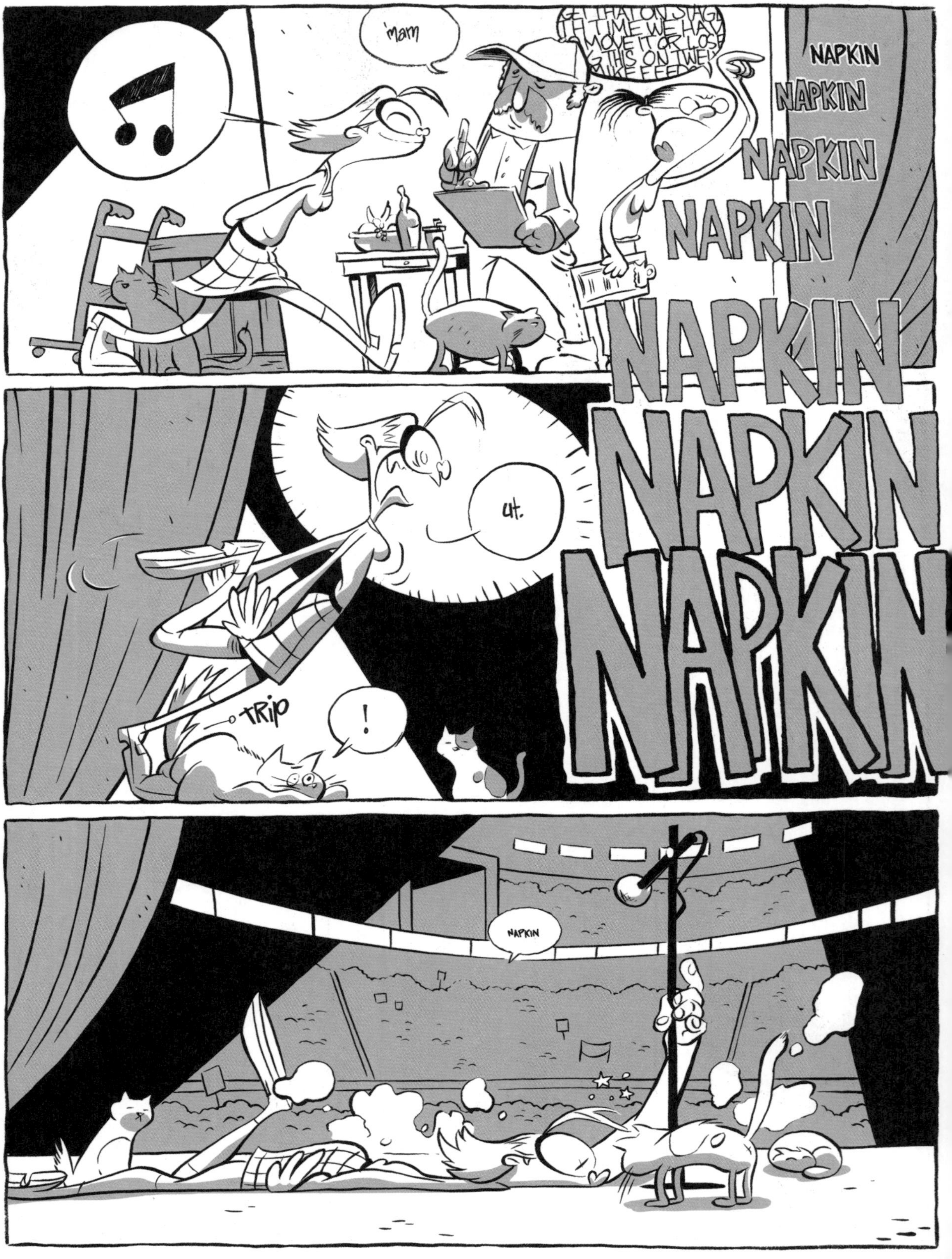

'mam
GET THAT ON STAG
H TIME WE HAV
MOVE IT OR LOS
G THIS ON TWE
MIKE FEED
NAPKIN
NAPKIN
NAPKIN
NAPKIN
NAPKIN
NAPKIN
NAPKIN
uh.
TRIP
!
NAPKIN

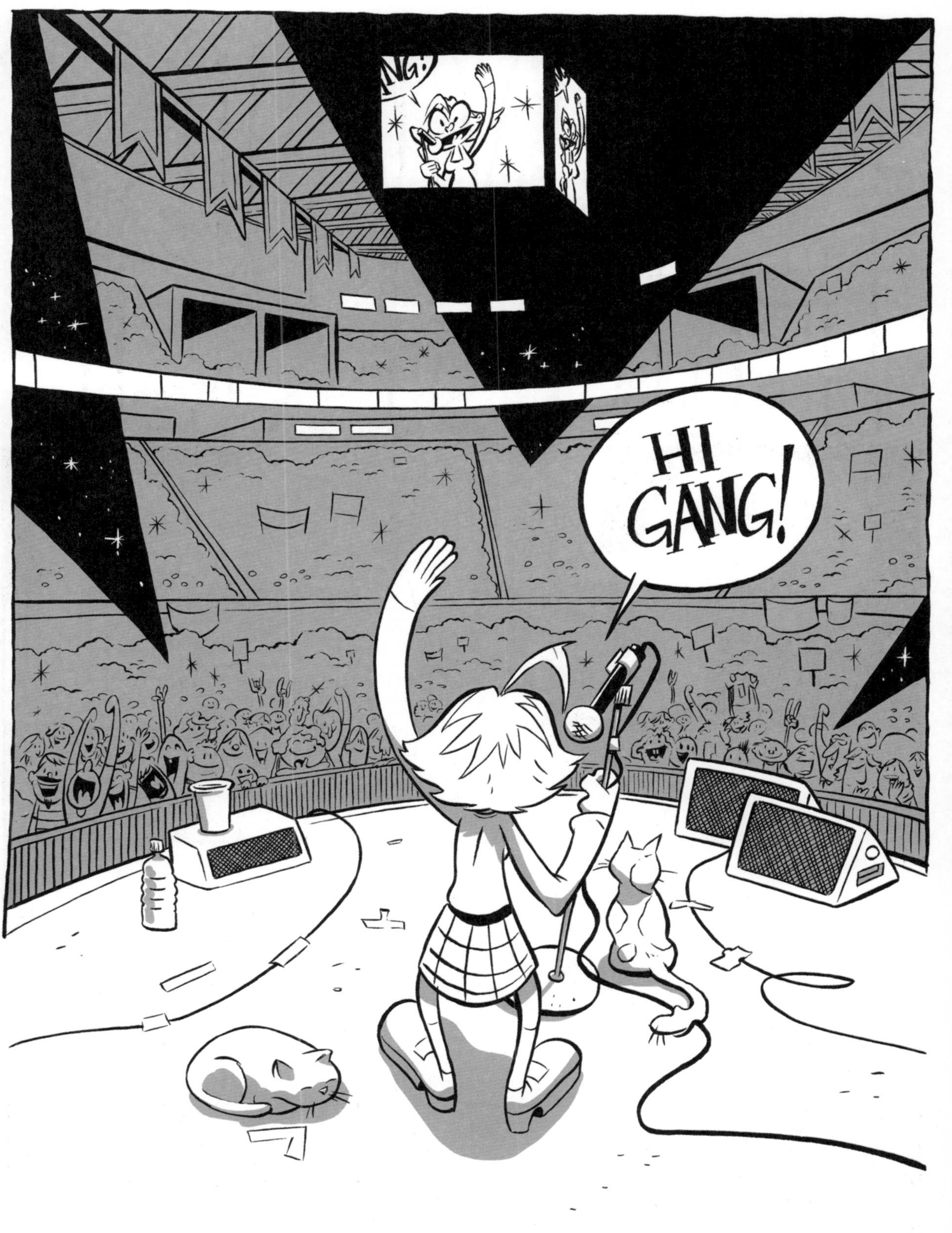
HI GANG!

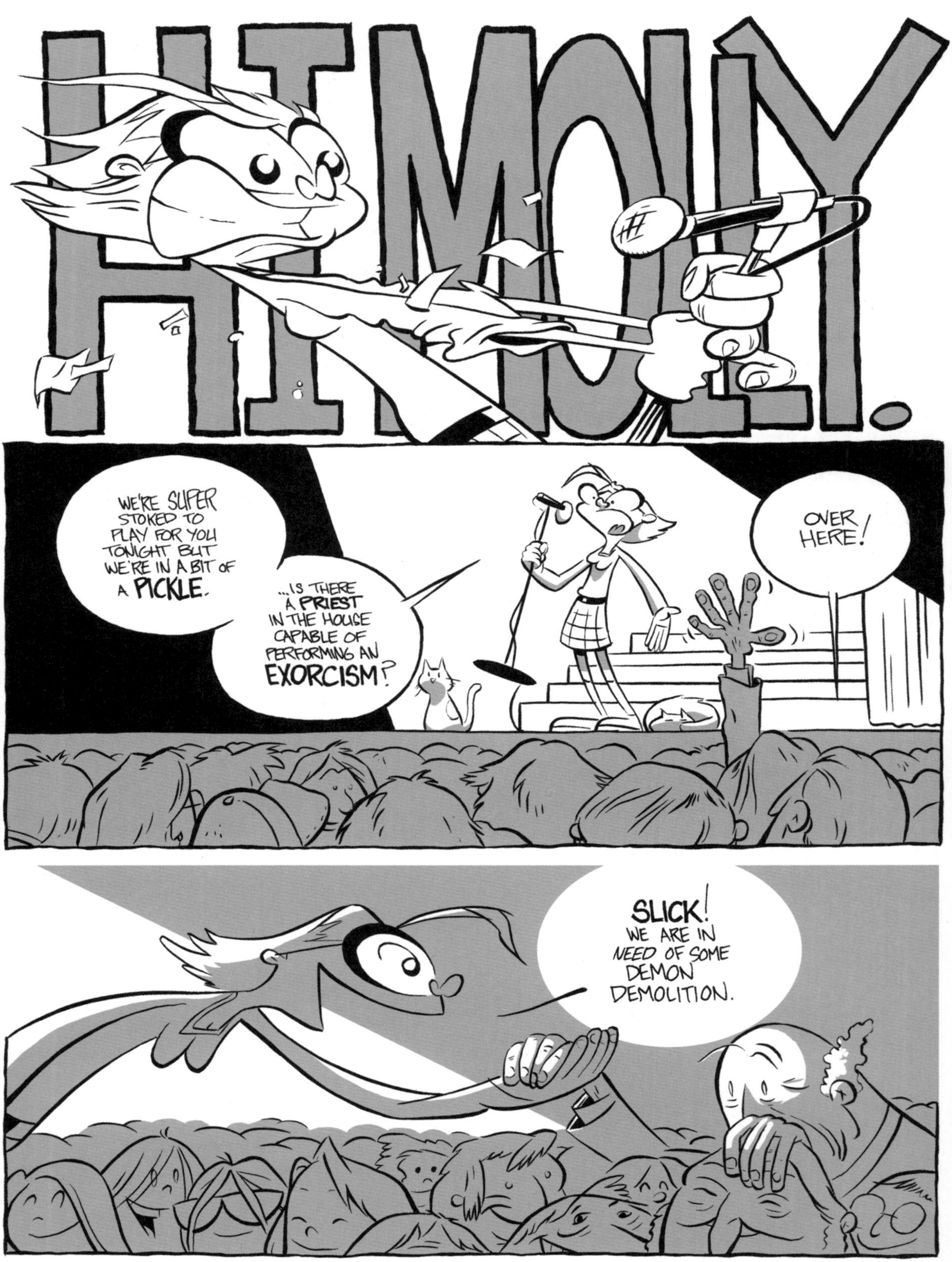
HI MOLLY.
WE'RE SUPER STOKED TO PLAY FOR YOU TONIGHT BUT WE'RE IN A BIT OF A PICKLE.
...IS THERE A PRIEST IN THE HOUSE CAPABLE OF PERFORMING AN EXORCISM?
OVER HERE!
SLICK! WE ARE IN NEED OF SOME DEMON DEMOLITION.

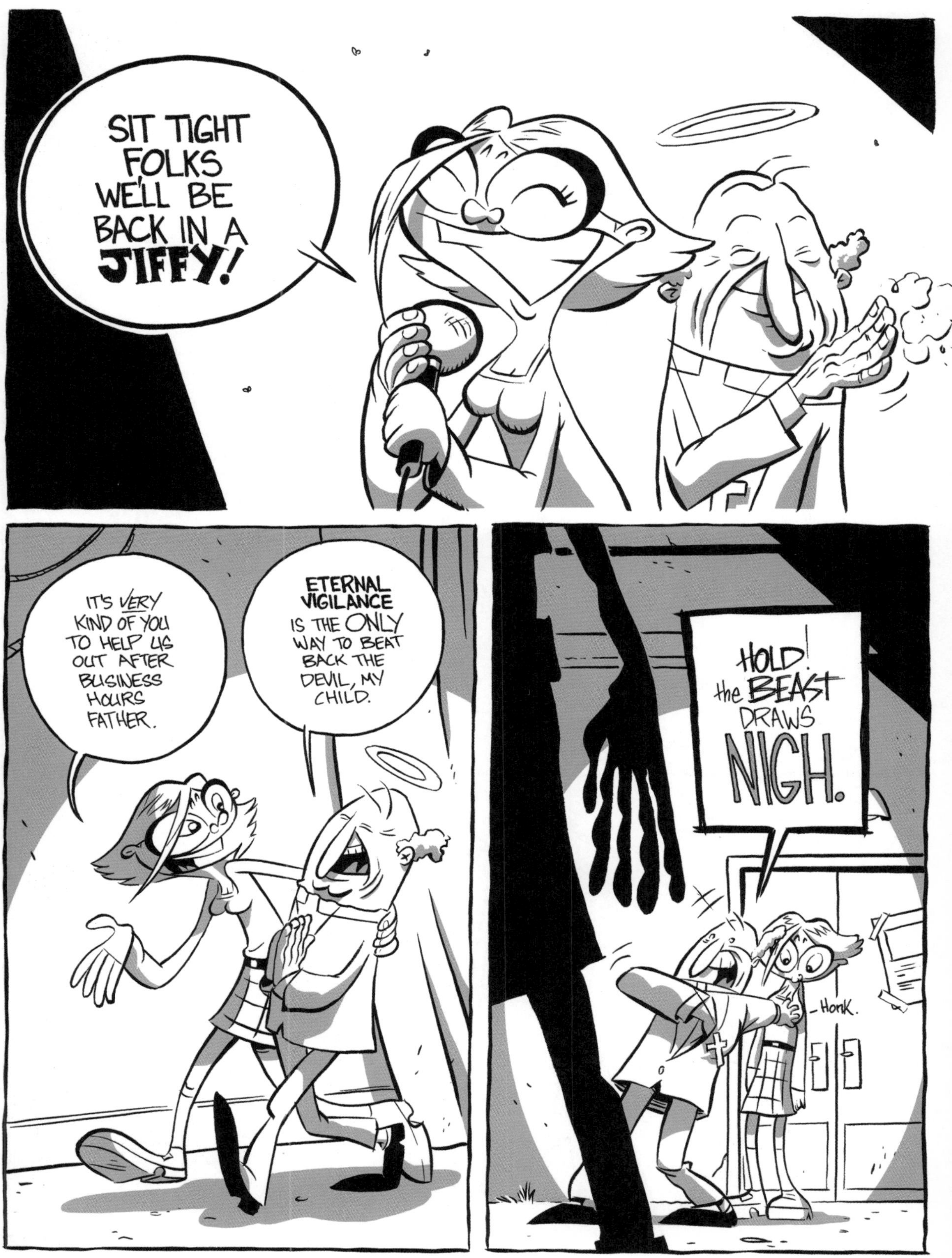
SIT TIGHT FOLKS WE'LL BE BACK IN A JIFFY!
IT'S VERY KIND OF YOU TO HELP US OUT AFTER BUSINESS HOURS FATHER.
ETERNAL VIGILANCE IS THE ONLY WAY TO BEAT BACK THE DEVIL, MY CHILD.
HOLD! the BEAST DRAWS NIGH.
-Honk.

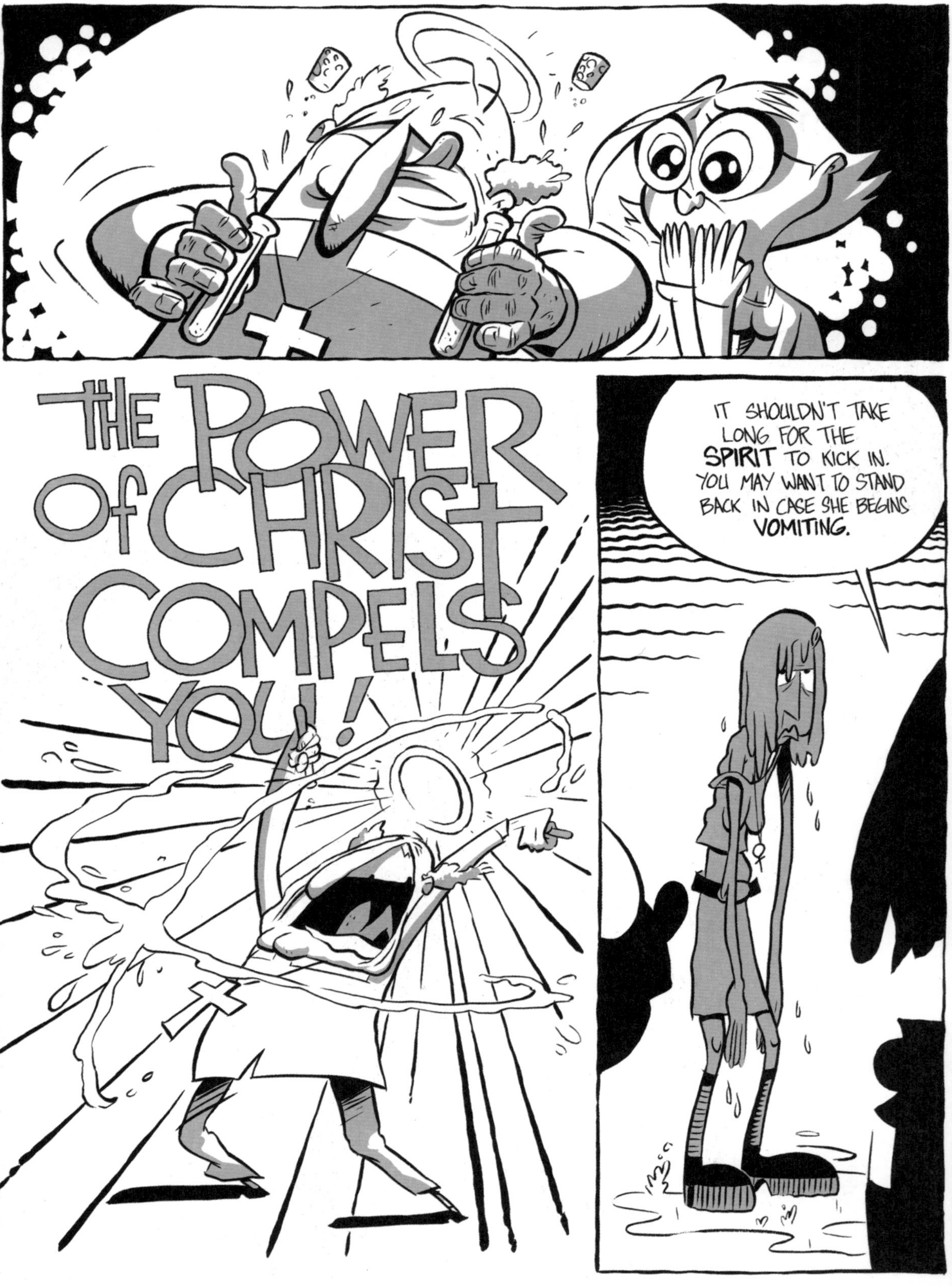
THE POWER OF CHRIST COMPELS YOU!
IT SHOULDN'T TAKE LONG FOR THE SPIRIT TO KICK IN. YOU MAY WANT TO STAND BACK IN CASE SHE BEGINS VOMITING.

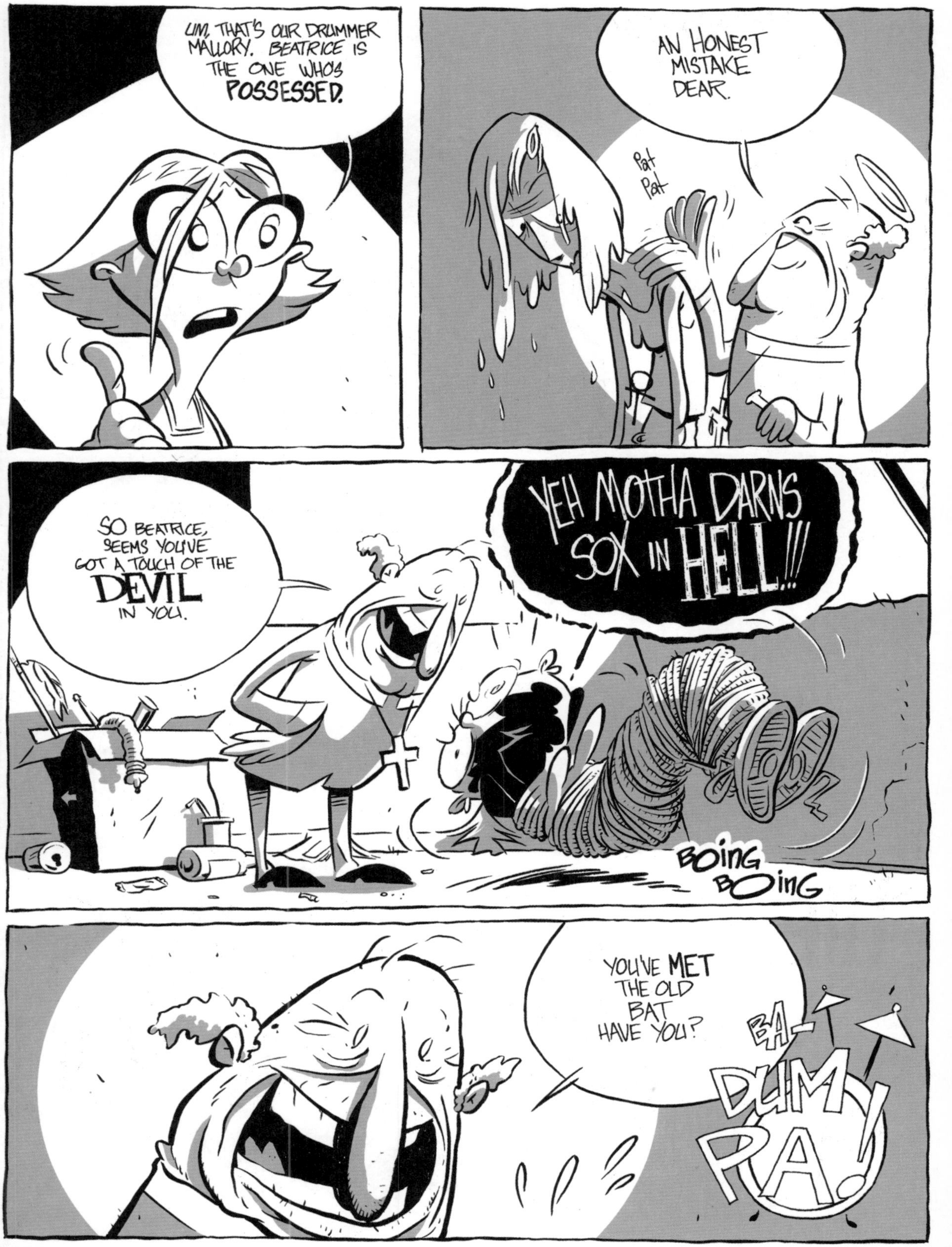
UM, THAT'S OUR DRUMMER MALLORY. BEATRICE IS THE ONE WHO'S POSSESSED.
AN HONEST MISTAKE DEAR.
Pat Pat
SO BEATRICE, SEEMS YOU'VE GOT A TOUCH OF THE DEVIL IN YOU.
YEH MOTHA DARNS SOX IN HELL!!!
BOING BOING
YOU'VE MET THE OLD BAT HAVE YOU?
BA-DUM PA!

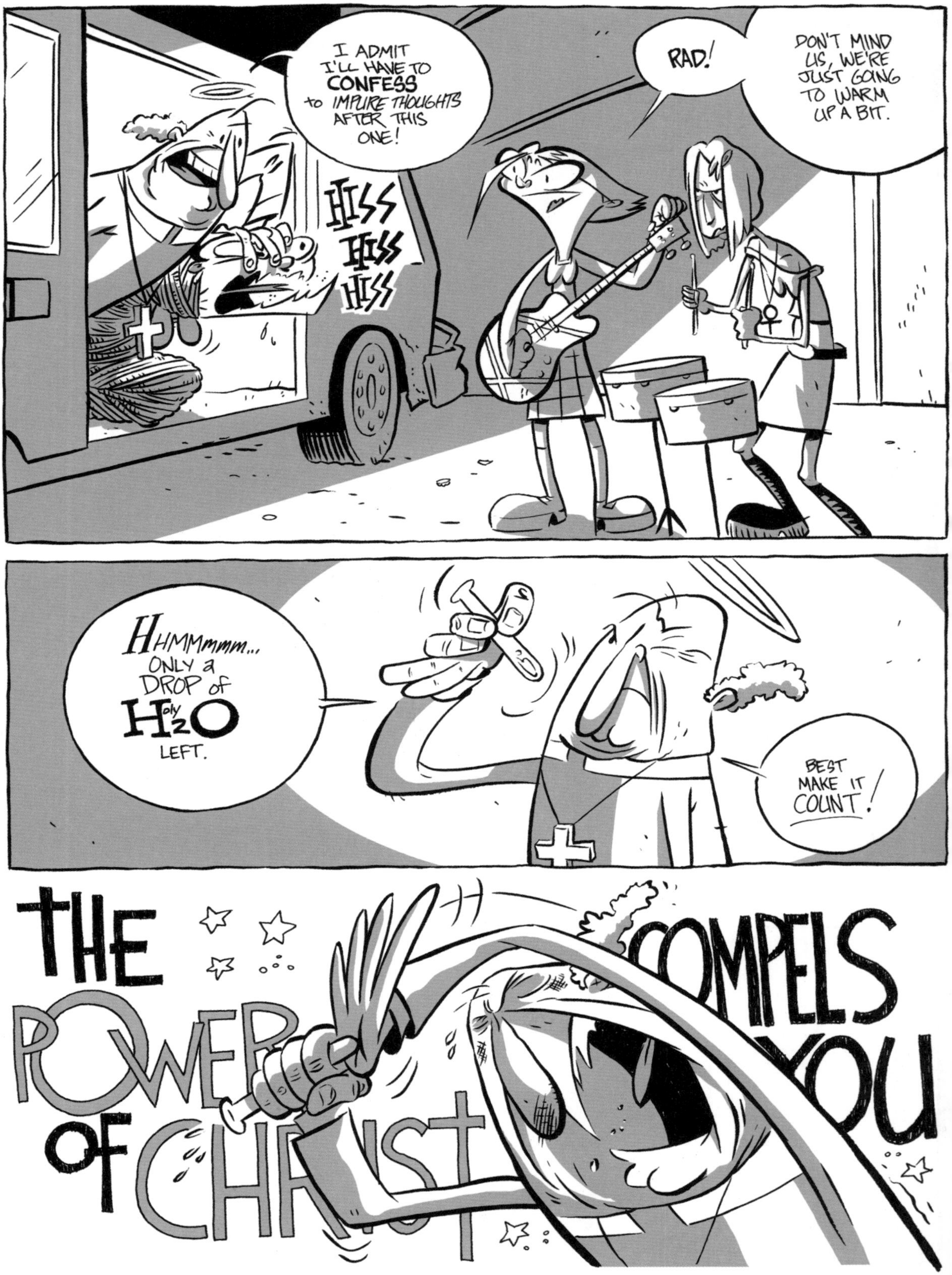
I ADMIT I'LL HAVE TO CONFESS to IMPURE THOUGHTS AFTER THIS ONE!
HISS HISS HISS
RAD!
DON'T MIND US, WE'RE JUST GOING TO WARM UP A BIT.
HHMMmmm... ONLY a DROP of H(oly)2O LEFT.
BEST MAKE IT COUNT!
THE POWER OF CHRIST COMPELS YOU

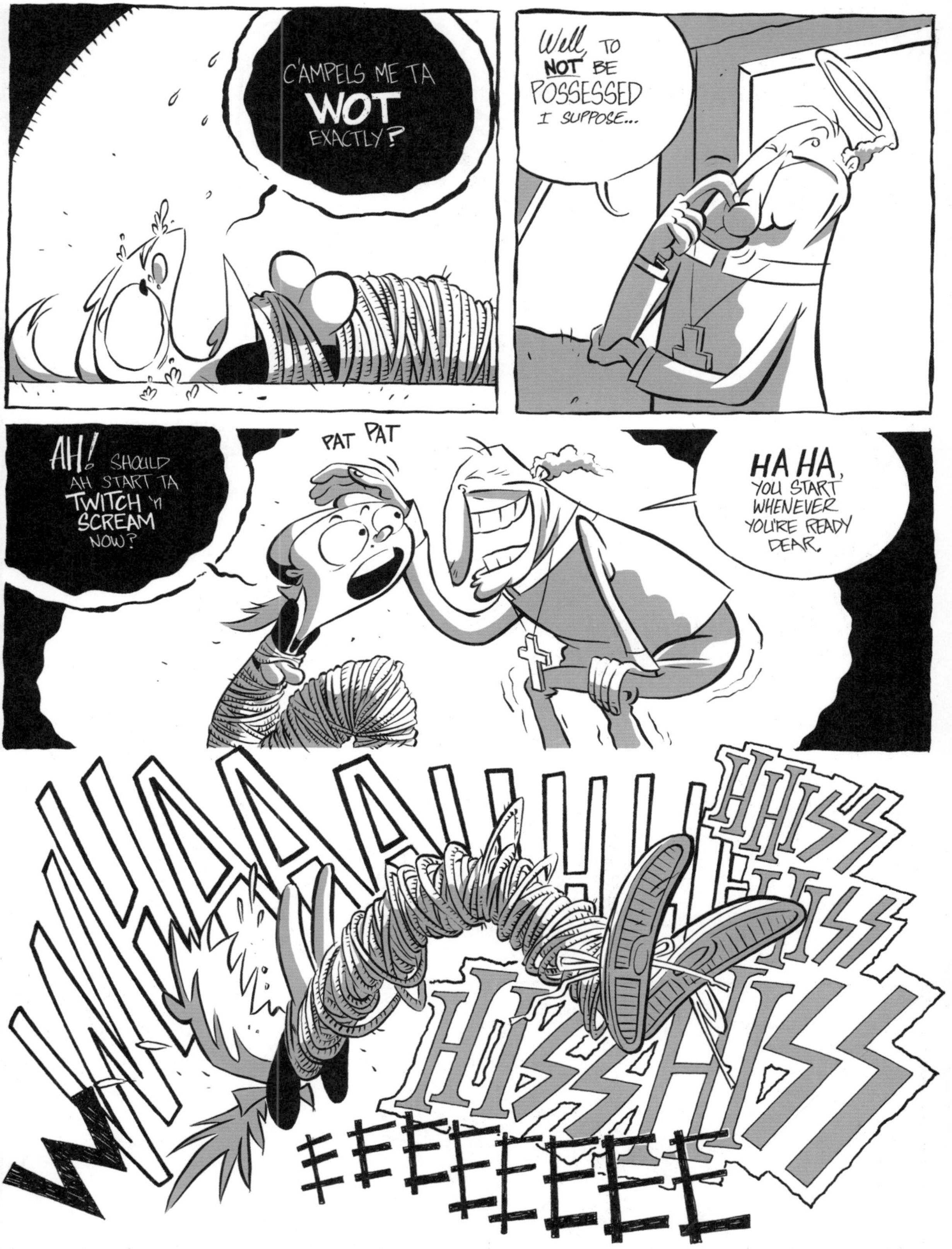

C'AMPELS ME TA WOT EXACTLY?
Well, TO NOT BE POSSESSED I SUPPOSE...
AH! SHOULD AH START TA TWITCH 'N SCREAM NOW?
PAT PAT
HA HA, YOU START WHENEVER YOU'RE READY DEAR.
HHISS HISS HISS HISS
EEEEEEEE

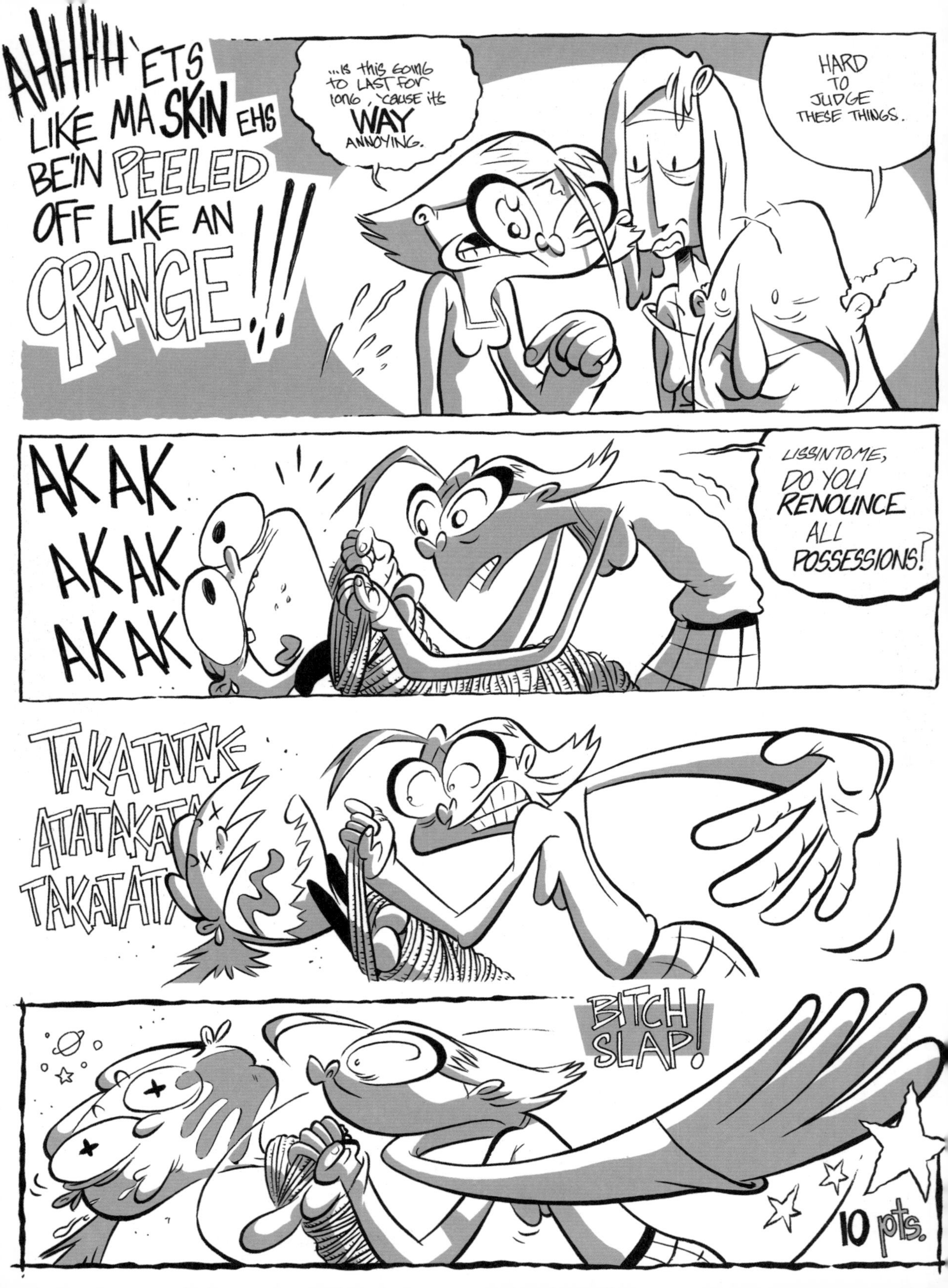
AHHHH `ETS LIKE MA SKIN EHS BE'IN PEELED OFF LIKE AN ORANGE!!
...is this going to LAST for long, 'cause it's WAY ANNOYING.
HARD TO JUDGE THESE THINGS.
AK AK AKAK AKAK
LISSINTOME, DO YOU RENOUNCE ALL POSSESSIONS?
TAKATATAK-ATATAKATA TAKATATA
BITCH SLAP!
10 pts.

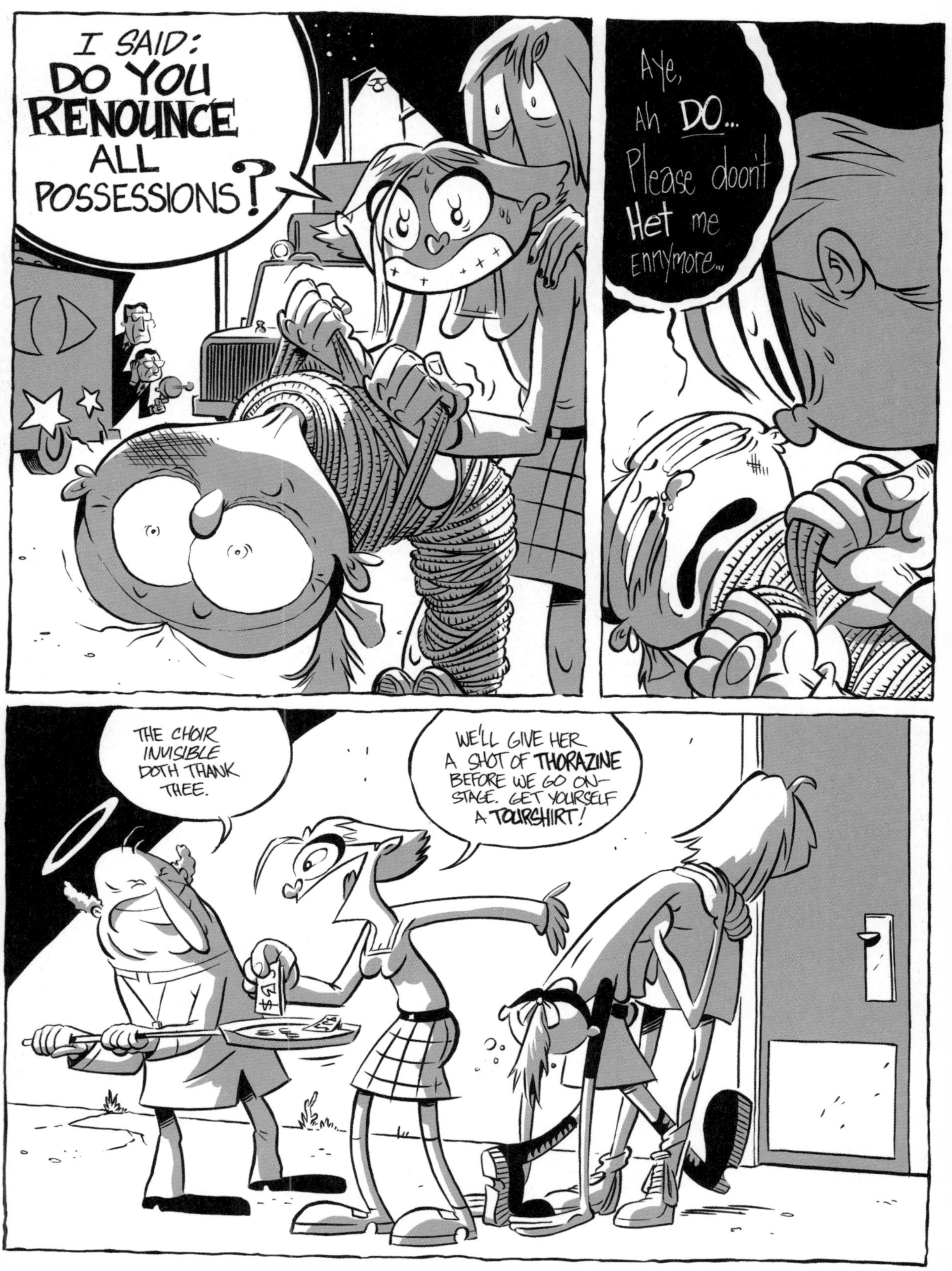
I SAID: DO YOU RENOUNCE ALL POSSESSIONS?
Aye, Ah DO... Please doon't Het me ennymore...
THE CHOIR INVISIBLE DOTH THANK THEE.
WE'LL GIVE HER A SHOT OF THORAZINE BEFORE WE GO ON-STAGE. GET YOURSELF A TOURSHIRT!

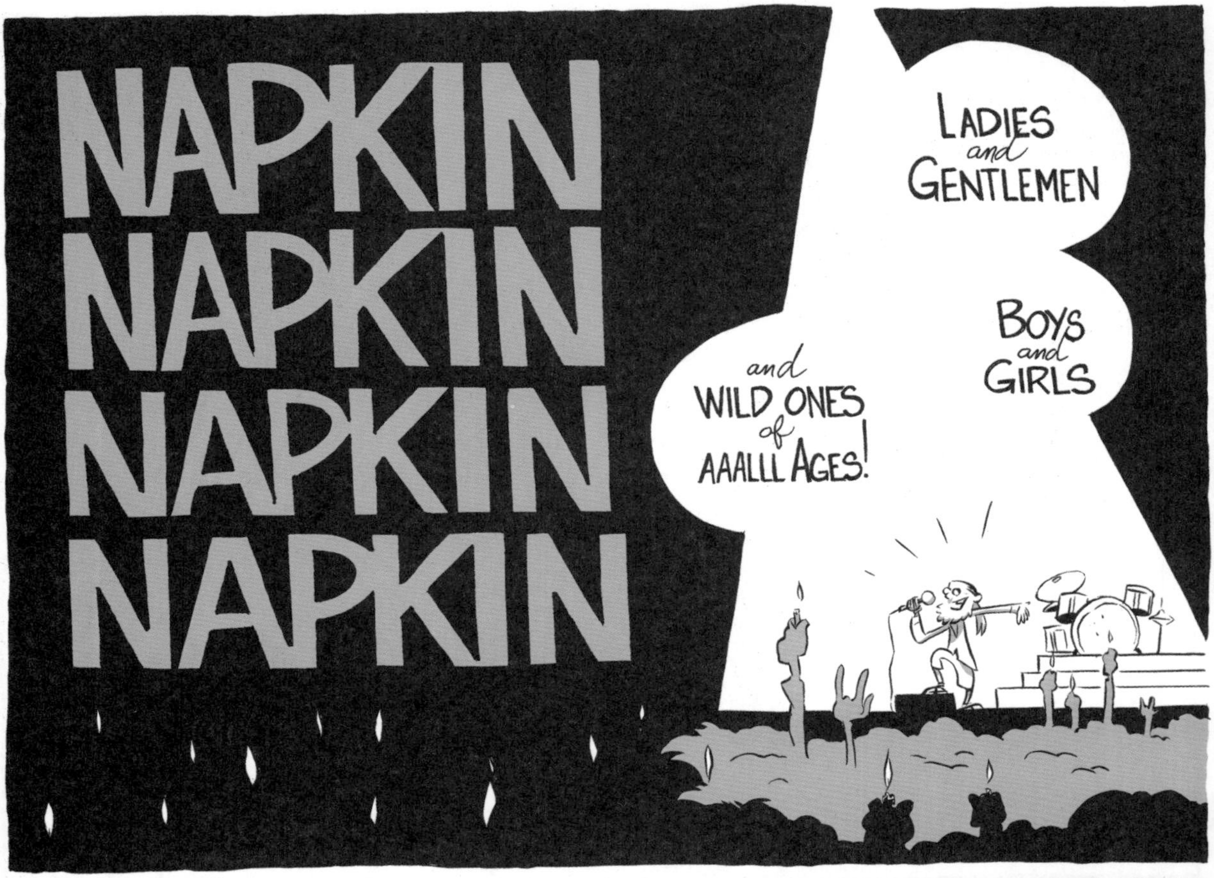
NAPKIN NAPKIN NAPKIN NAPKIN
LADIES and GENTLEMEN
BOYS and GIRLS
and WILD ONES of AAALLL AGES!

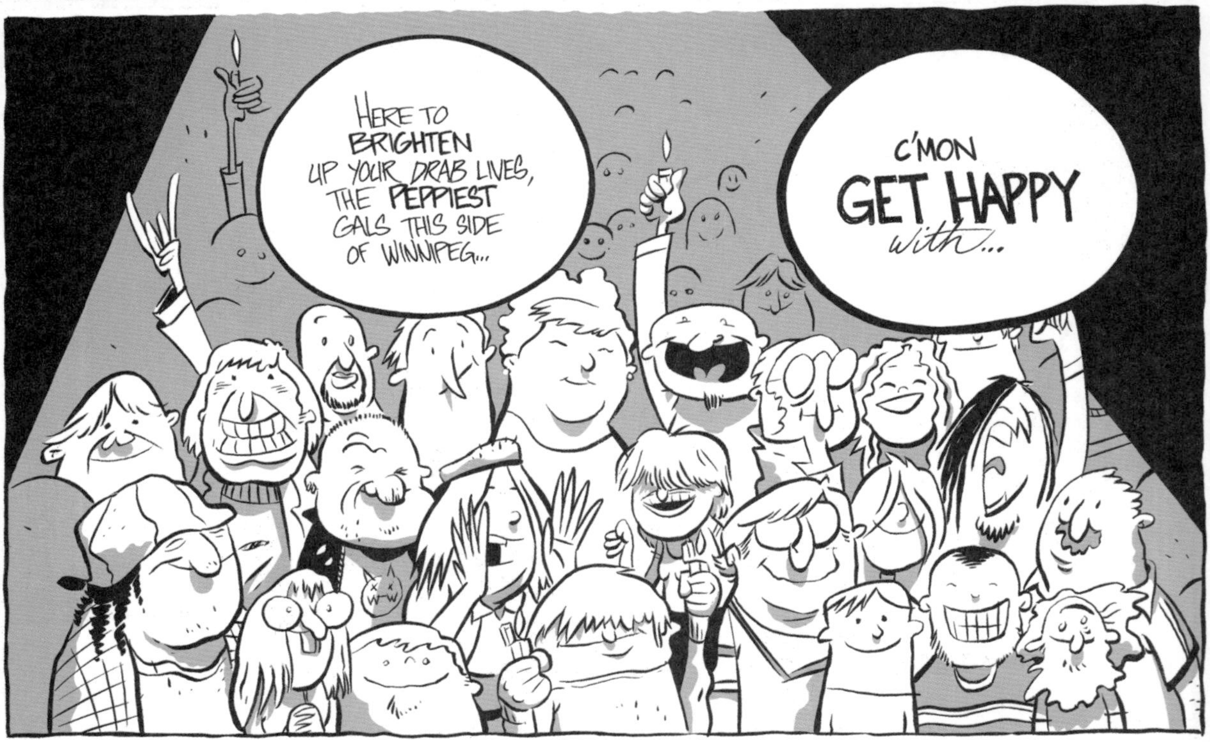
HERE TO BRIGHTEN UP YOUR DRAB LIVES, THE PEPPIEST GALS THIS SIDE OF WINNIPEG...
C'MON GET HAPPY with...

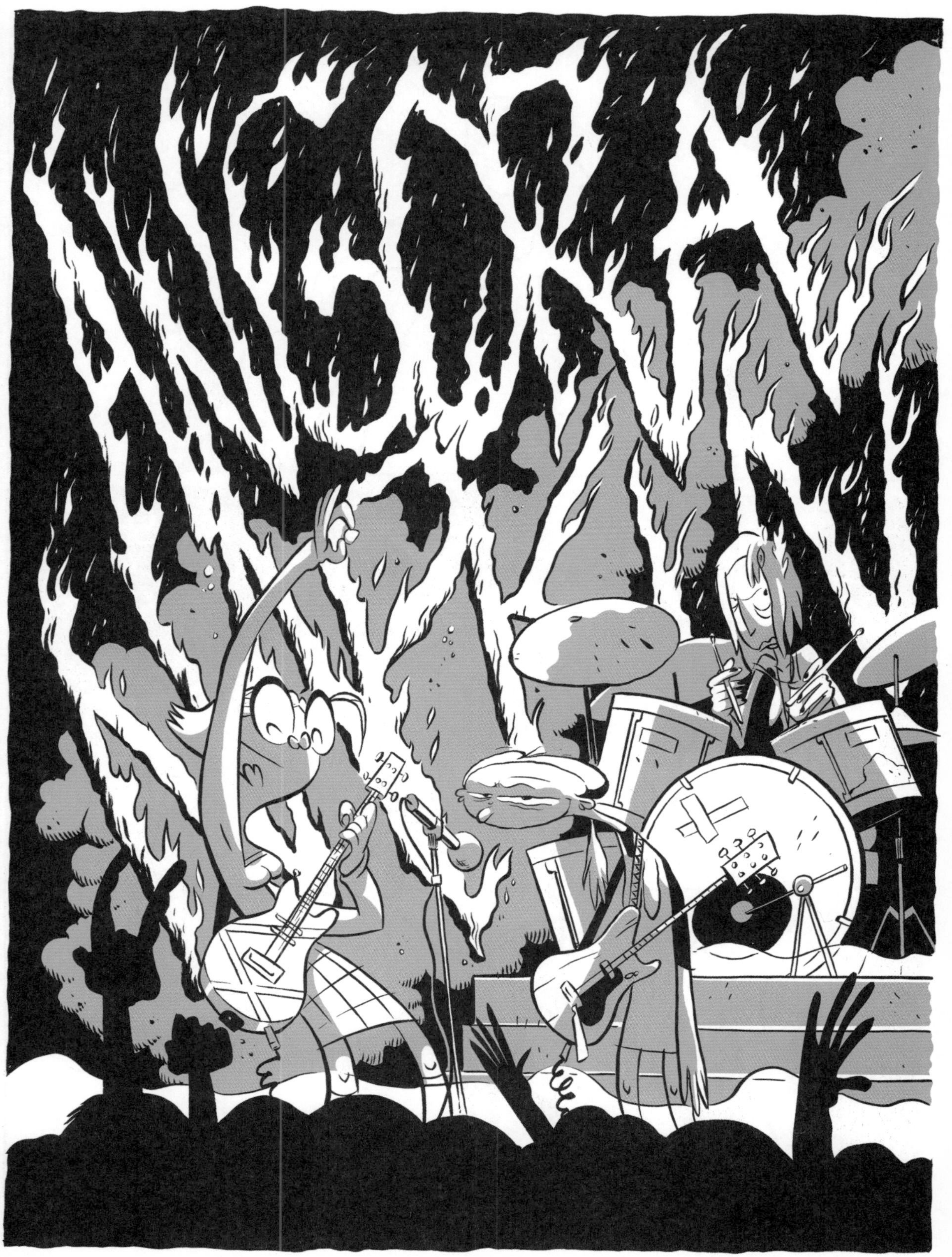

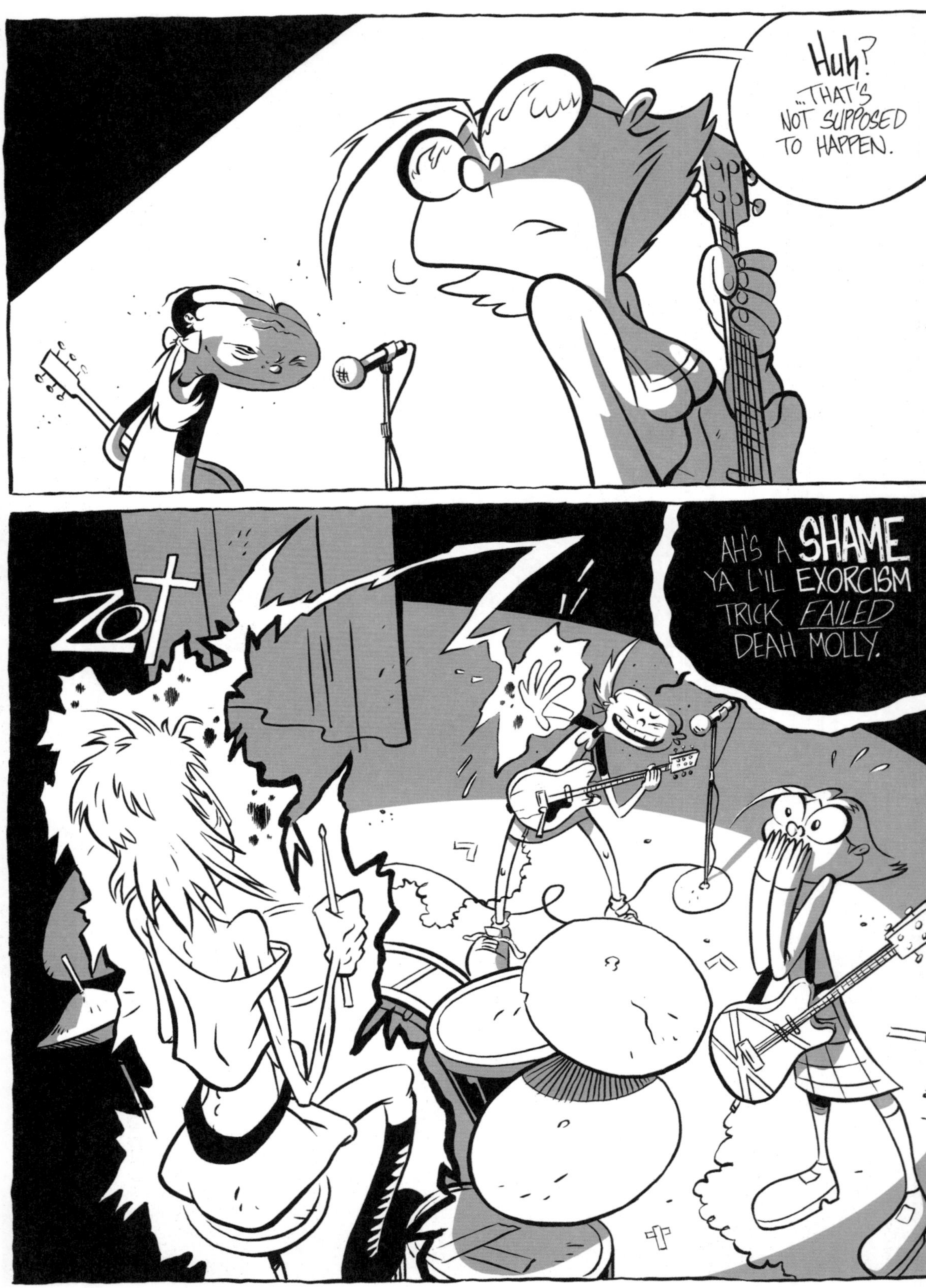
Huh? ...THAT'S NOT SUPPOSED TO HAPPEN.
ZOT
AH'S A SHAME YA L'IL EXORCISM TRICK FAILED DEAH MOLLY.

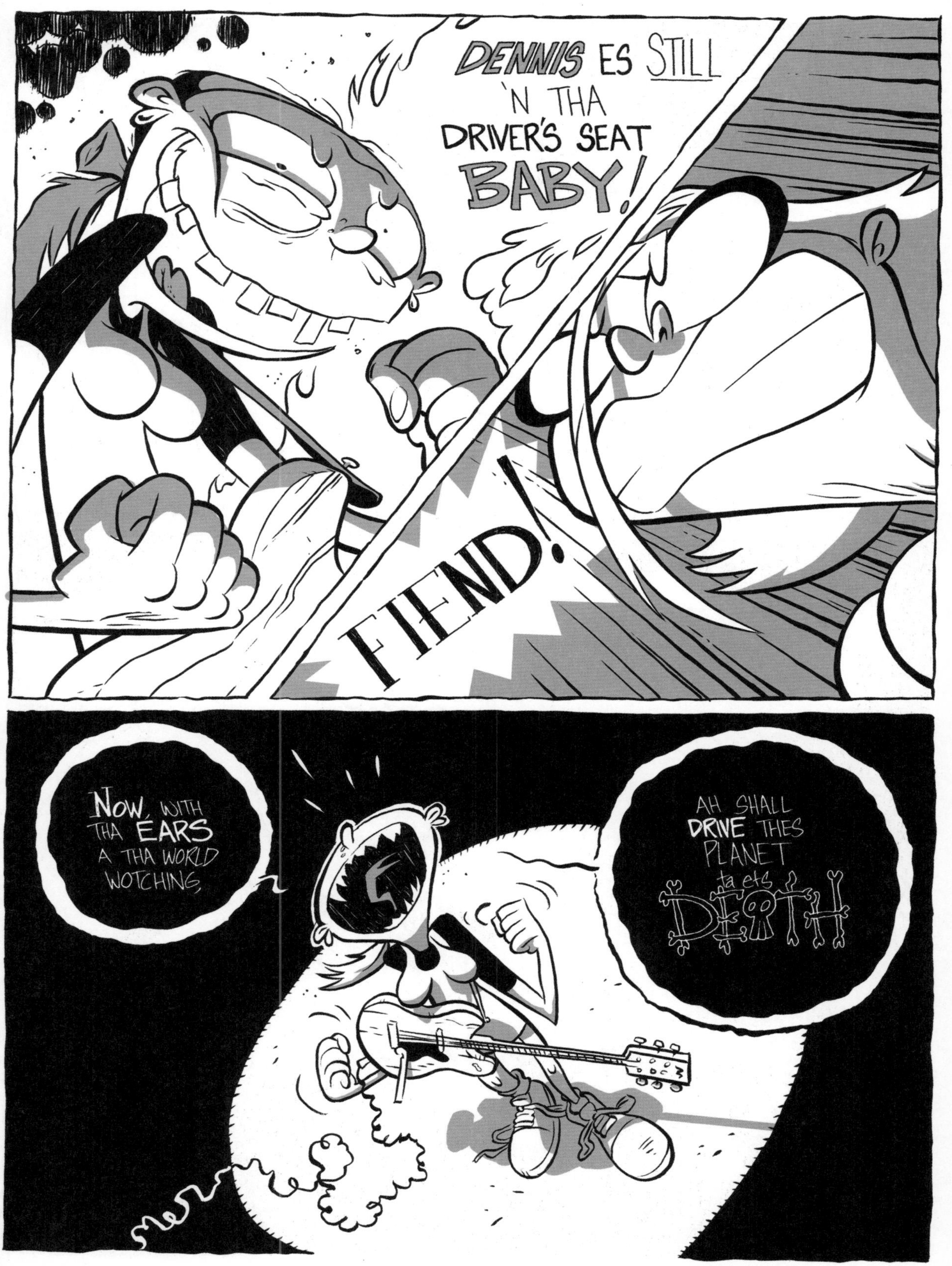
DENNIS ES STILL 'N THA DRIVER'S SEAT BABY!
FIEND!
NOW, WITH THA EARS A THA WORLD WOTCHING,
AH SHALL DRIVE THES PLANET ta ets DEATH

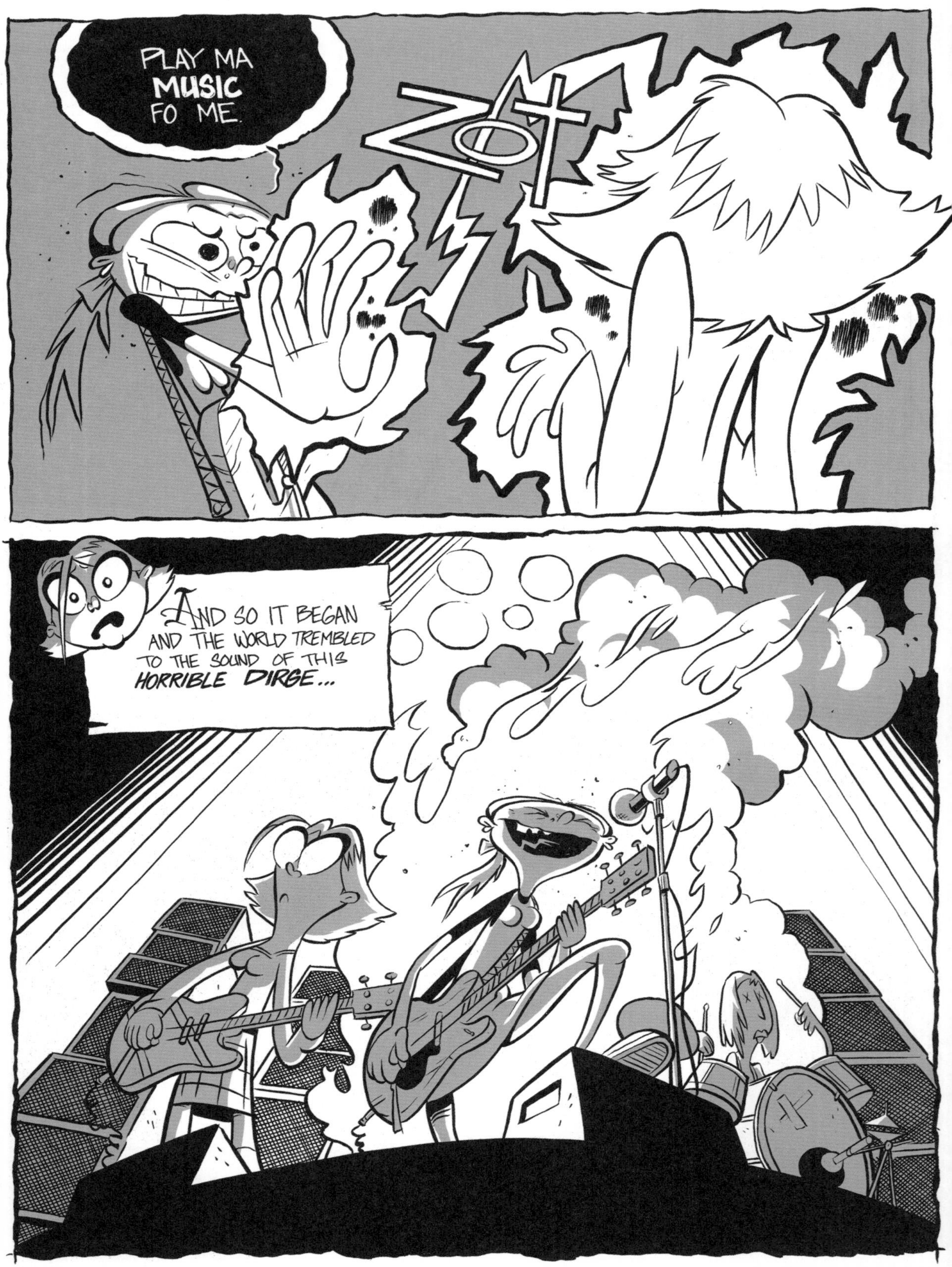

PLAY MA **MUSIC** FO ME.
ZOT
AND SO IT BEGAN AND THE WORLD TREMBLED TO THE SOUND OF THIS *HORRIBLE DIRGE...*

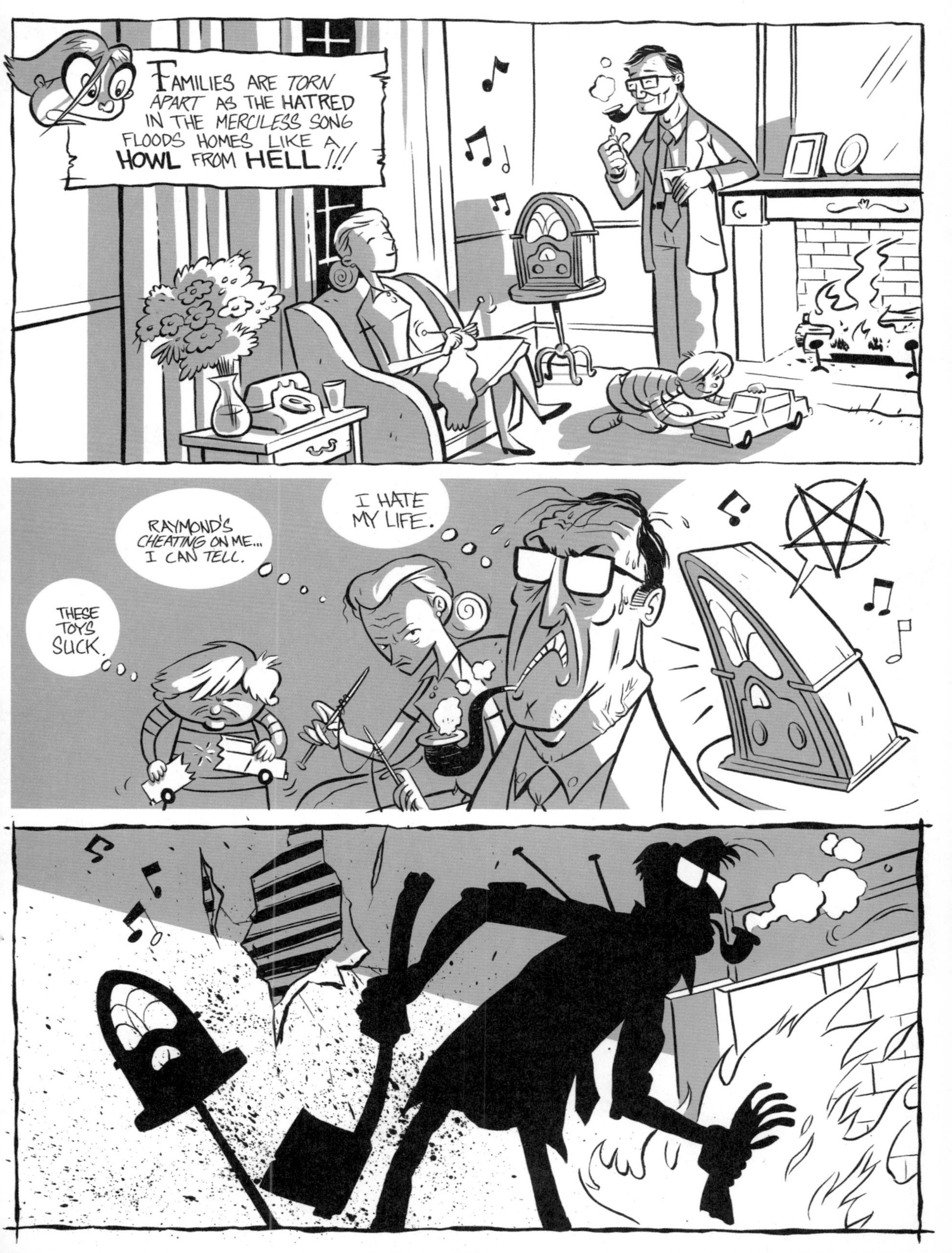
FAMILIES ARE TORN APART AS THE HATRED IN THE MERCILESS SONG FLOODS HOMES LIKE A HOWL FROM HELL!!!
I HATE MY LIFE.
RAYMOND'S CHEATING ON ME... I CAN TELL.
THESE TOYS SUCK.

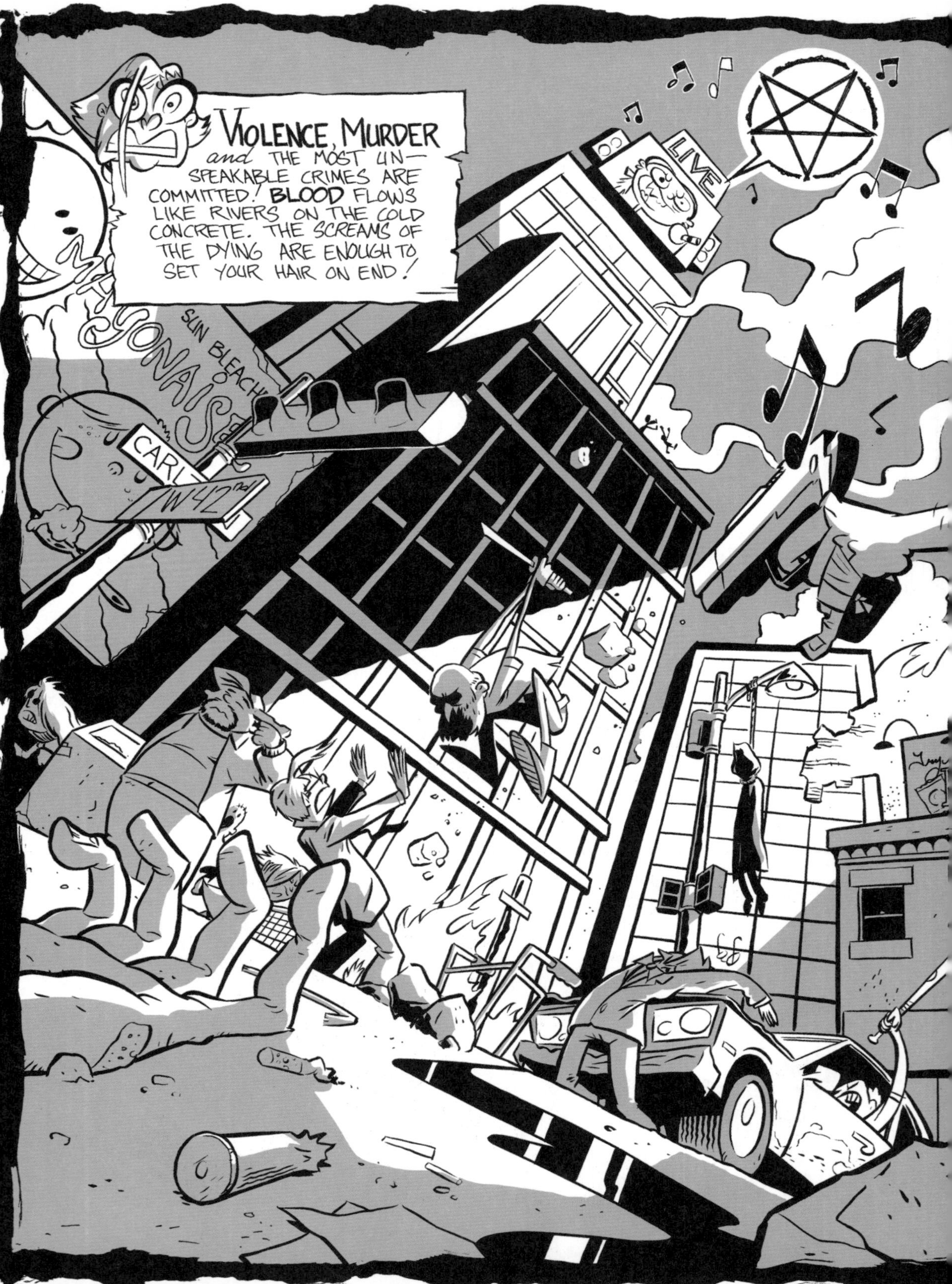

VIOLENCE, MURDER and THE MOST UN-SPEAKABLE CRIMES ARE COMMITTED! BLOOD FLOWS LIKE RIVERS ON THE COLD CONCRETE. THE SCREAMS OF THE DYING ARE ENOUGH TO SET YOUR HAIR ON END!
LIVE
MAYONAISE
SLIN BLEACH
CARL
W 42

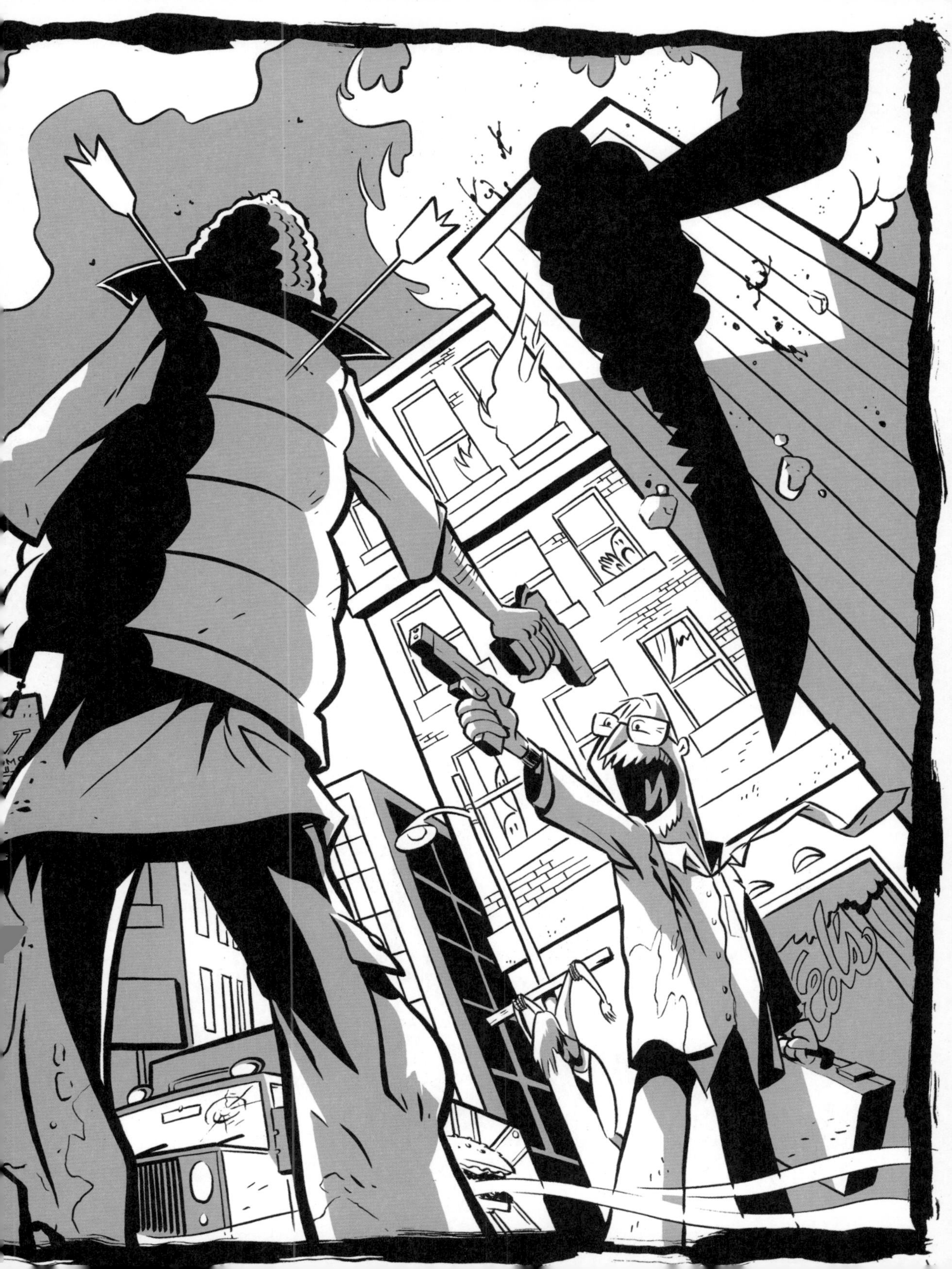

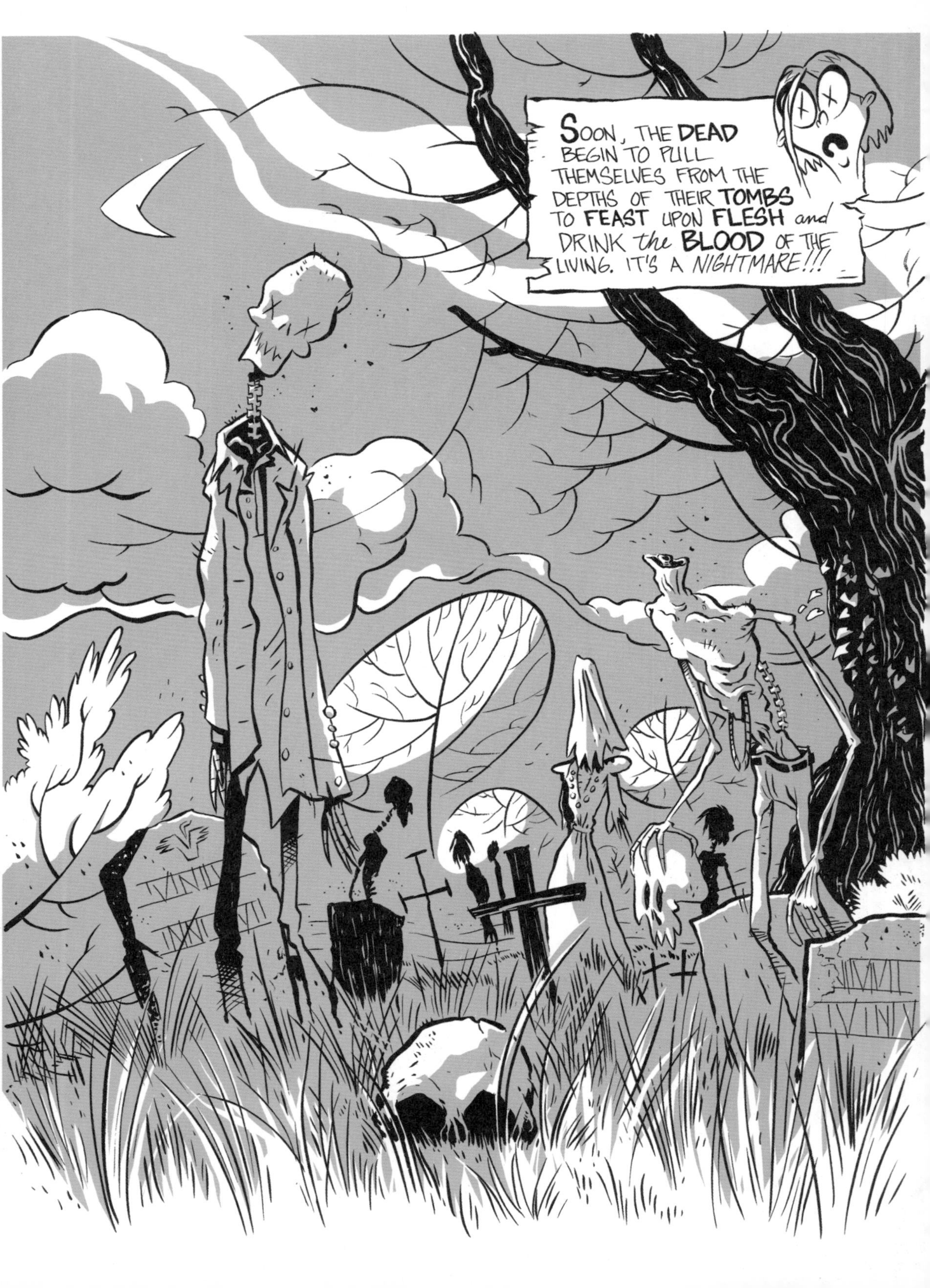
SOON, THE DEAD BEGIN TO PULL THEMSELVES FROM THE DEPTHS OF THEIR TOMBS TO FEAST UPON FLESH and DRINK the BLOOD OF THE LIVING. IT'S A NIGHTMARE!!!

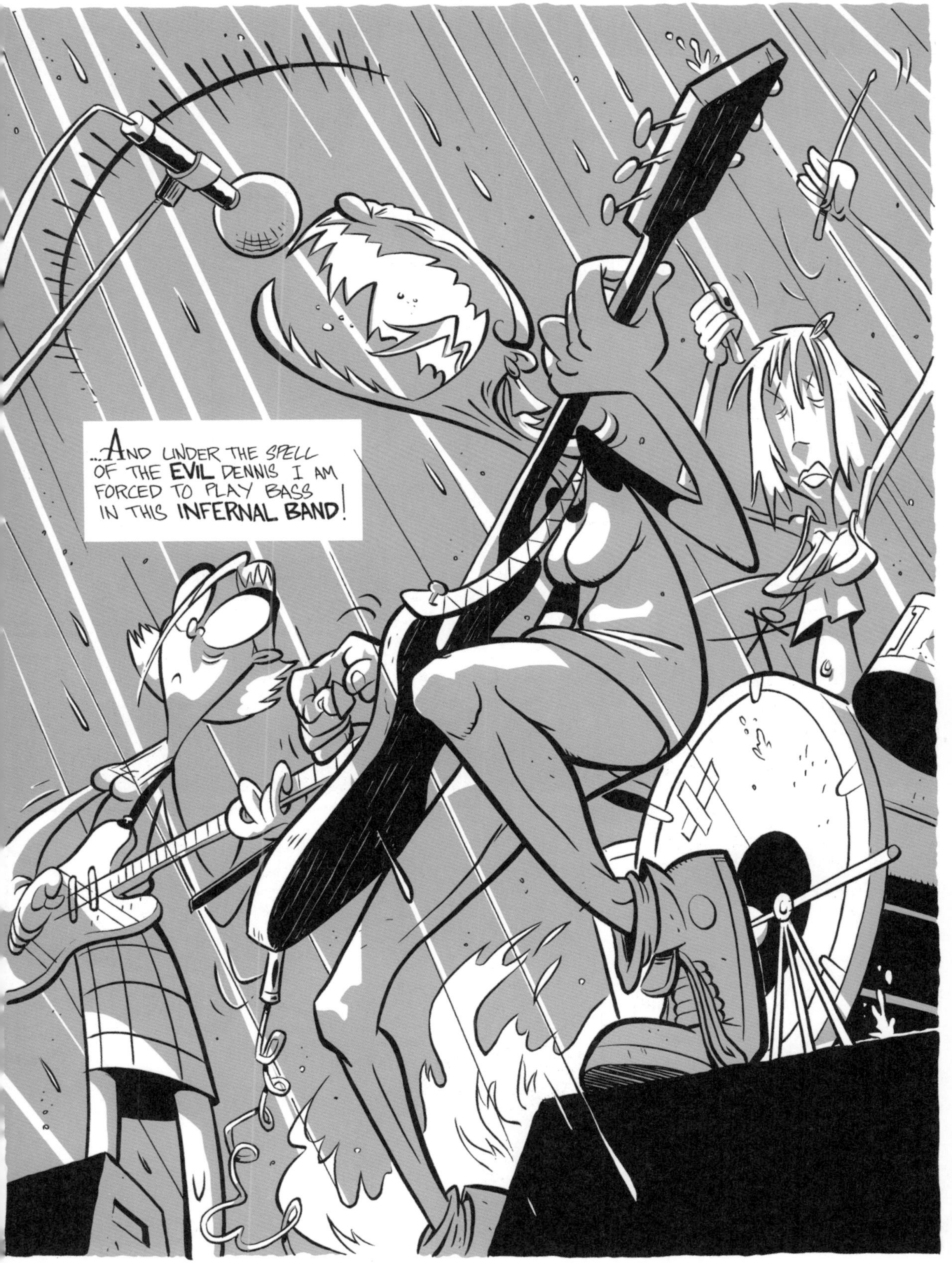
...AND UNDER THE SPELL OF THE EVIL DENNIS I AM FORCED TO PLAY BASS IN THIS INFERNAL BAND!

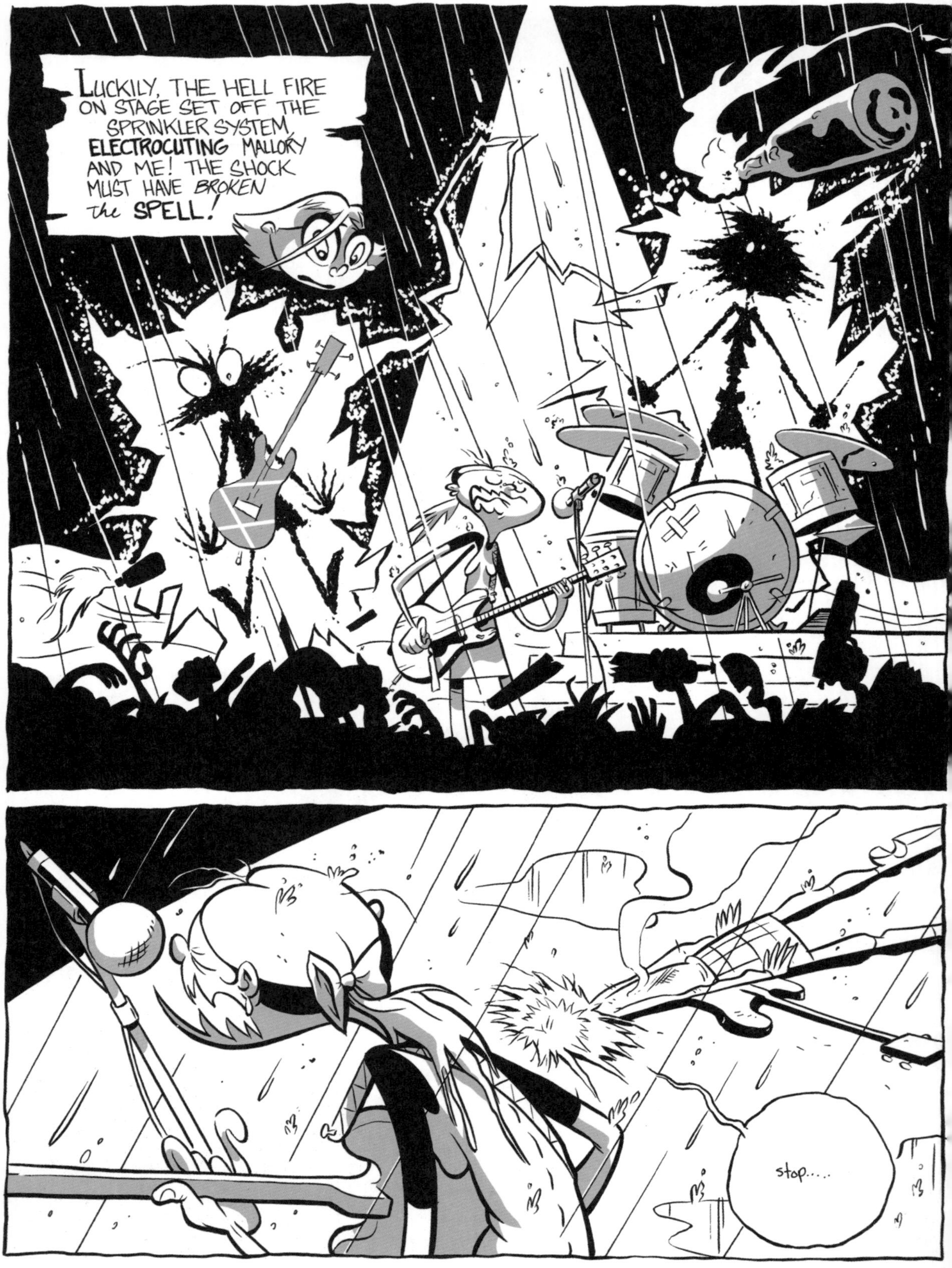
LUCKILY, THE HELL FIRE ON STAGE SET OFF THE SPRINKLER SYSTEM, ELECTROCUTING MALLORY AND ME! THE SHOCK MUST HAVE BROKEN the SPELL!
stop.....

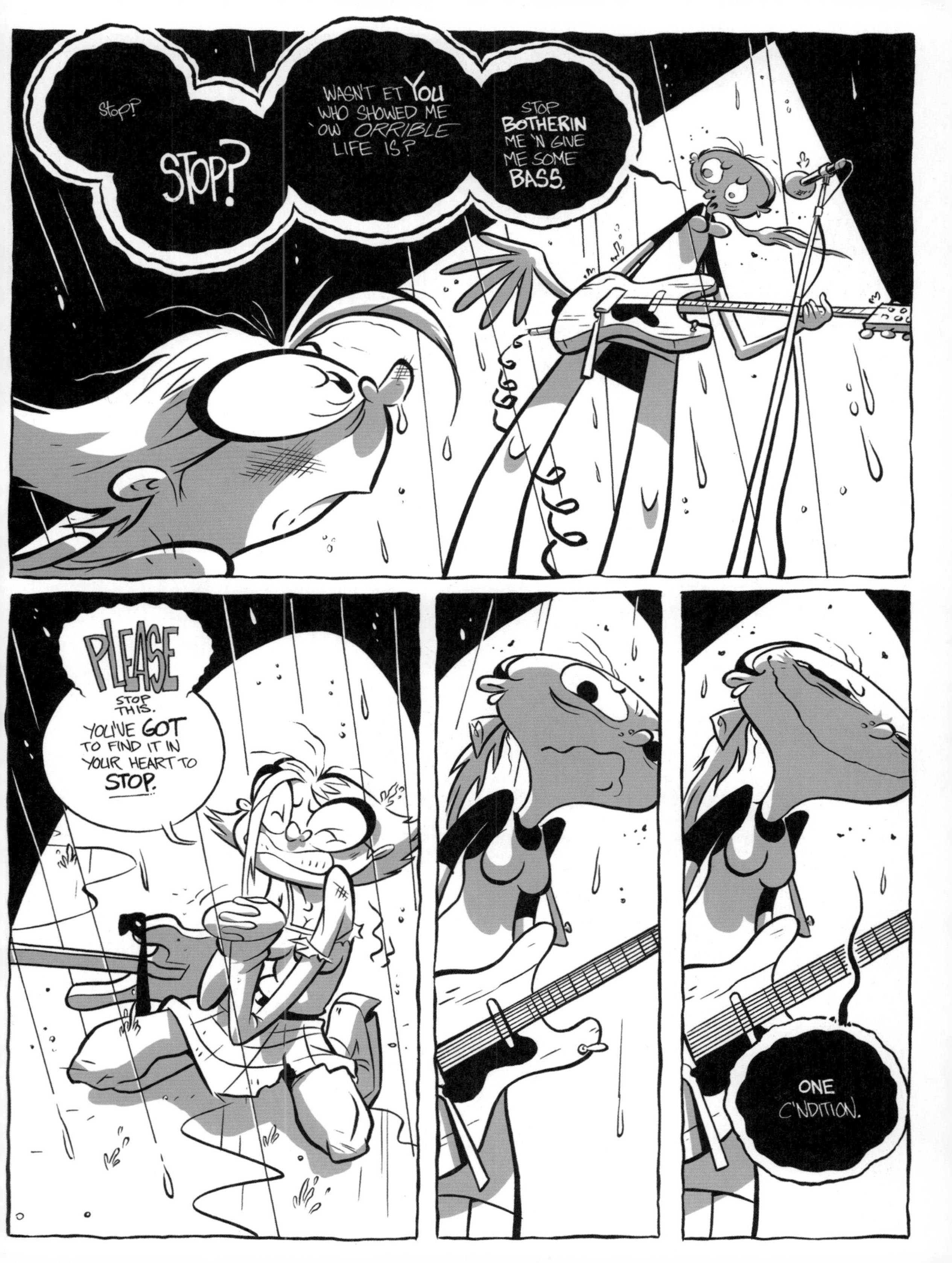

STOP? STOP?
WASN'T ET YOU WHO SHOWED ME 'OW ORRIBLE LIFE IS?
STOP BOTHERIN ME 'N GIVE ME SOME BASS.
PLEASE STOP THIS. YOU'VE GOT TO FIND IT IN YOUR HEART TO STOP.
ONE C'NDITION.

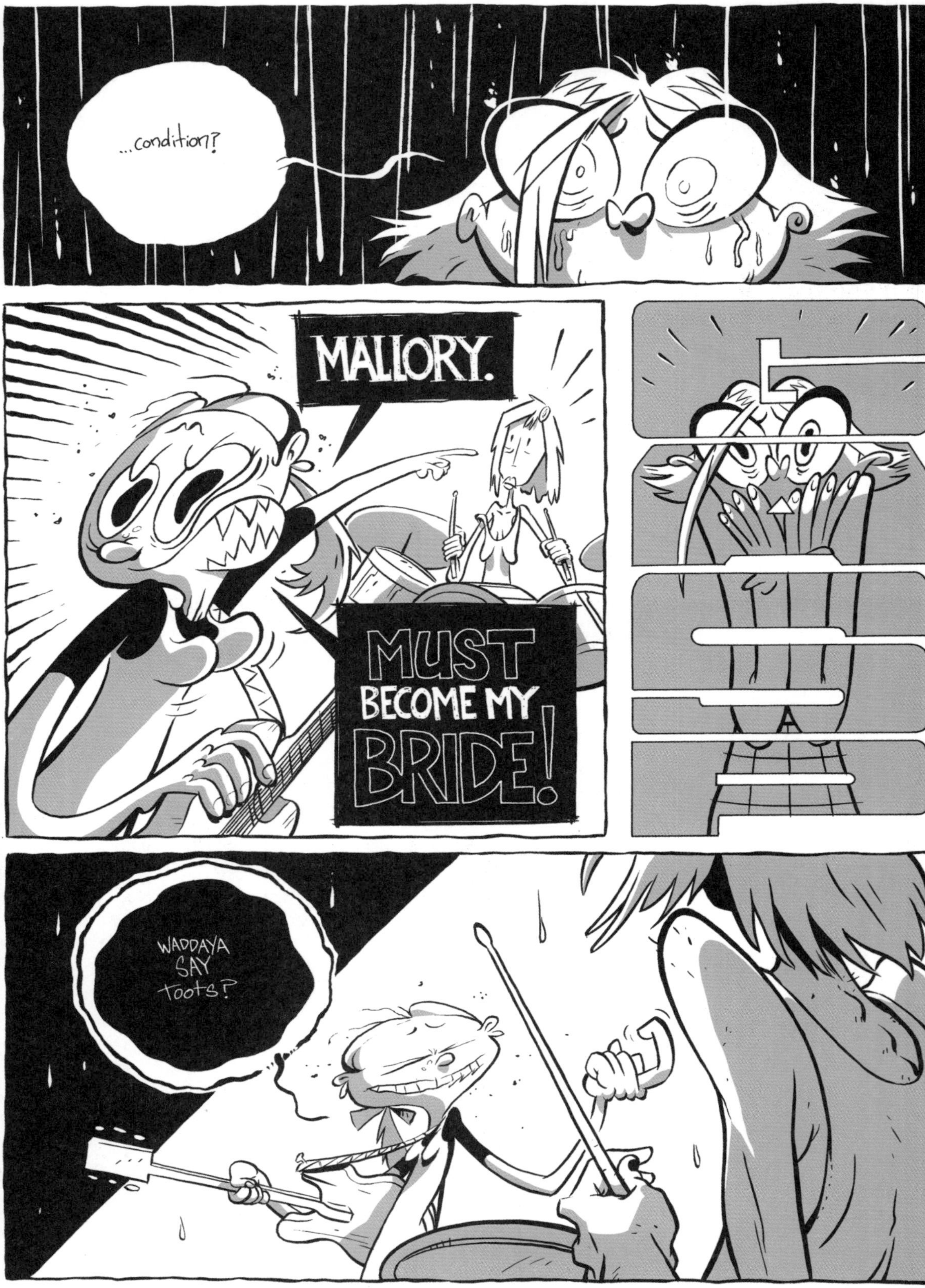

...condition?
MALLORY.
MUST BECOME MY BRIDE!
WADDAYA SAY toots?

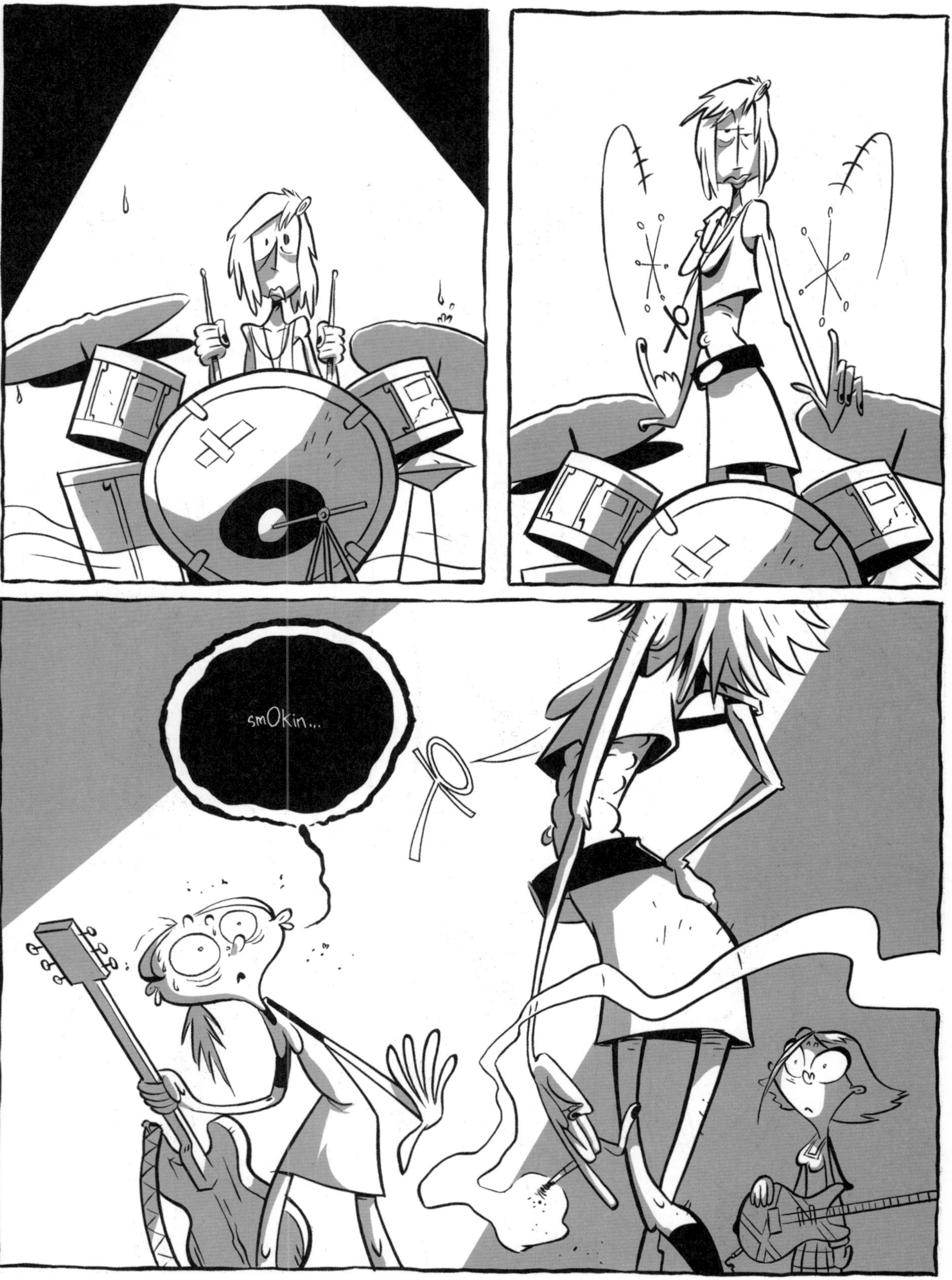
smOkin...

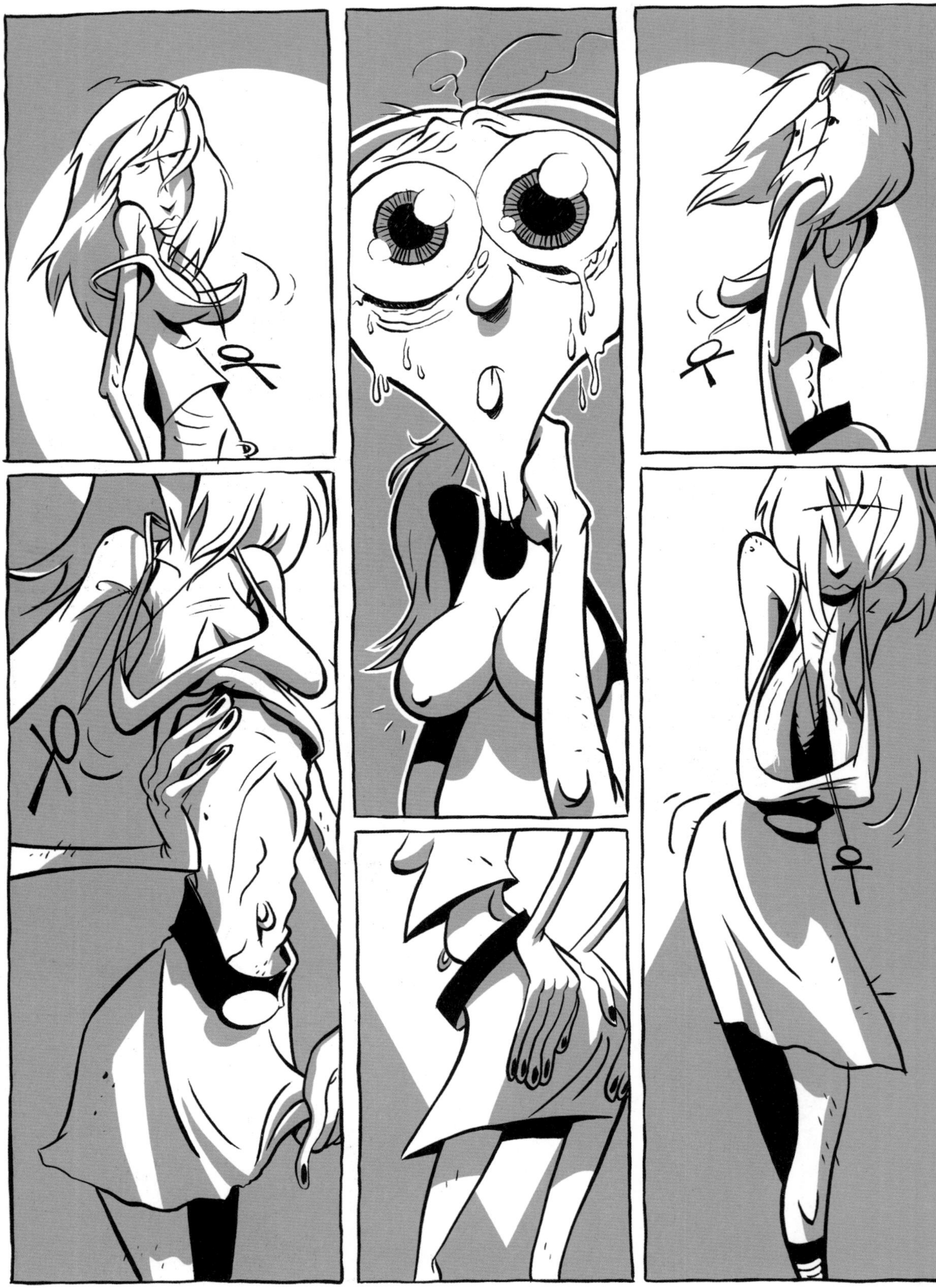

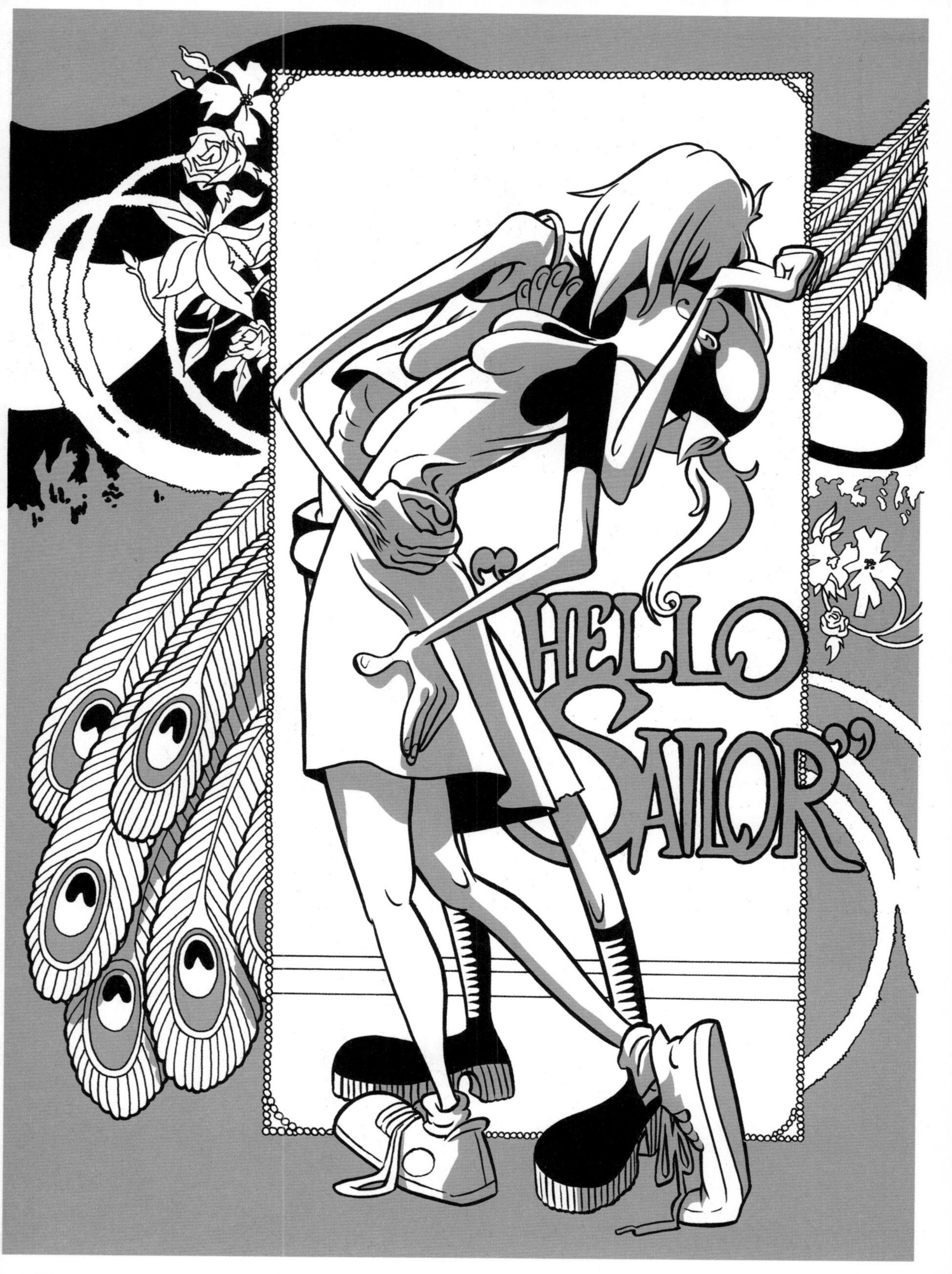
"HELLO SAILOR"

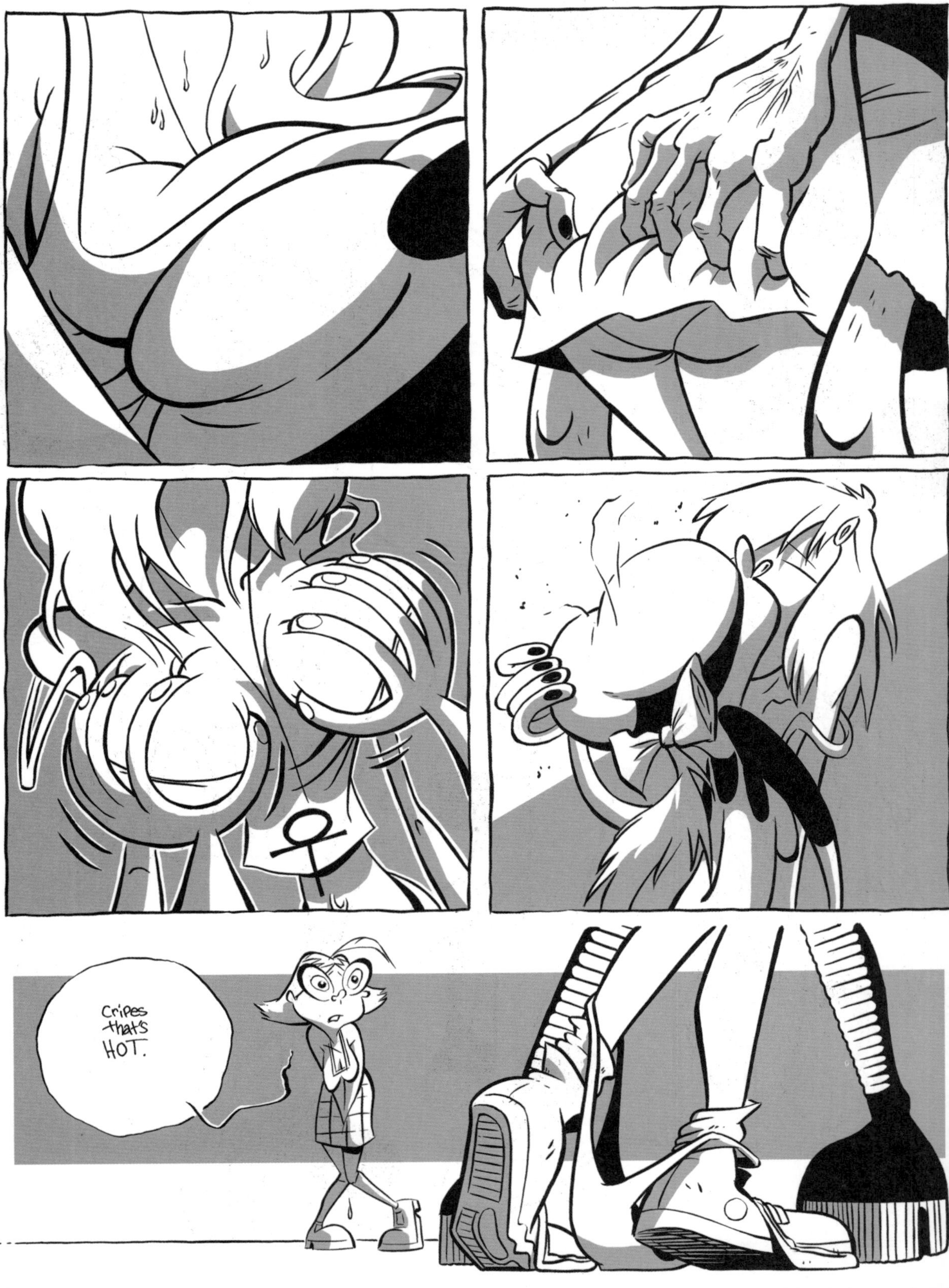
Cripes that's HOT.

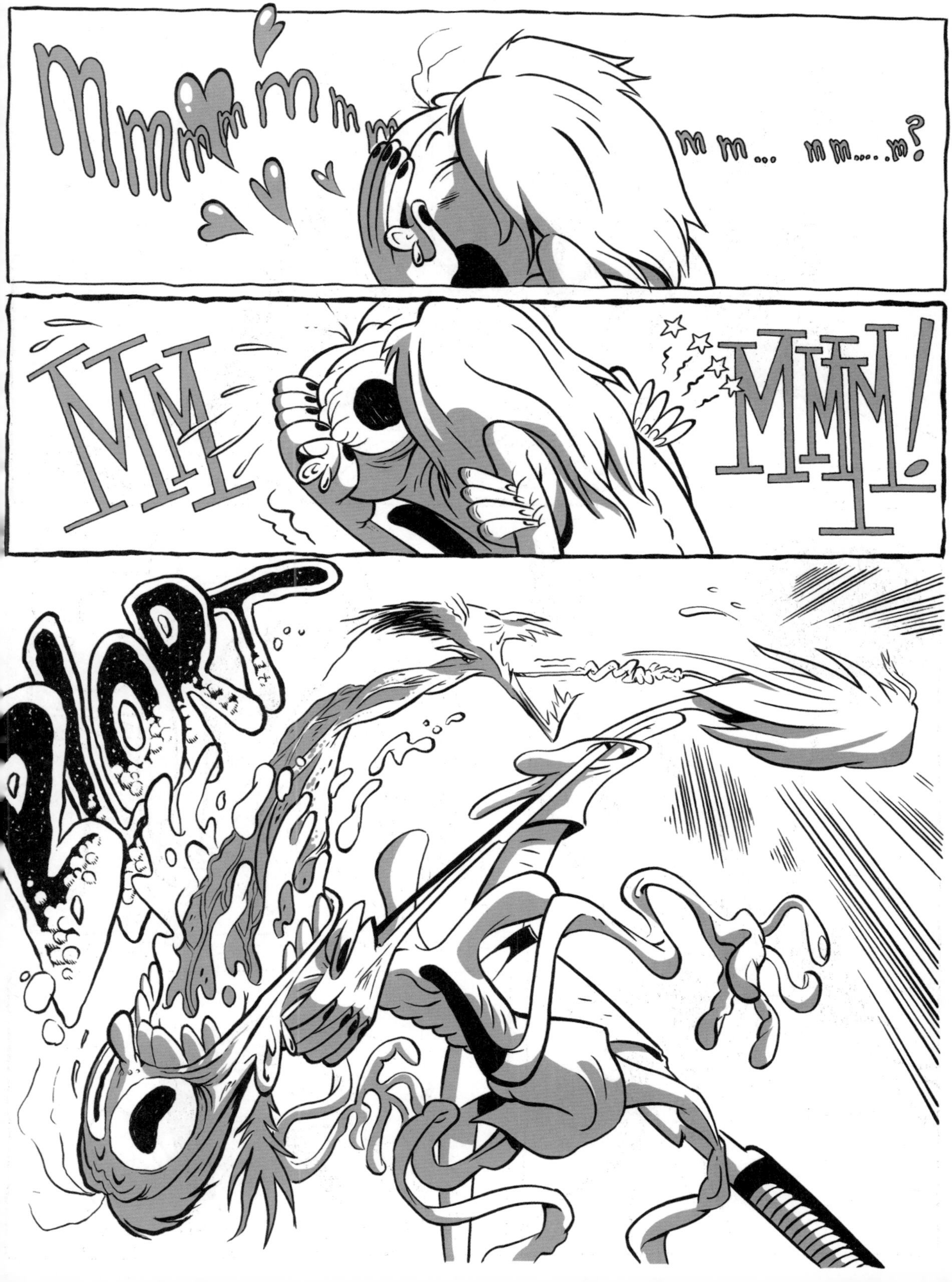
Mmmmmmmm
mm... mm....m?
MM
MMM!

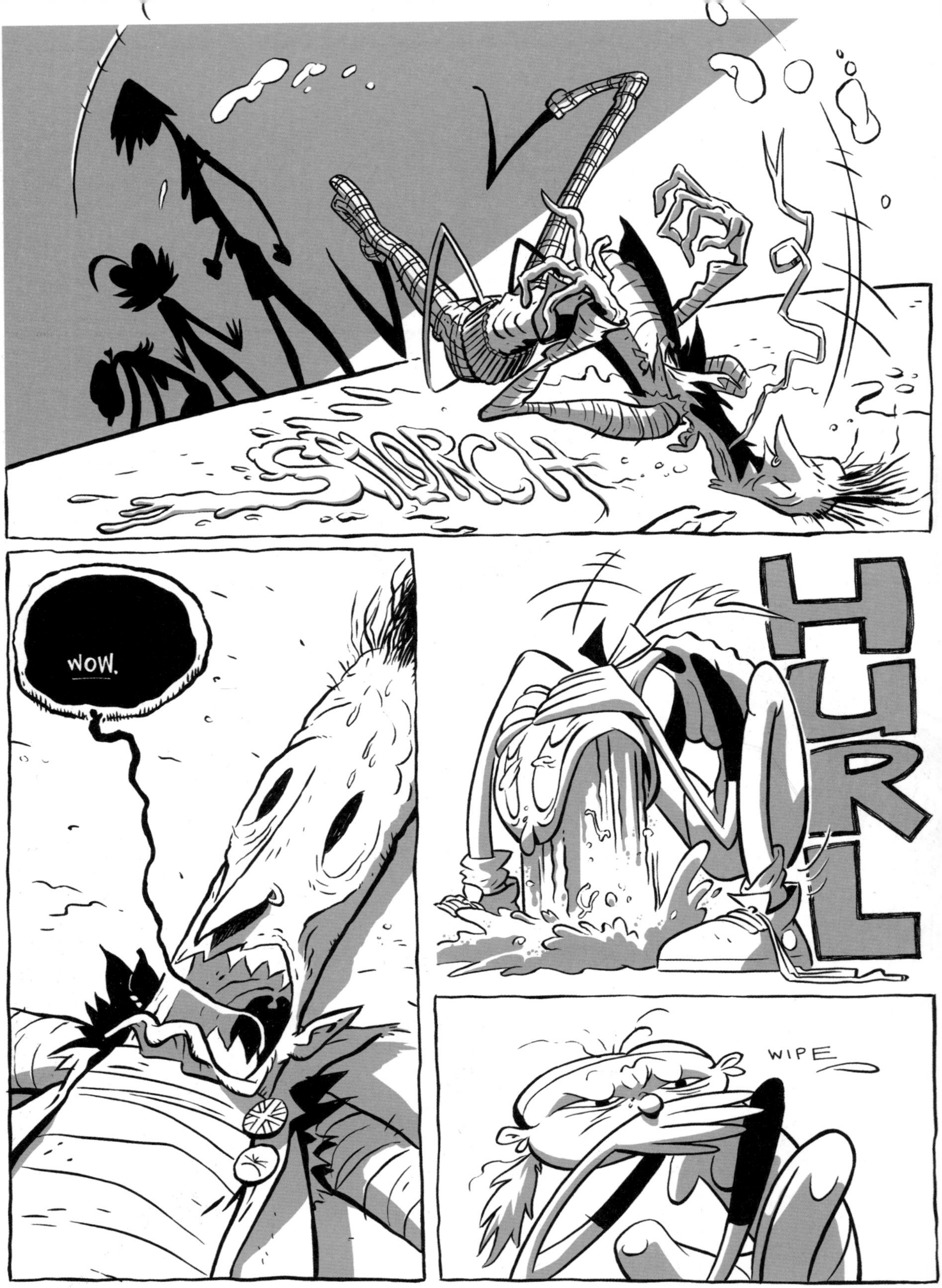
SPLORCH
WOW.
HURL
WIPE

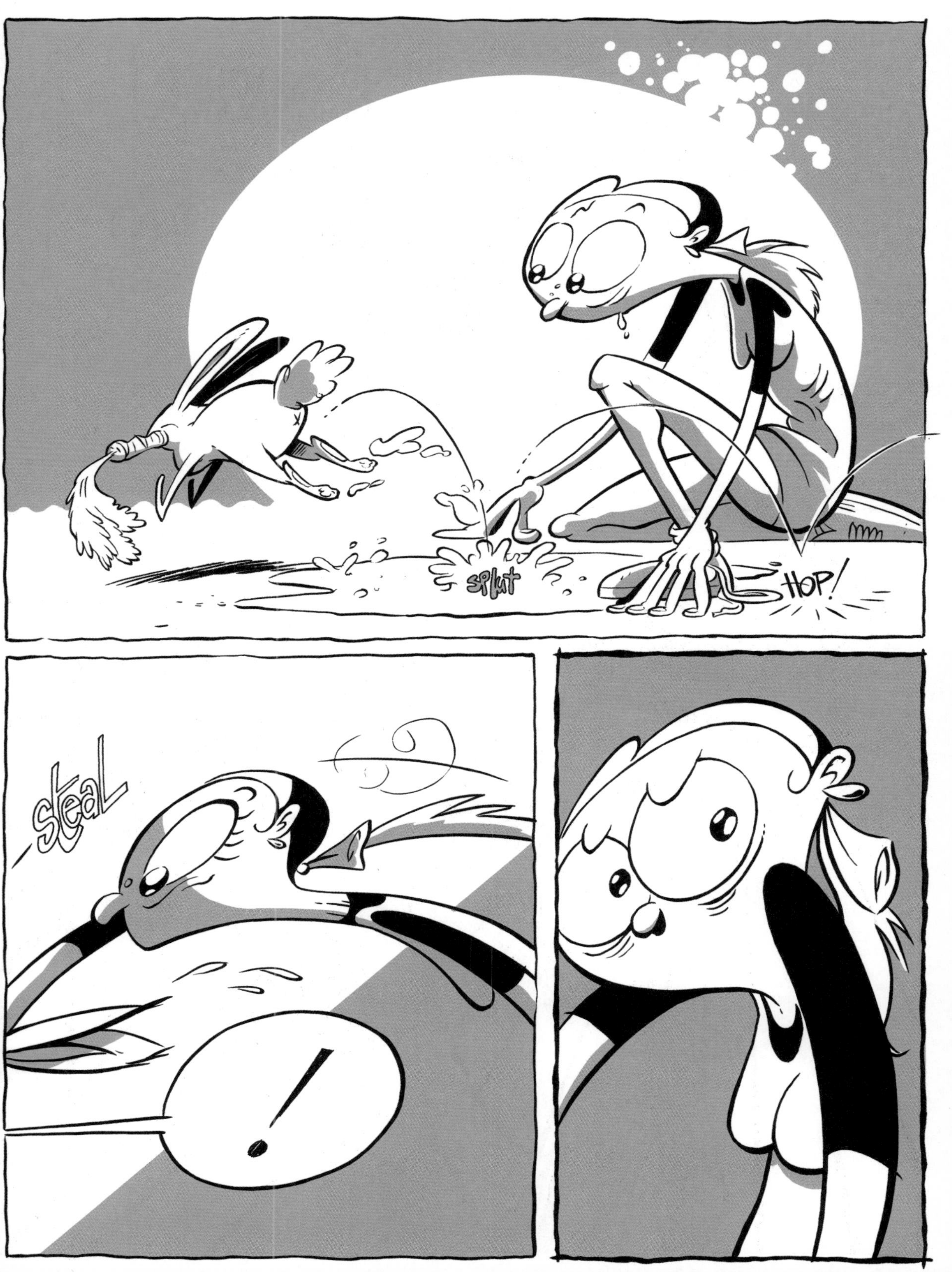
SPLUT
HOP!
steal
!

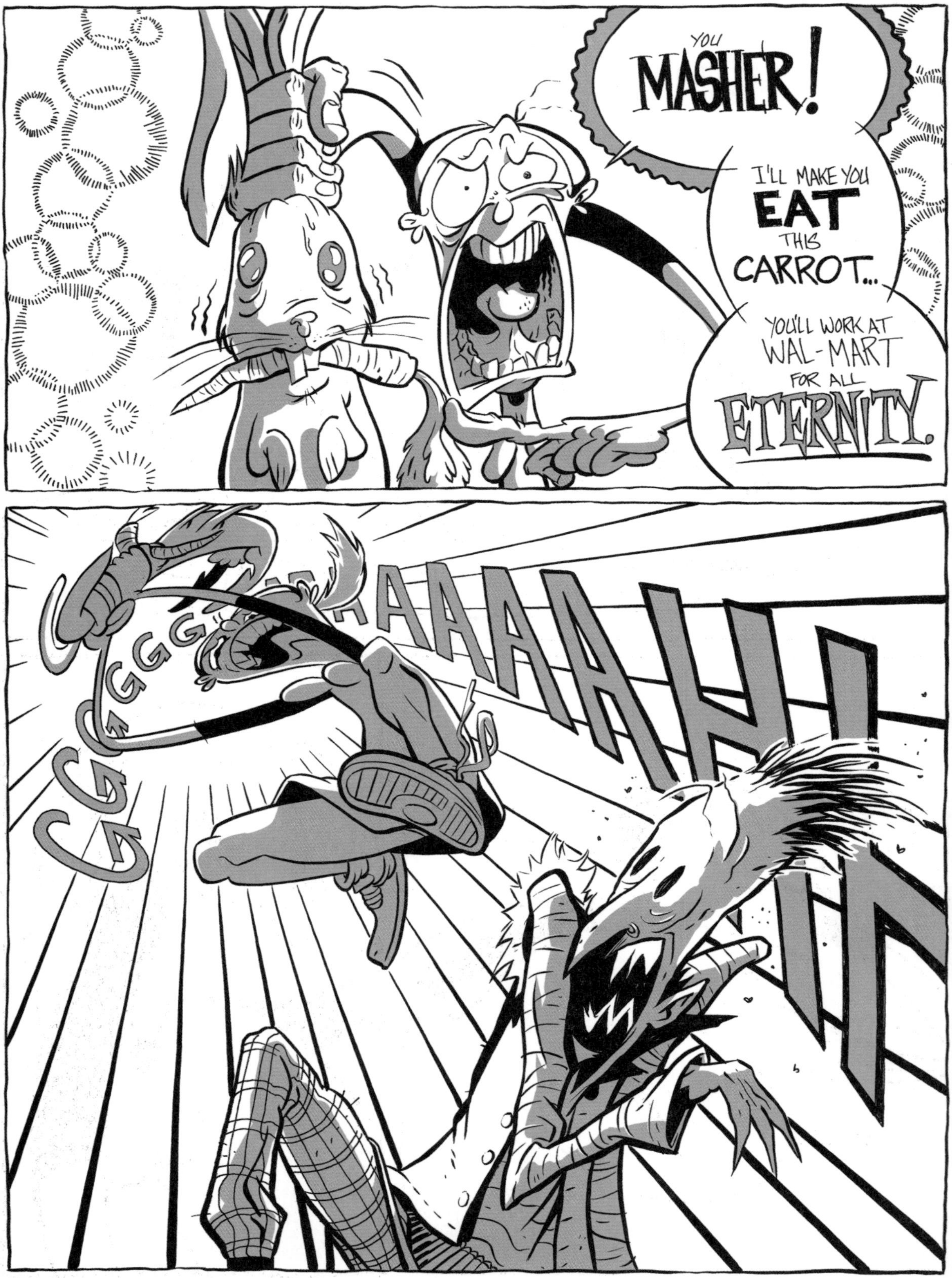
YOU MASHER!
I'LL MAKE YOU EAT THIS CARROT...
YOU'LL WORK AT WAL-MART FOR ALL ETERNITY.
GGGGGGAAAAAAAHH!

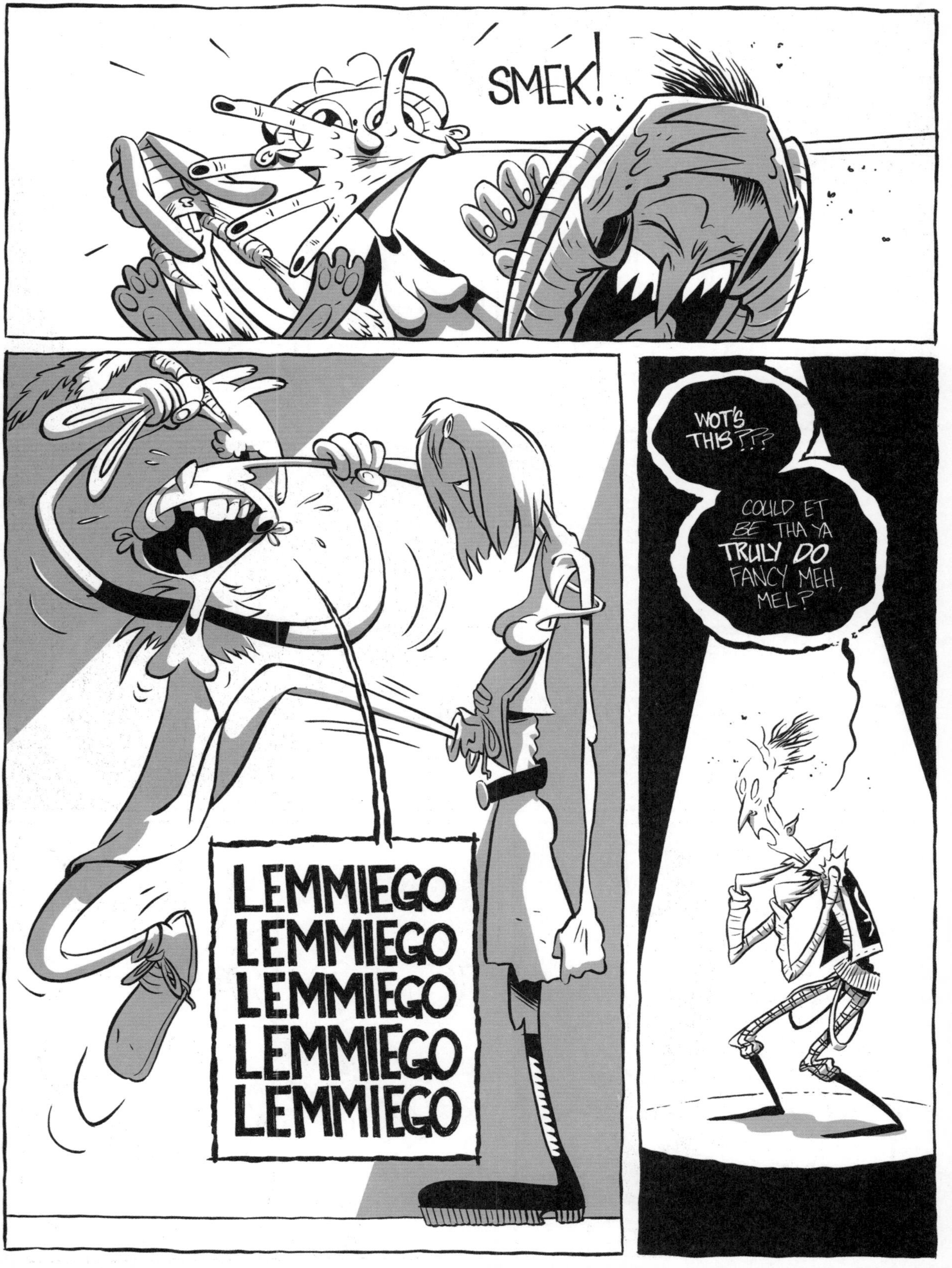
SMEK!
LEMMIEGO LEMMIEGO LEMMIEGO LEMMIEGO LEMMIEGO
WOT'S THIS???
COULD ET BE THA YA TRULY DO FANCY MEH, MEL?

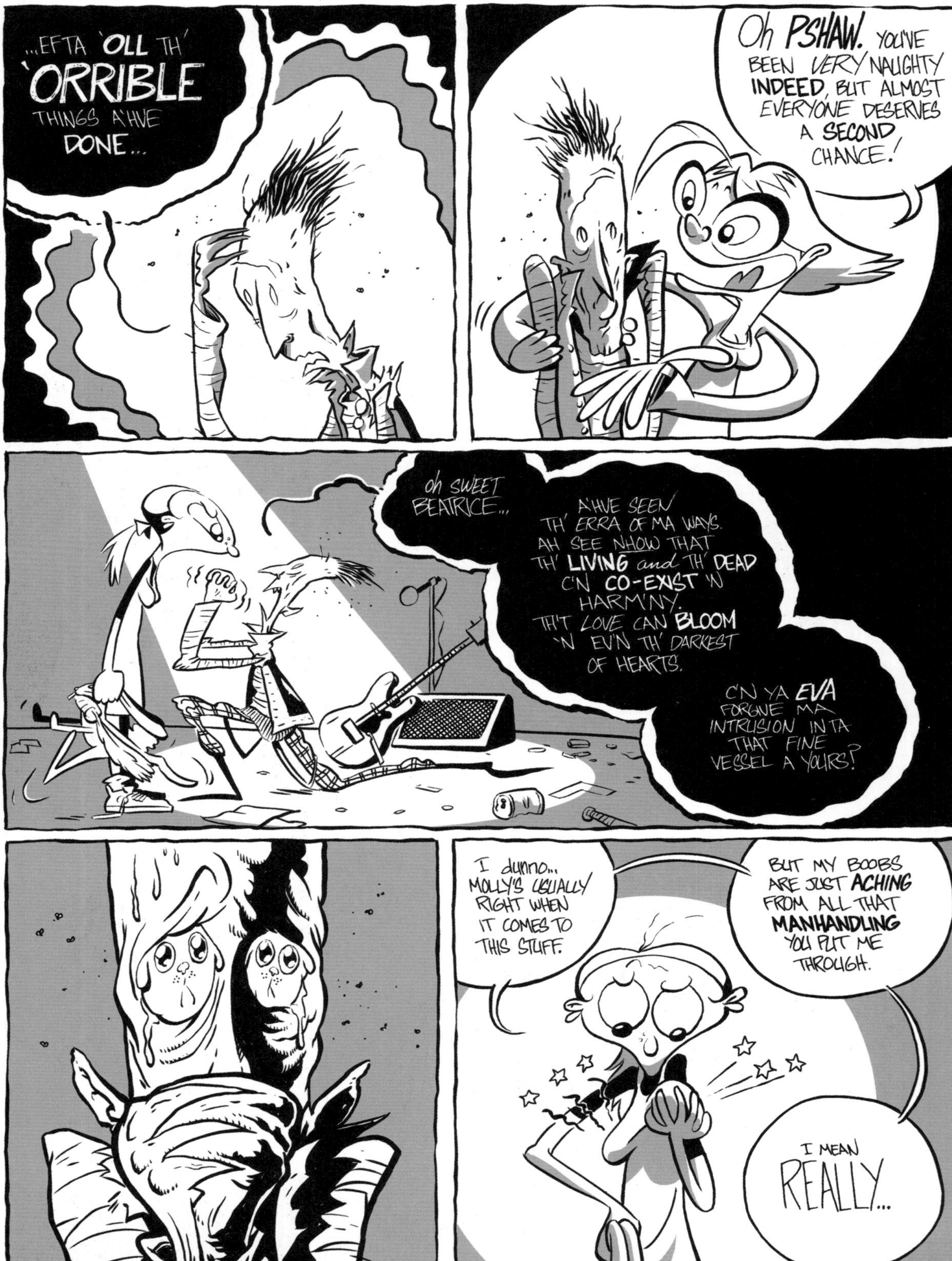

...EFTA 'OLL TH' 'ORRIBLE THINGS A'HVE DONE...
Oh PSHAW. YOU'VE BEEN VERY NAUGHTY INDEED, BUT ALMOST EVERYONE DESERVES A SECOND CHANCE!
oh SWEET BEATRICE...
A'HVE SEEN TH' ERRA OF MA WAYS. AH SEE NHOW THAT TH' LIVING and TH' DEAD C'N CO-EXIST 'N HARM'NY. TH'T LOVE CAN BLOOM 'N EV'N TH' DARKEST OF HEARTS.
C'N YA EVA FORGIVE MA INTRUSION INTA THAT FINE VESSEL A YOURS?
I dunno... MOLLY'S USUALLY RIGHT WHEN IT COMES TO THIS STUFF.
BUT MY BOOBS ARE JUST ACHING FROM ALL THAT MANHANDLING YOU PUT ME THROUGH.
I MEAN REALLY...

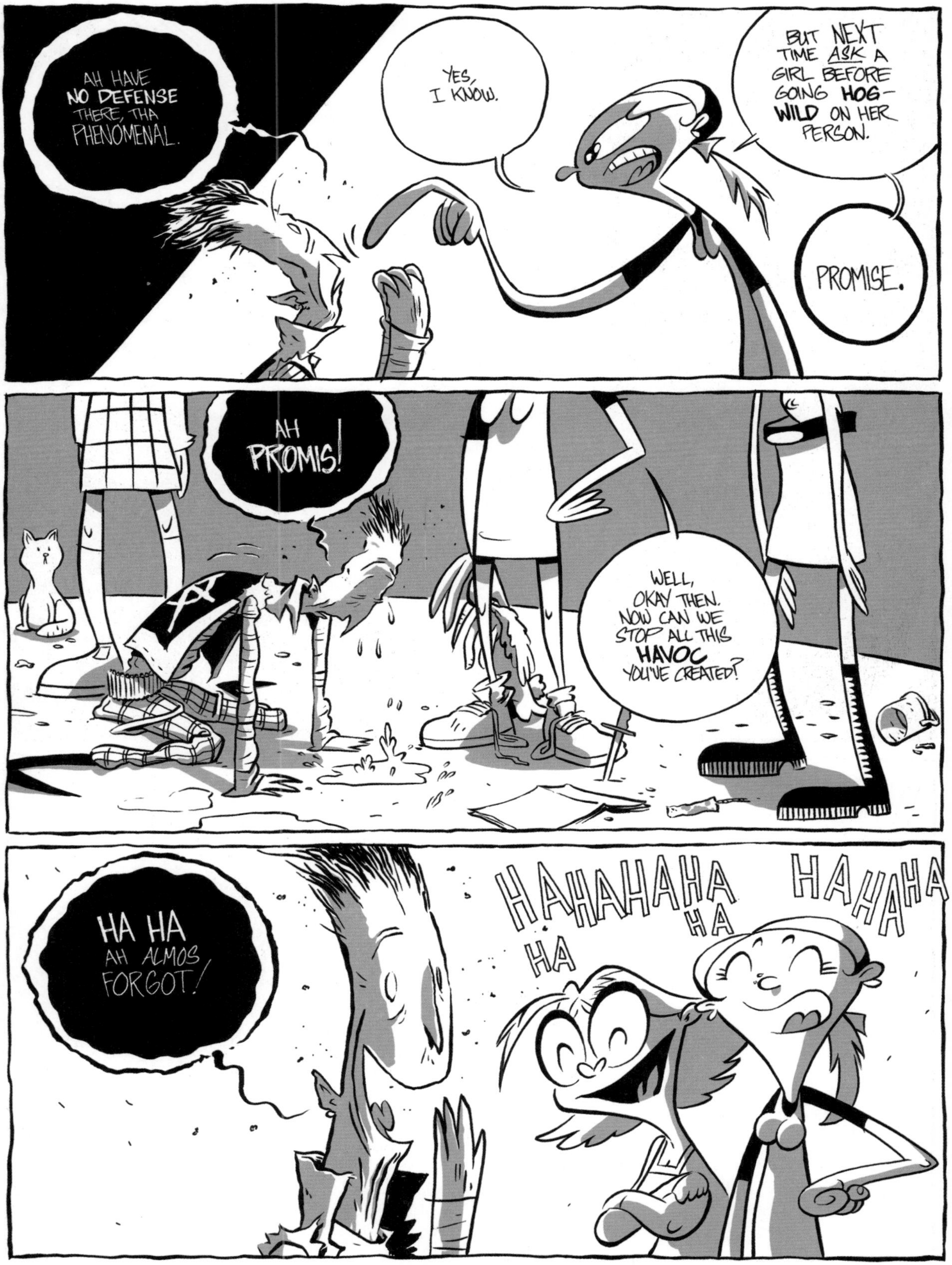

AH HAVE NO DEFENSE THERE, THA PHENOMENAL.
YES, I KNOW.
BUT NEXT TIME ASK A GIRL BEFORE GOING HOG-WILD ON HER PERSON.
PROMISE.
AH PROMIS!
WELL, OKAY THEN. NOW CAN WE STOP ALL THIS HAVOC YOU'VE CREATED?
HA HA AH ALMOS FORGOT!
HAHAHAHAHA HA HA
HAHAHAHA

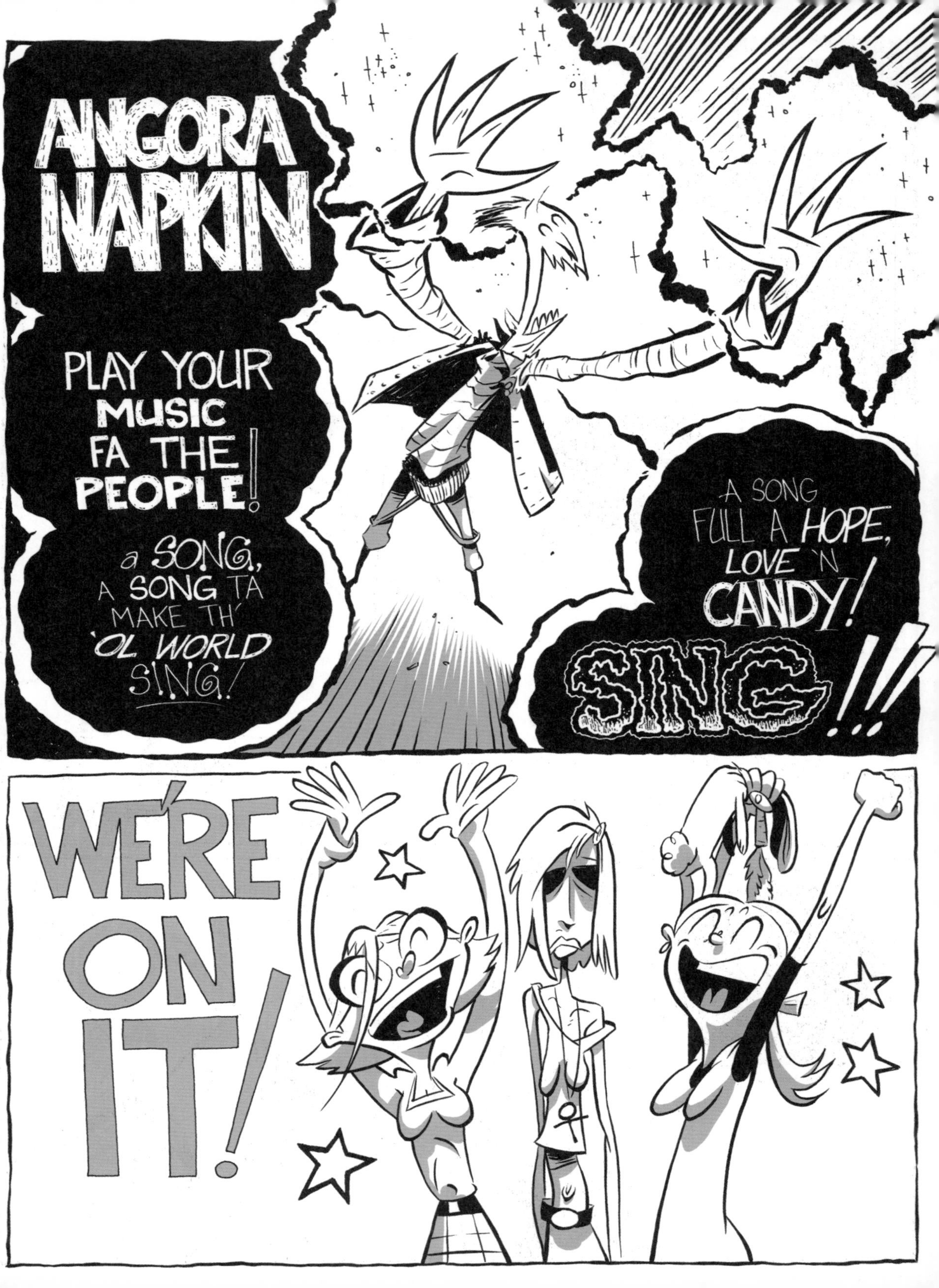

ANGORA NAPKIN
PLAY YOUR MUSIC FA THE PEOPLE!
a SONG, A SONG TA MAKE TH' 'OL WORLD SING!
A SONG FULL A HOPE, LOVE 'N CANDY!
SING!!!
WE'RE ON IT!

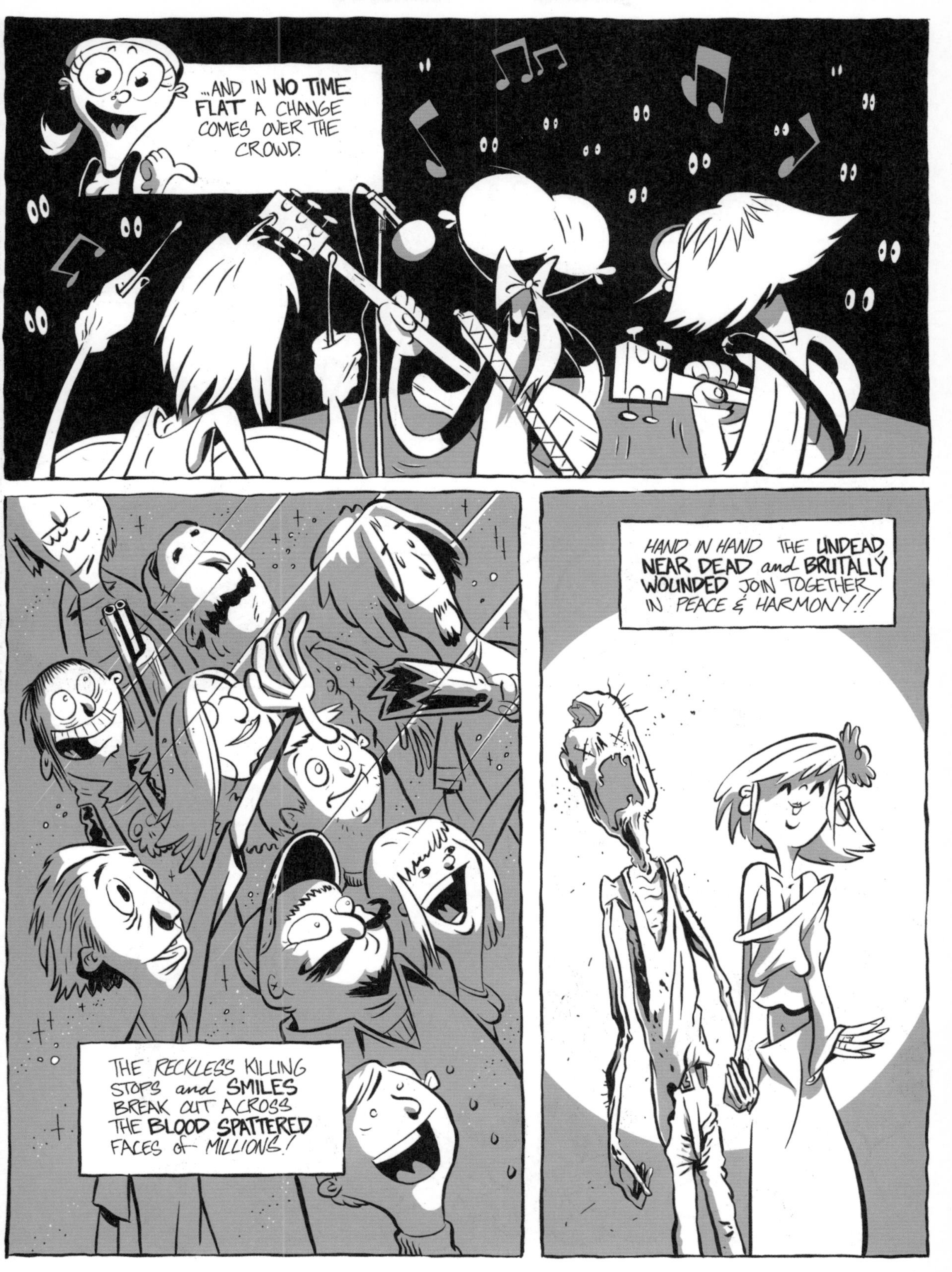
...AND IN NO TIME FLAT A CHANGE COMES OVER THE CROWD.
THE RECKLESS KILLING STOPS and SMILES BREAK OUT ACROSS THE BLOOD SPATTERED FACES of MILLIONS!
HAND IN HAND THE UNDEAD, NEAR DEAD and BRUTALLY WOUNDED JOIN TOGETHER IN PEACE & HARMONY!!

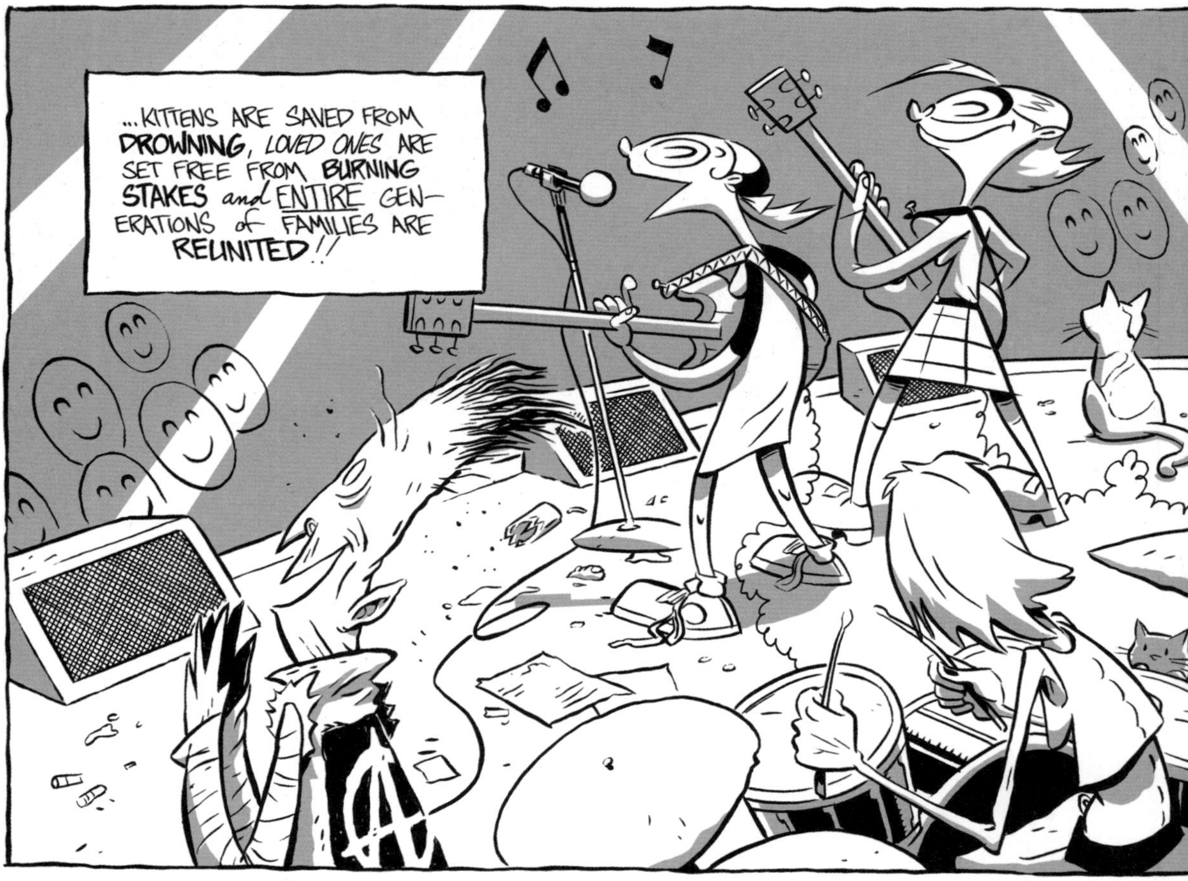
...KITTENS ARE SAVED FROM DROWNING, LOVED ONES ARE SET FREE FROM BURNING STAKES and ENTIRE GENERATIONS of FAMILIES ARE REUNITED!!

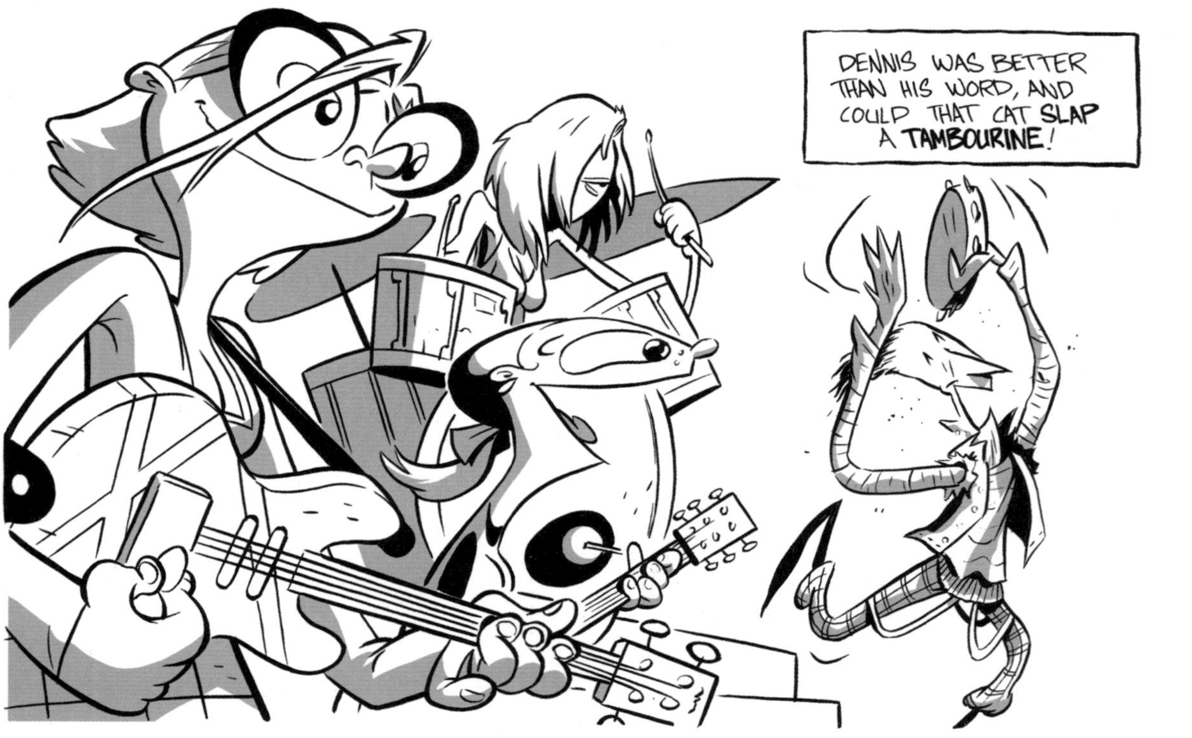
DENNIS WAS BETTER THAN HIS WORD, AND COULD THAT CAT SLAP A TAMBOURINE!

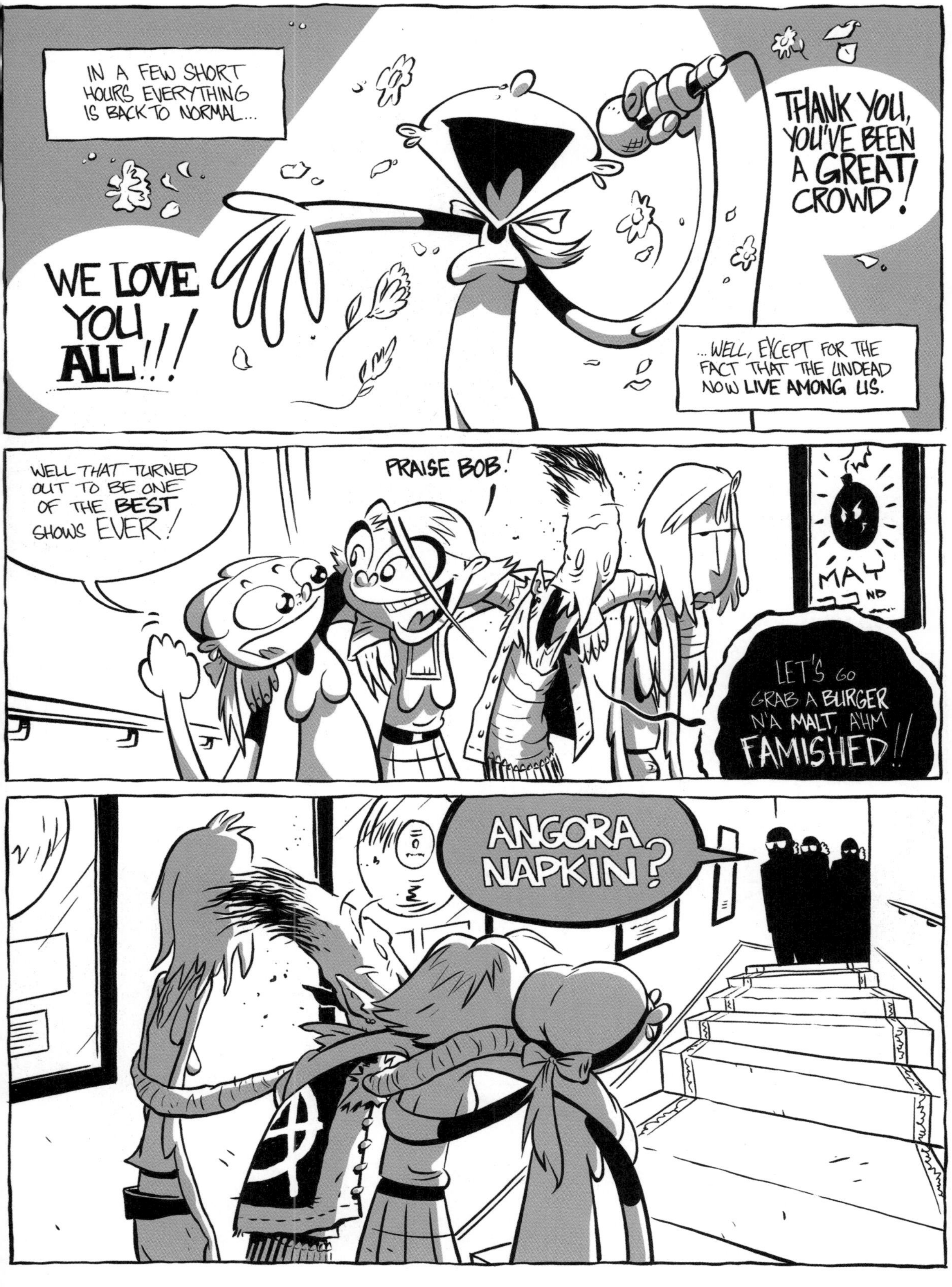

IN A FEW SHORT HOURS EVERYTHING IS BACK TO NORMAL...
THANK YOU, YOU'VE BEEN A GREAT CROWD!
WE LOVE YOU ALL!!!
...WELL, EXCEPT FOR THE FACT THAT THE UNDEAD NOW LIVE AMONG US.
WELL THAT TURNED OUT TO BE ONE OF THE BEST SHOWS EVER!
PRAISE BOB!
LET'S GO GRAB A BURGER N'A MALT, A'HM FAMISHED!!
ANGORA NAPKIN?

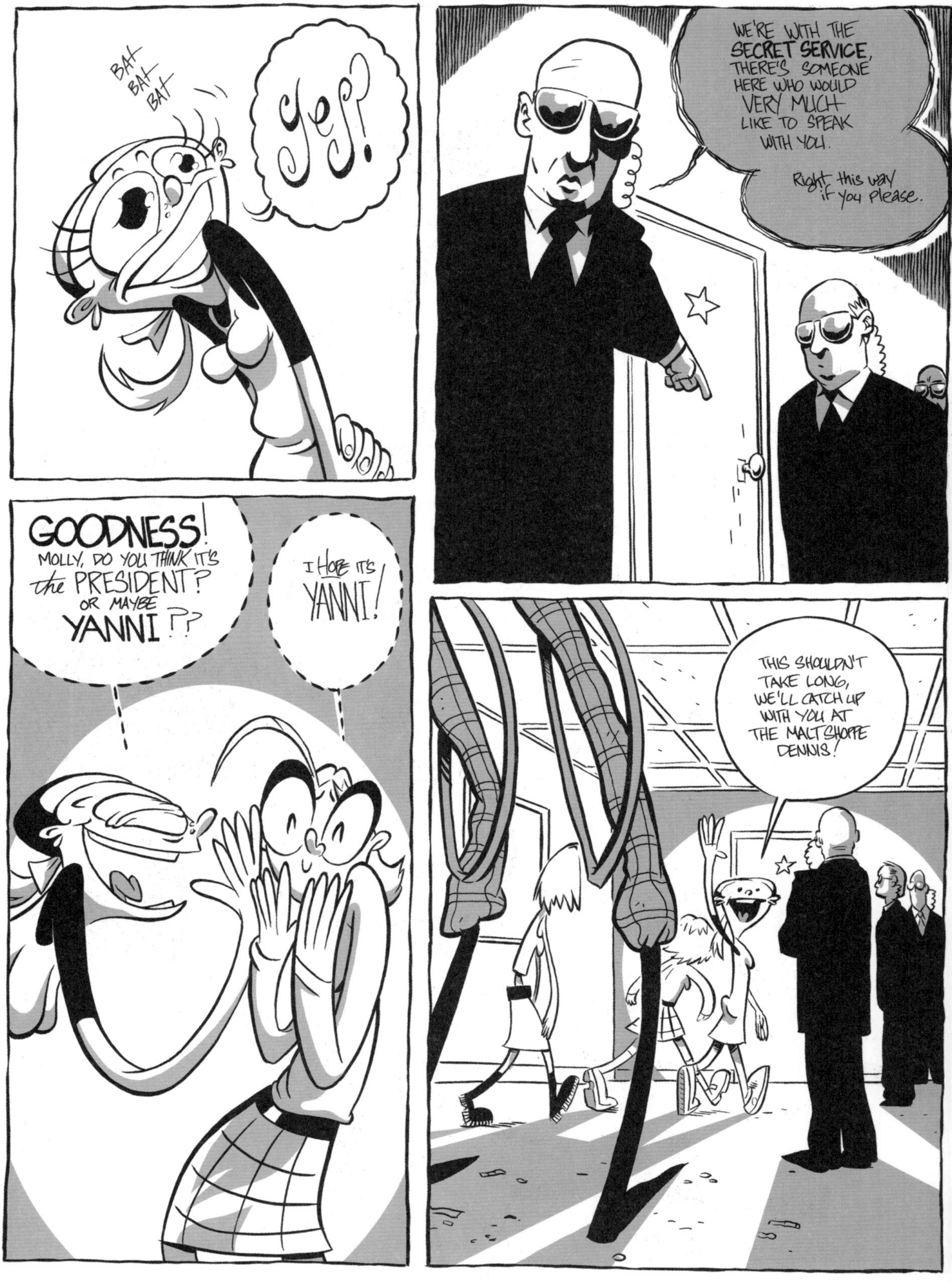
BAT BAT BAT
Yep!
WE'RE WITH THE SECRET SERVICE, THERE'S SOMEONE HERE WHO WOULD VERY MUCH LIKE TO SPEAK WITH YOU.
Right this way if you please.
GOODNESS! MOLLY, DO YOU THINK IT'S the PRESIDENT? OR MAYBE YANNI?
I HOPE IT'S YANNI!
THIS SHOULDN'T TAKE LONG, WE'LL CATCH UP WITH YOU AT THE MALTSHOPPE DENNIS!

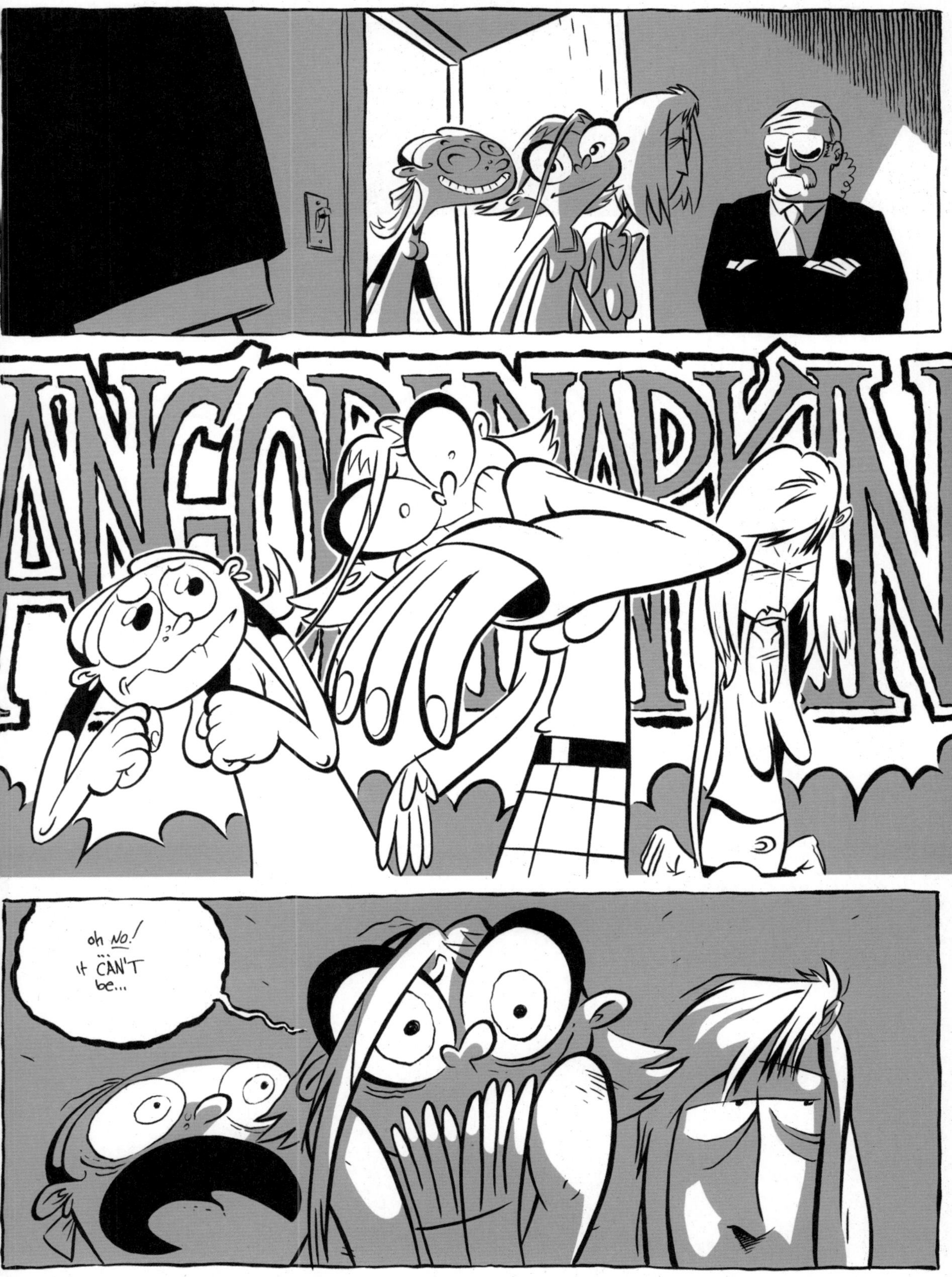
oh NO! ... it CAN'T be...

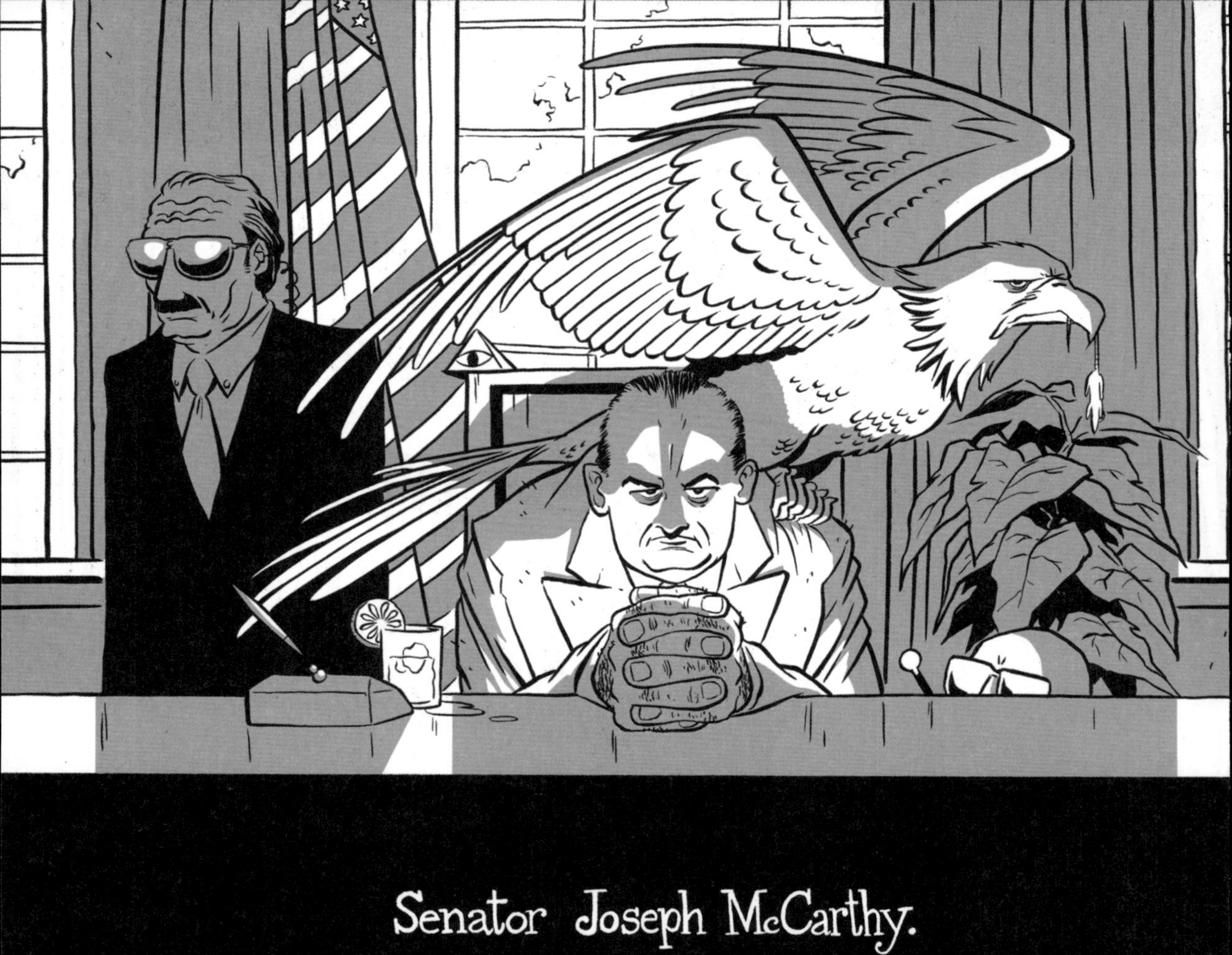
Senator Joseph McCarthy.

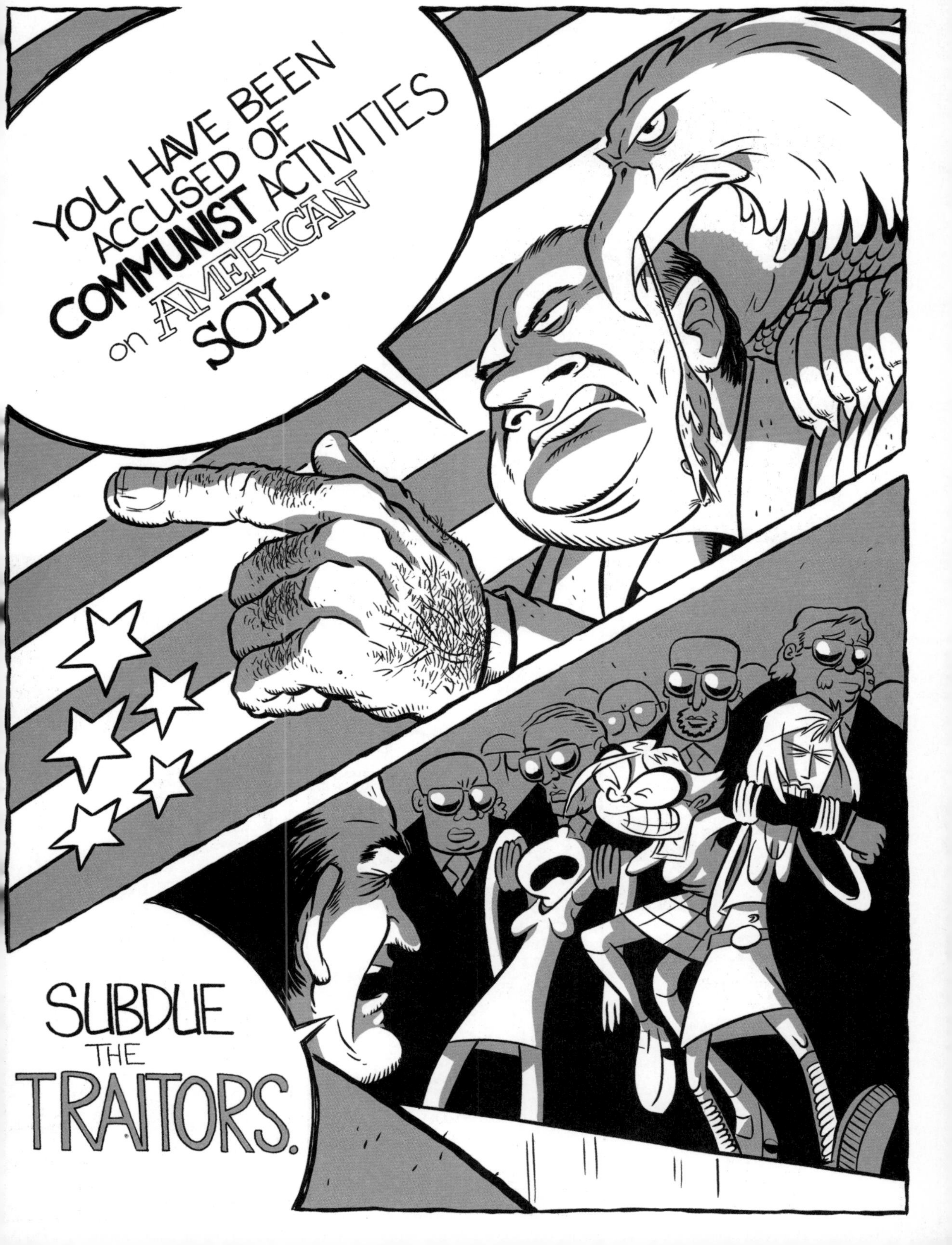

YOU HAVE BEEN ACCUSED OF COMMUNIST ACTIVITIES on AMERICAN SOIL.
SUBDUE THE TRAITORS.

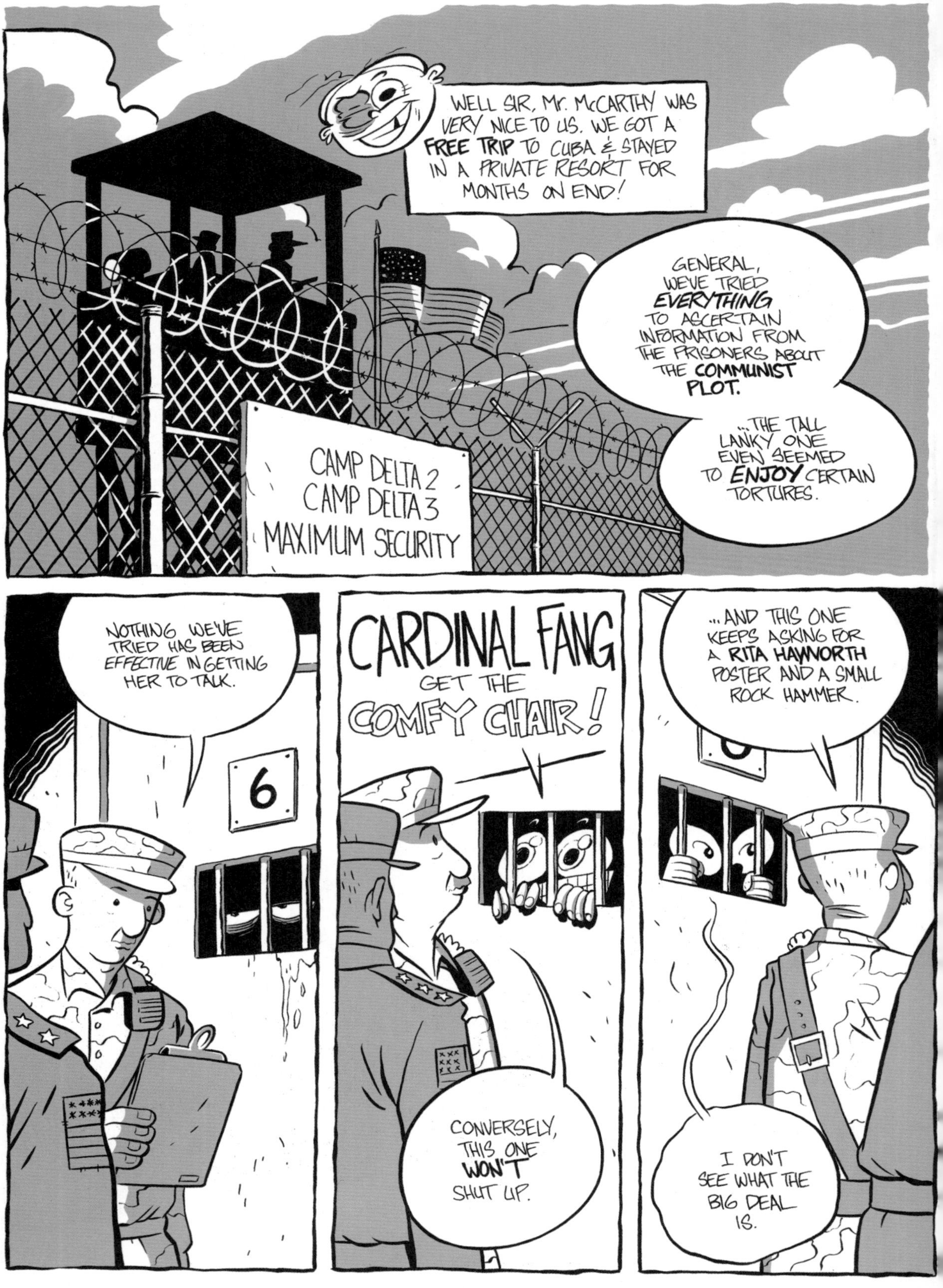
WELL SIR, Mr. McCARTHY WAS VERY NICE TO US. WE GOT A FREE TRIP TO CUBA & STAYED IN A PRIVATE RESORT FOR MONTHS ON END!
GENERAL, WE'VE TRIED EVERYTHING TO ASCERTAIN INFORMATION FROM THE PRISONERS ABOUT THE COMMUNIST PLOT.
...THE TALL LANKY ONE EVEN SEEMED TO ENJOY CERTAIN TORTURES.
CAMP DELTA 2
CAMP DELTA 3
MAXIMUM SECURITY
NOTHING WE'VE TRIED HAS BEEN EFFECTIVE IN GETTING HER TO TALK.
6
CARDINAL FANG GET THE COMFY CHAIR!
CONVERSELY, THIS ONE WON'T SHUT UP.
...AND THIS ONE KEEPS ASKING FOR A RITA HAYWORTH POSTER AND A SMALL ROCK HAMMER.
I DON'T SEE WHAT THE BIG DEAL IS.

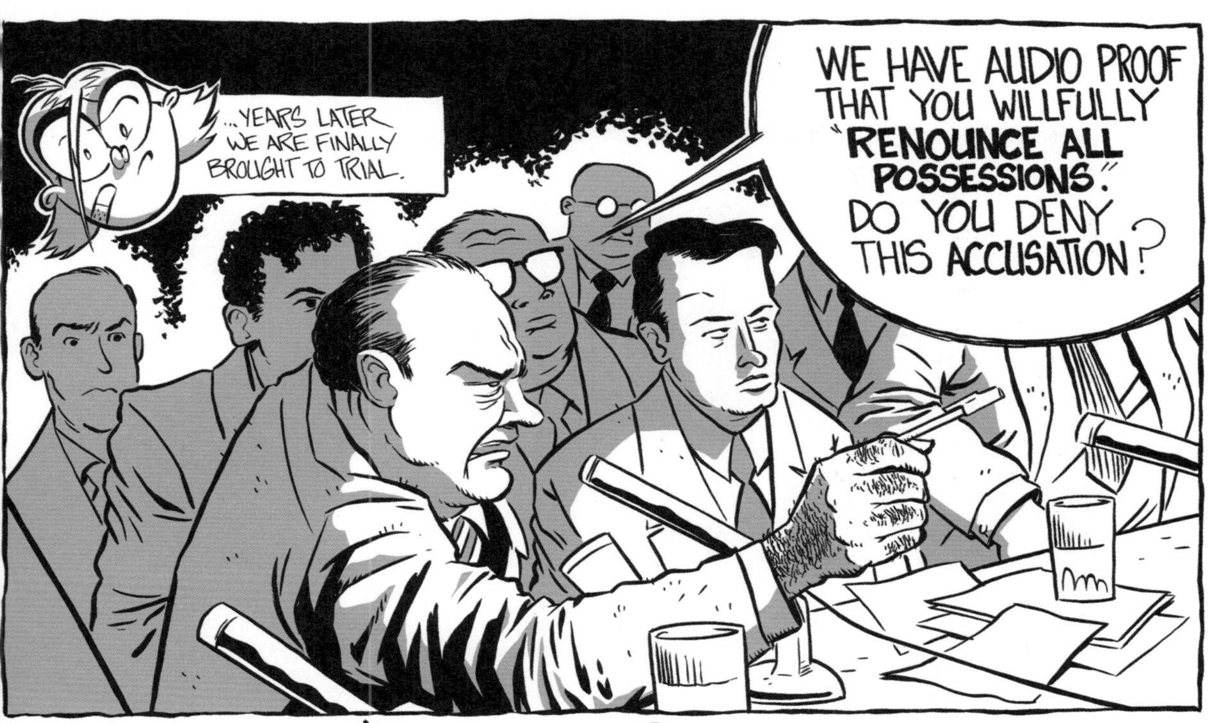
...YEARS LATER WE ARE FINALLY BROUGHT TO TRIAL.
WE HAVE AUDIO PROOF THAT YOU WILLFULLY "RENOUNCE ALL POSSESSIONS." DO YOU DENY THIS ACCUSATION?

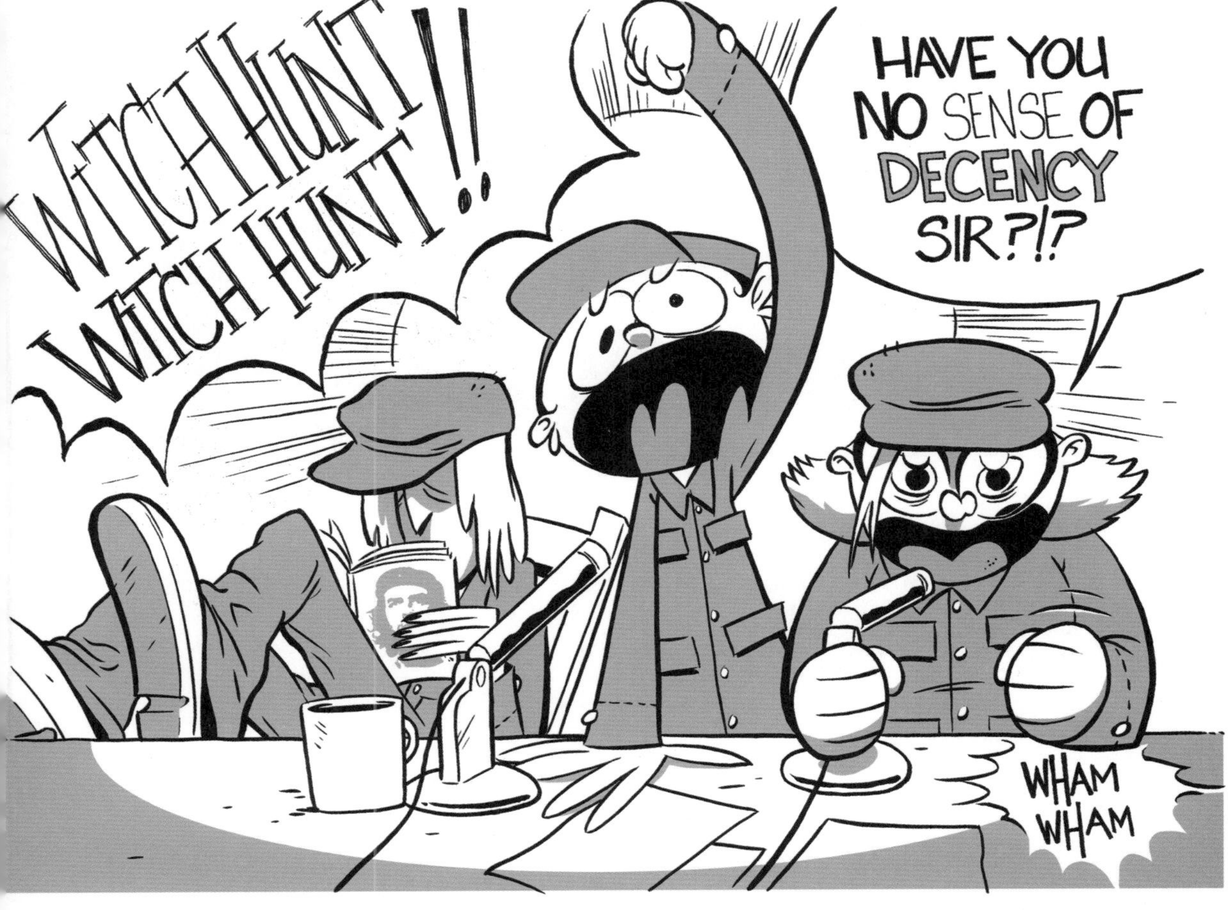
WITCH HUNT WITCH HUNT!!
HAVE YOU NO SENSE OF DECENCY SIR?!?
WHAM WHAM

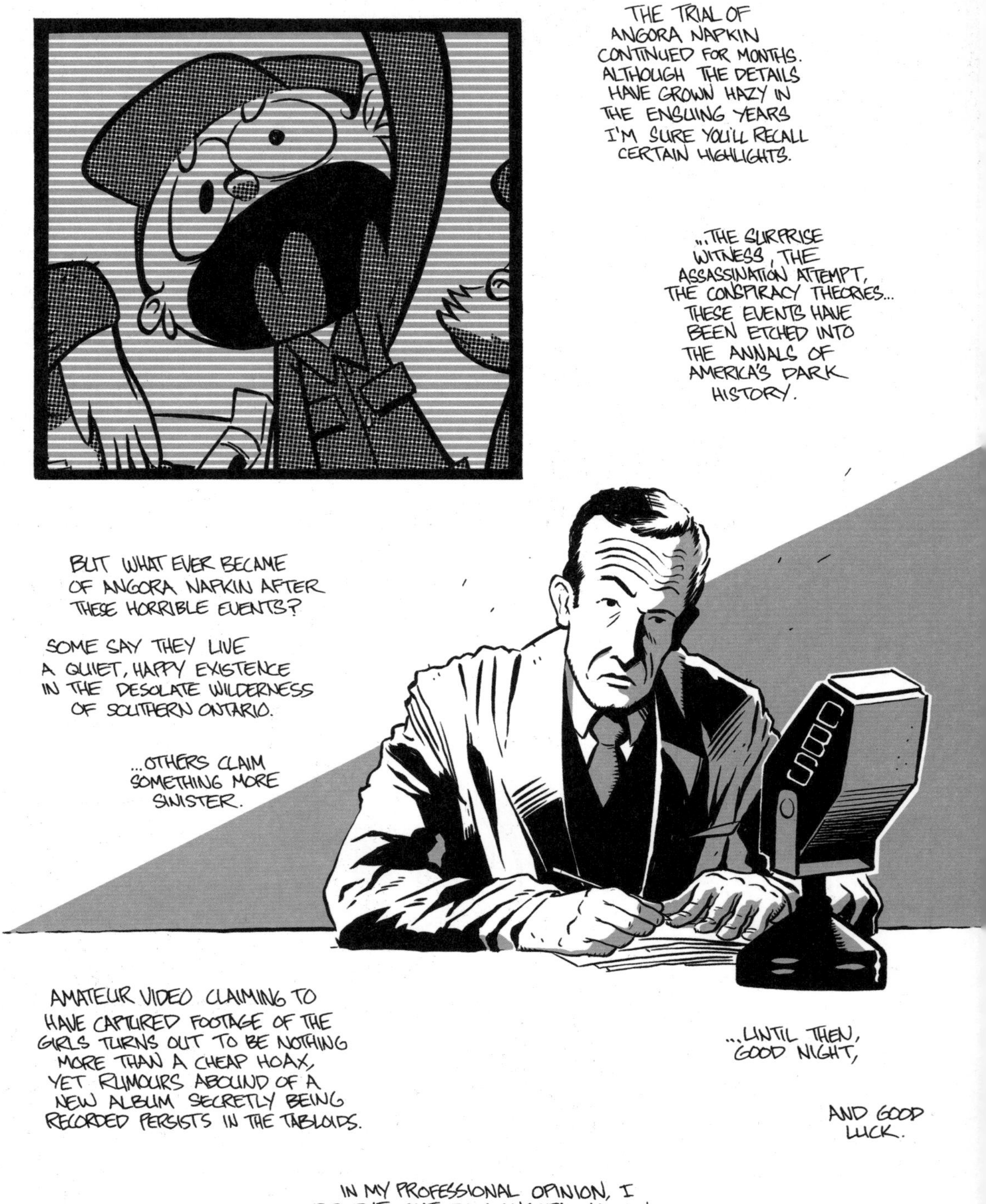
THE TRIAL OF ANGORA NAPKIN CONTINUED FOR MONTHS. ALTHOUGH THE DETAILS HAVE GROWN HAZY IN THE ENSUING YEARS I'M SURE YOU'LL RECALL CERTAIN HIGHLIGHTS.
...THE SURPRISE WITNESS, THE ASSASSINATION ATTEMPT, THE CONSPIRACY THEORIES... THESE EVENTS HAVE BEEN ETCHED INTO THE ANNALS OF AMERICA'S DARK HISTORY.
BUT WHAT EVER BECAME OF ANGORA NAPKIN AFTER THESE HORRIBLE EVENTS?
SOME SAY THEY LIVE A QUIET, HAPPY EXISTENCE IN THE DESOLATE WILDERNESS OF SOUTHERN ONTARIO.
...OTHERS CLAIM SOMETHING MORE SINISTER.
AMATEUR VIDEO CLAIMING TO HAVE CAPTURED FOOTAGE OF THE GIRLS TURNS OUT TO BE NOTHING MORE THAN A CHEAP HOAX, YET RUMOURS ABOUND OF A NEW ALBUM SECRETLY BEING RECORDED PERSISTS IN THE TABLOIDS.
...UNTIL THEN, GOOD NIGHT,
AND GOOD LUCK.
IN MY PROFESSIONAL OPINION, I BELIEVE ONE DAY ANGORA NAPKIN WILL RETURN TO RIGHT THE WRONGS OF THIS FAIR NATION, DESTROYING US ALL IN THE PROCESS.

THE
END.

Afterword

Angora Napkin was an idea my friend Nick Cross and I came up with for an animated series back in 1997. We needed an outlet to cope with being a cog in the syrupy-sweet world of animated children's programming which we worked in all day long. So we decided to create a show that would appeal to our jaded, subversive natures and Beatrice, Molly, and Mallory became that outlet.

We spent a lot of time developing the show, writing scripts and drawing storyboards, but in the end the show amounted to a nice idea that had ostensibly been collecting dust in a few binders.

I recall having coffee with Nick at a Starbucks in Ottawa before I moved back to Prince Edward Island in '03 and we discussed the fate of Angora Napkin. By now Nick had become a force to be reckoned with in Independent Animation circles and I was doing my best to break into comics with my self-published opus Chiaroscuro. I really liked the characters, and hated the idea that they may fester on a shelf, so we agreed to leave their future open for either of us to tackle should one of us desire to do something with them. I always knew I'd make this book, but I didn't know when.

The 'when' began in 2005; I had just completed the first volume of Chiaroscuro and wanted to take a break from the cross-hatched noir world of Steven Patch and do something quick and fun (and without a 102 Crowquill). Angora Napkin seemed like the perfect choice and so I began working on some story ideas.

Originally, I believed this book would take me about a year to complete and then I'd be back to *Chiaroscuro* but the process hit a few bumps. Two in fact; the birth of my beautiful twin daughters Alicen & Hayden in August of 2006!

Through late nights and blinding exhaustion I somehow managed to finish the book when another strange twist in the story began.

There was a Canada-wide call for new late night animation programming and *Teletoon* (Canada's answer to the *Cartoon Network*) green lit *Angora Napkin* for a pilot! I called Nick and we found ourselves dusting off those old binders and picking up where we left off years before. 2009 looks like a very good year for the return of Cuddle-Core.

As a special bonus, I've included a few *Angora Napkin* rarities. The short comic "Oscillating Retriever" appeared in the back of *Chiaroscuro #5* and was the first time *Angora Napkin* appeared in comic book form. That was followed in issue #7 with "Zesty Pineapple Sprig" (incidentally the final self published issue of *Chiaroscuro*). I'm also pleased to present for the first time "What's the Rhubarb?"—an *Angora Napkin* comic by Nick Cross.

Troy Little – October 2008

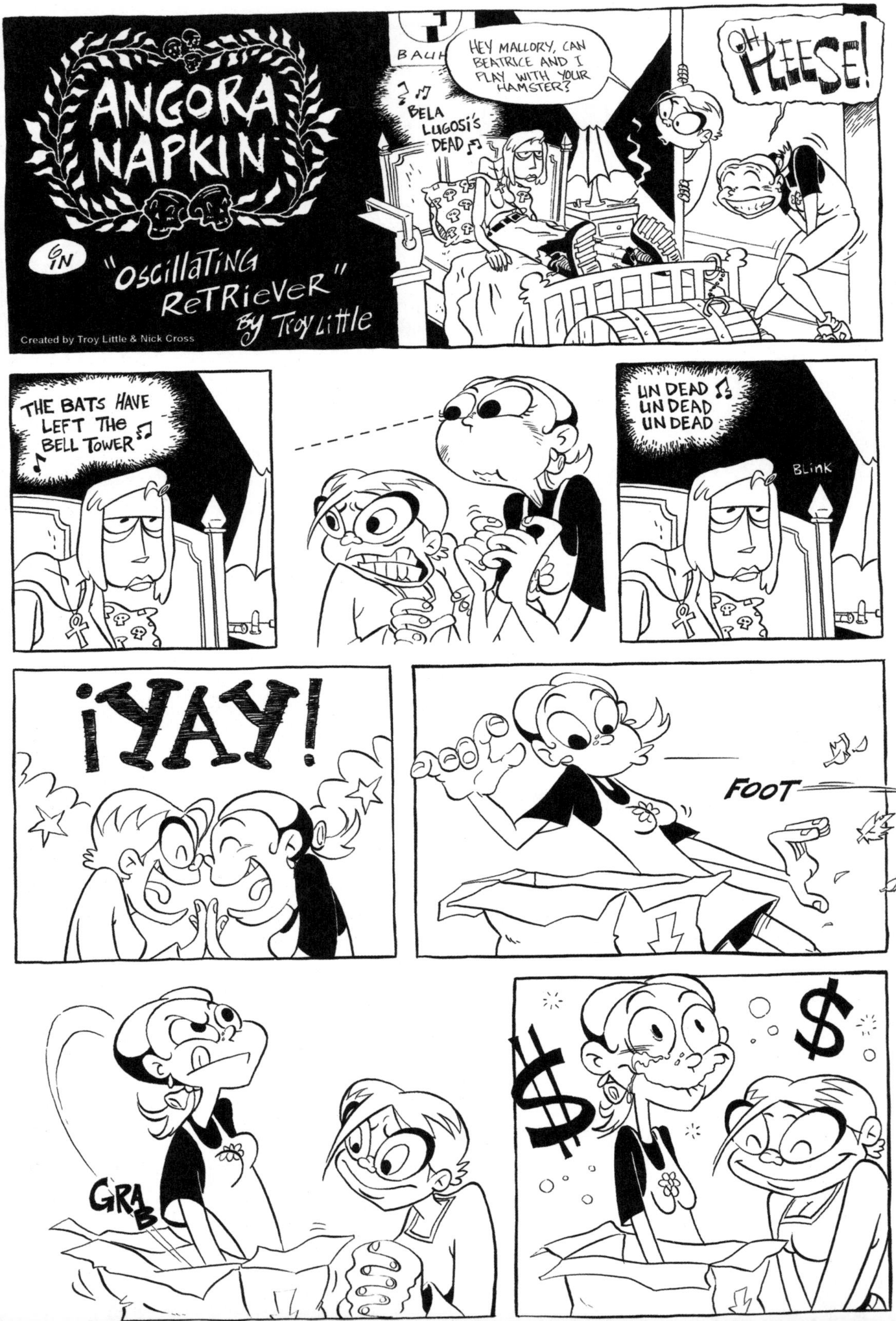

ANGORA NAPKIN
in
"Oscillating Retriever"
By Troy Little
Created by Troy Little & Nick Cross
BAUH
HEY MALLORY, CAN BEATRICE AND I PLAY WITH YOUR HAMSTER?
BELA LUGOSI'S DEAD
OH PLEESE!
THE BATS HAVE LEFT THE BELL TOWER
UN DEAD UN DEAD UN DEAD
BLINK
¡YAY!
FOOT
GRAB
$
$

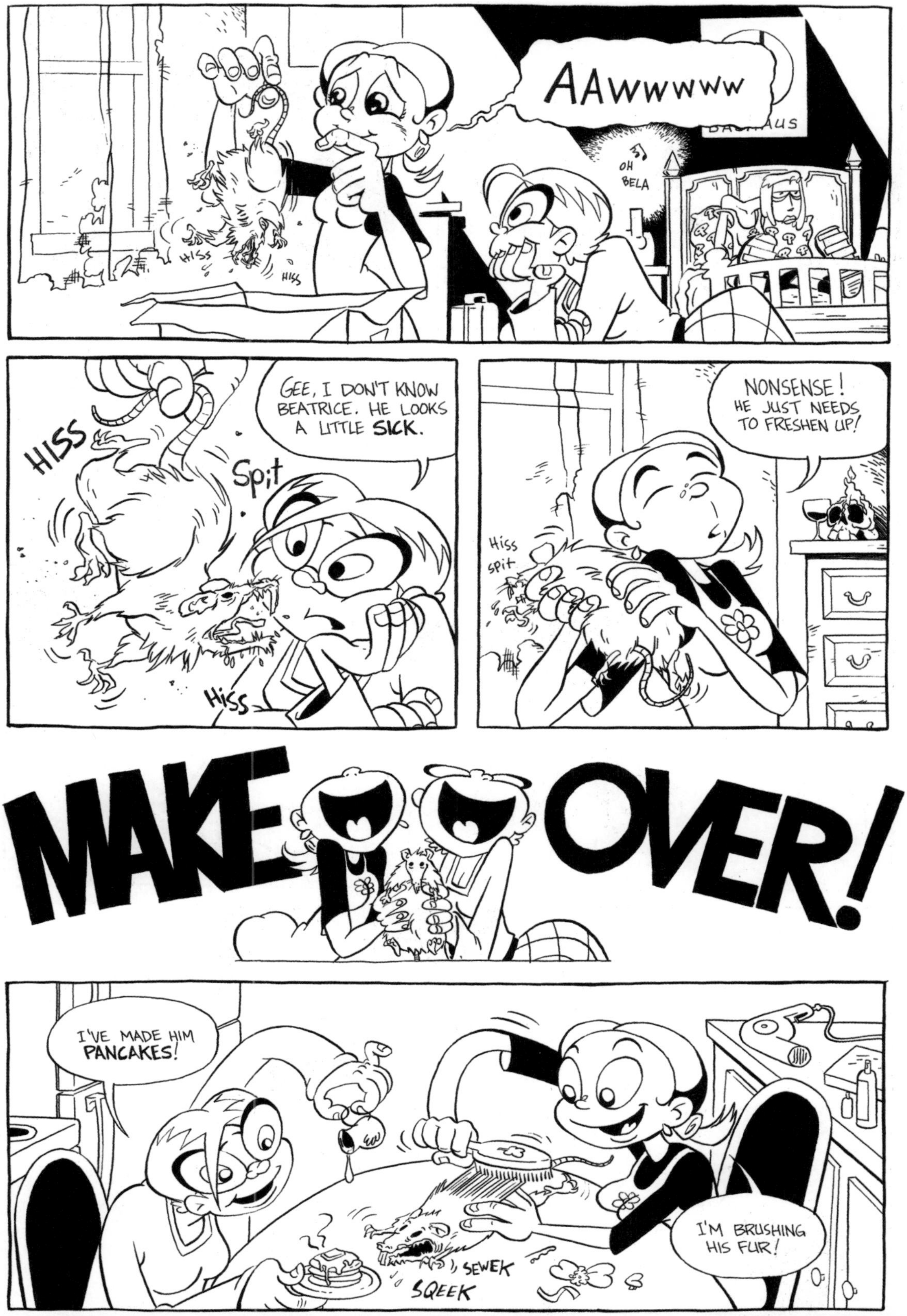

HISS
HISS
AAwwwww
OH BELA
HISS
Spit
HISS
GEE, I DON'T KNOW BEATRICE. HE LOOKS A LITTLE SICK.
NONSENSE! HE JUST NEEDS TO FRESHEN UP!
Hiss
spit
MAKE OVER!
I'VE MADE HIM PANCAKES!
SEWEK
SQEEK
I'M BRUSHING HIS FUR!

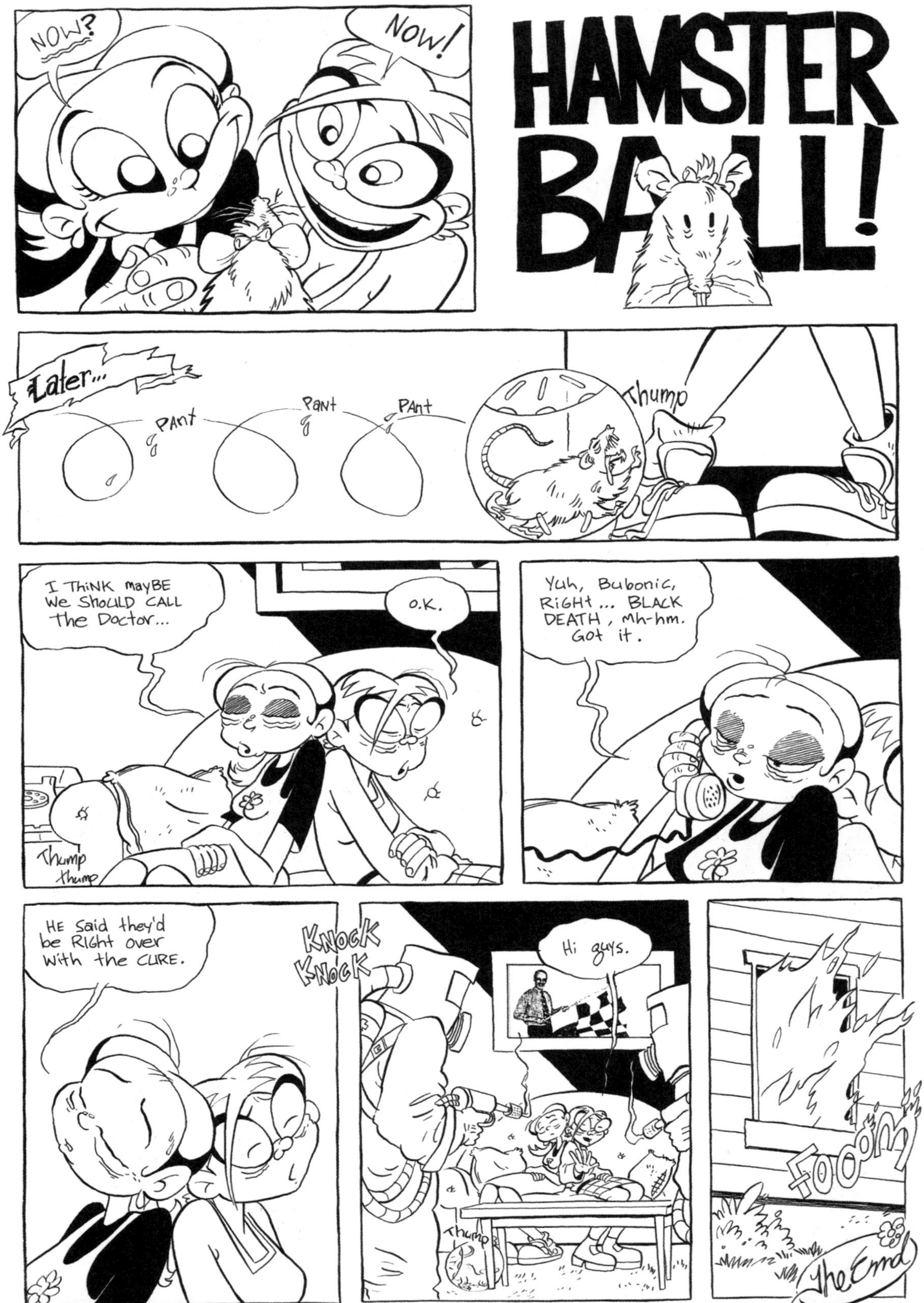
NOW?
Now!
HAMSTER BALL!
Later...
PANT
PAnt
PAnt
Thump
I ThiNK mayBE We SHOULD CALL The Doctor...
O.K.
Thump thump
Yuh, Bubonic, RiGHT... BLACK DEATH, Mh-hm. Got it.
HE Said they'd be RIGHT over With the CURE.
KNocK KNocK
Hi guys.
Thump
FOOOM
The End

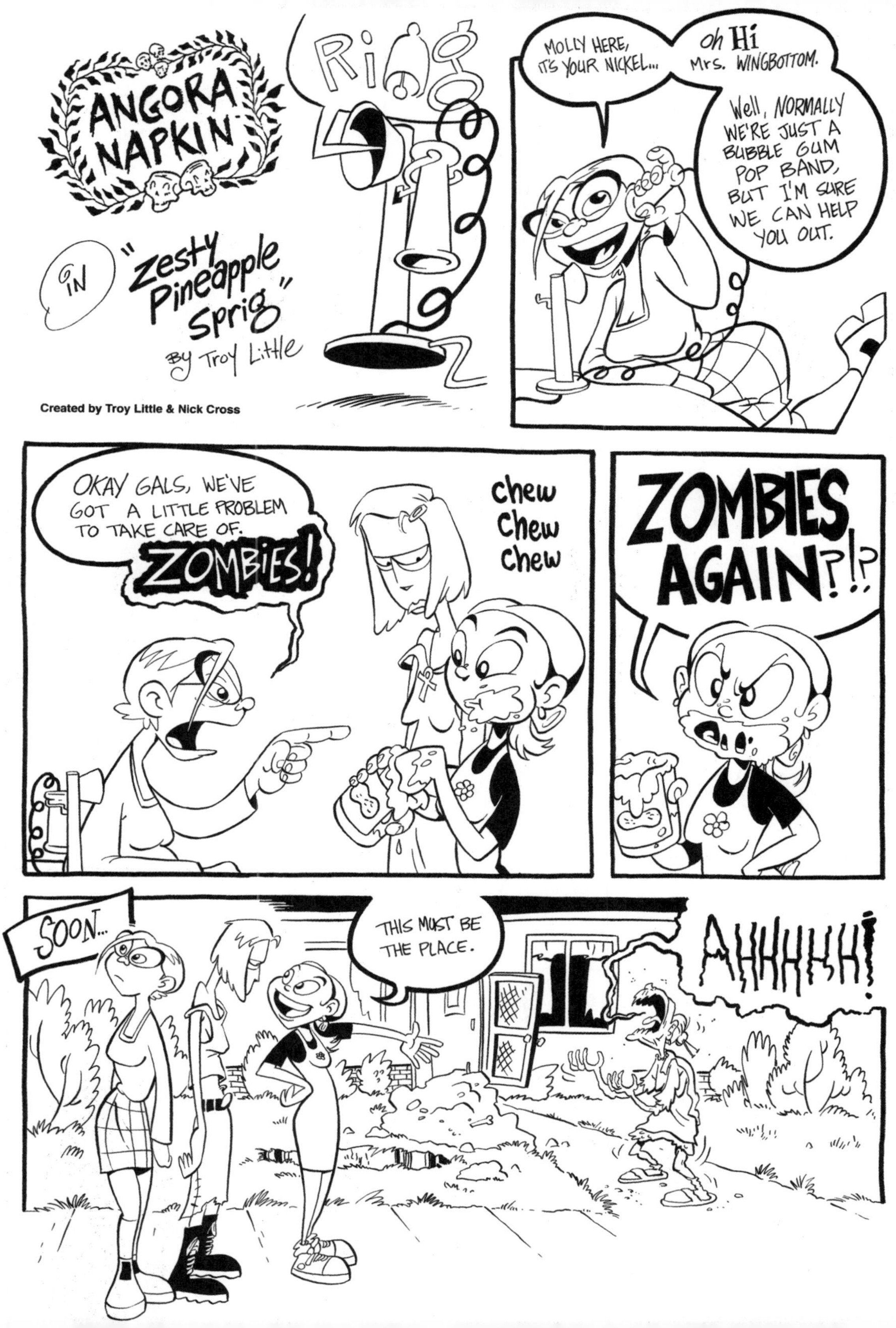

ANGORA NAPKIN
IN "Zesty Pineapple Sprig"
By Troy Little
Created by Troy Little & Nick Cross
Ring
MOLLY HERE, IT'S YOUR NICKEL...
oh Hi Mrs. WINGBOTTOM.
Well, NORMALLY WE'RE JUST A BUBBLE GUM POP BAND, BUT I'M SURE WE CAN HELP YOU OUT.
OKAY GALS, WE'VE GOT A LITTLE PROBLEM TO TAKE CARE OF. ZOMBIES!
chew chew chew
ZOMBIES AGAIN?!?
SOON...
THIS MUST BE THE PLACE.
AHHHHH!

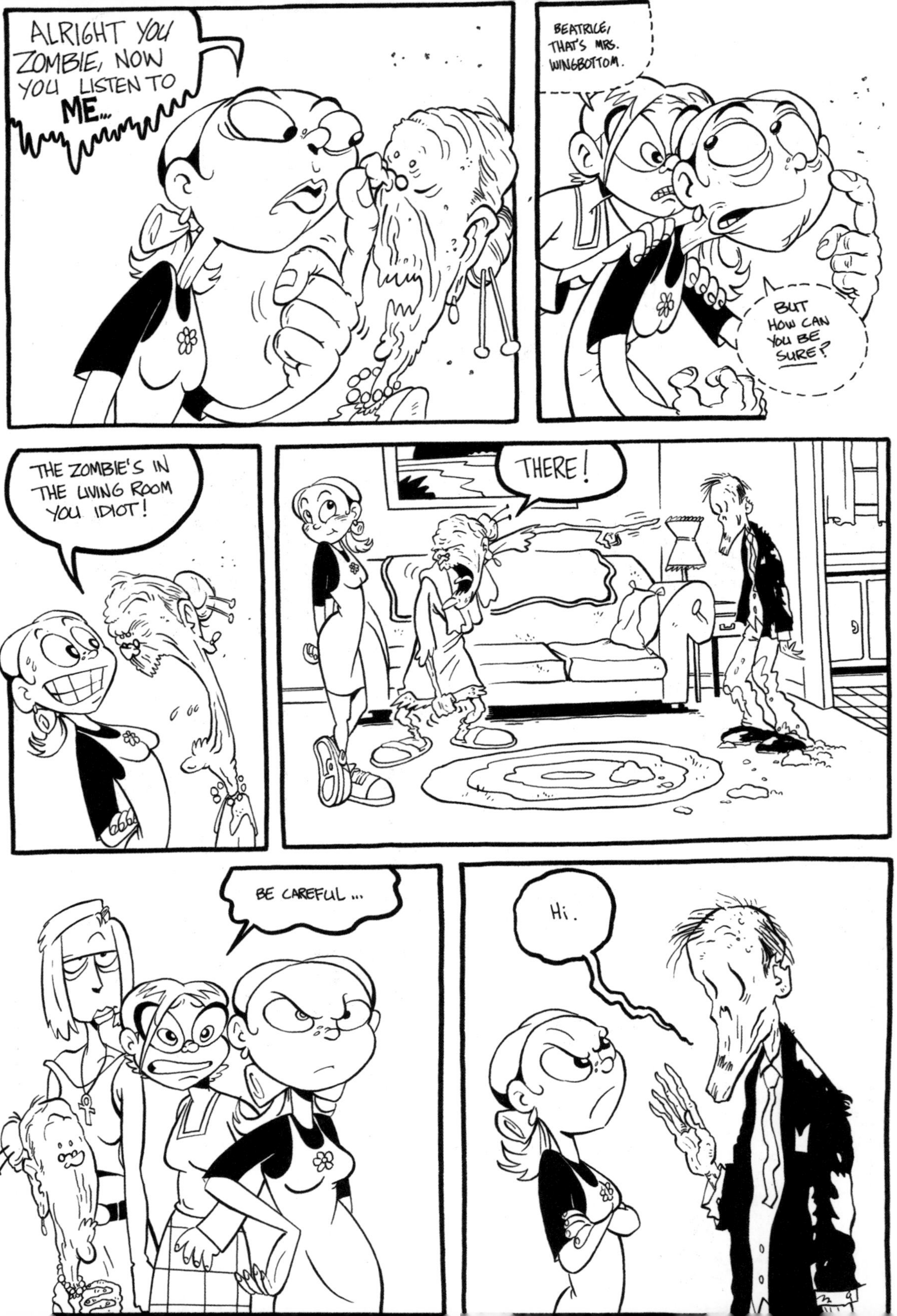
ALRIGHT YOU ZOMBIE, NOW YOU LISTEN TO ME...
BEATRICE, THAT'S MRS. WINGBOTTOM.
BUT HOW CAN YOU BE SURE?
THE ZOMBIE'S IN THE LIVING ROOM YOU IDIOT!
THERE!
BE CAREFUL ...
Hi.

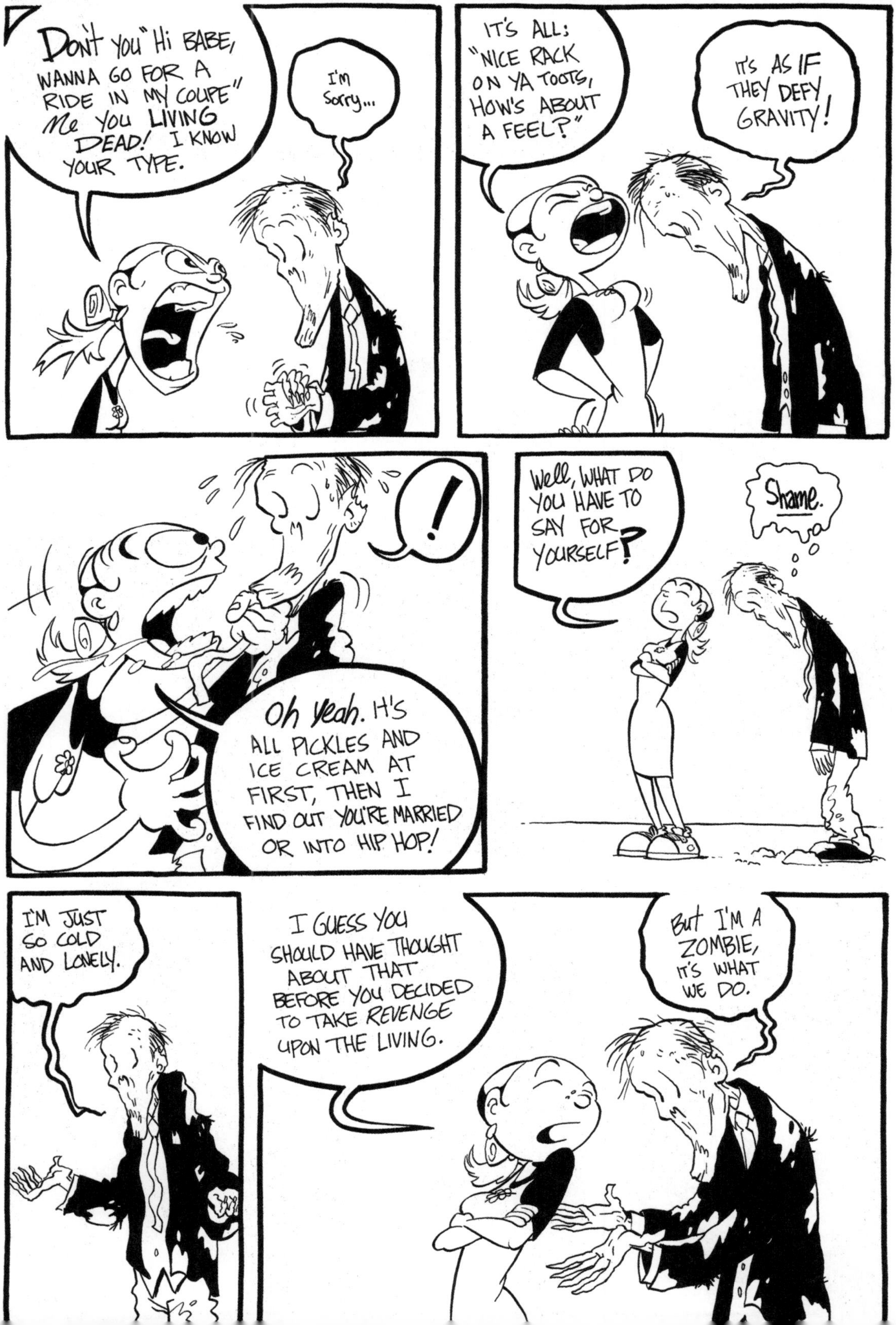

Don't you "Hi BABE, WANNA GO FOR A RIDE IN MY COUPE" Me YOU LIVING DEAD! I KNOW YOUR TYPE.
I'm Sorry...
IT'S ALL: "NICE RACK ON YA TOOTS, HOW'S ABOUT A FEEL?"
IT'S AS IF THEY DEFY GRAVITY!
!
Oh Yeah. It's ALL PICKLES AND ICE CREAM AT FIRST, THEN I FIND OUT YOU'RE MARRIED OR INTO HIP HOP!
Well, WHAT DO YOU HAVE TO SAY FOR YOURSELF?
Shame.
I'M JUST SO COLD AND LONELY.
I GUESS YOU SHOULD HAVE THOUGHT ABOUT THAT BEFORE YOU DECIDED TO TAKE REVENGE UPON THE LIVING.
But I'M A ZOMBIE, IT'S WHAT WE DO.

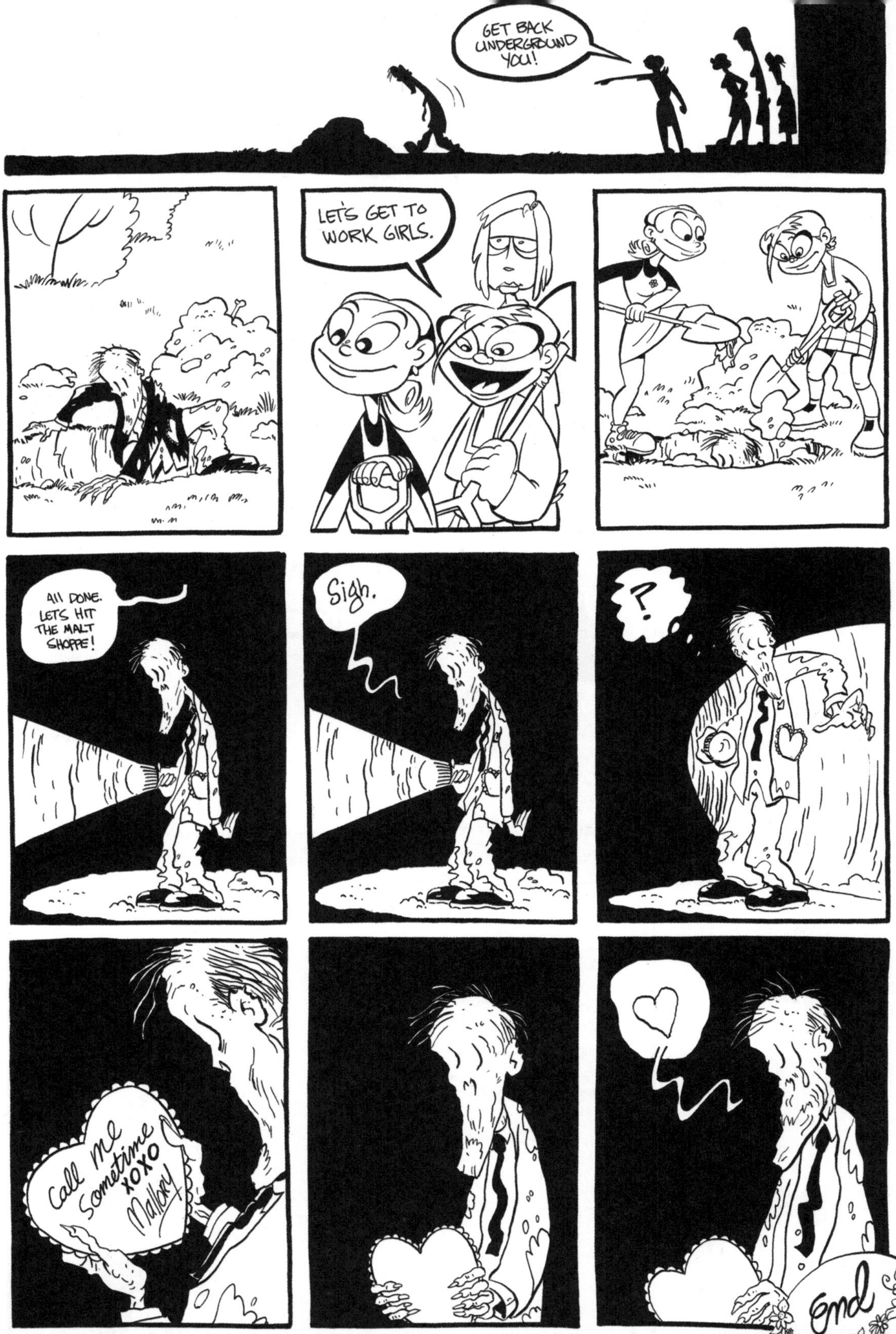
GET BACK UNDERGROUND YOU!
LET'S GET TO WORK GIRLS.
All DONE. LET'S HIT THE MALT SHOPPE!
Sigh.
?
Call me sometime XOXO Mallory
End

ANGORA NAPKIN

in

WHAT'S THE RHUBARB?

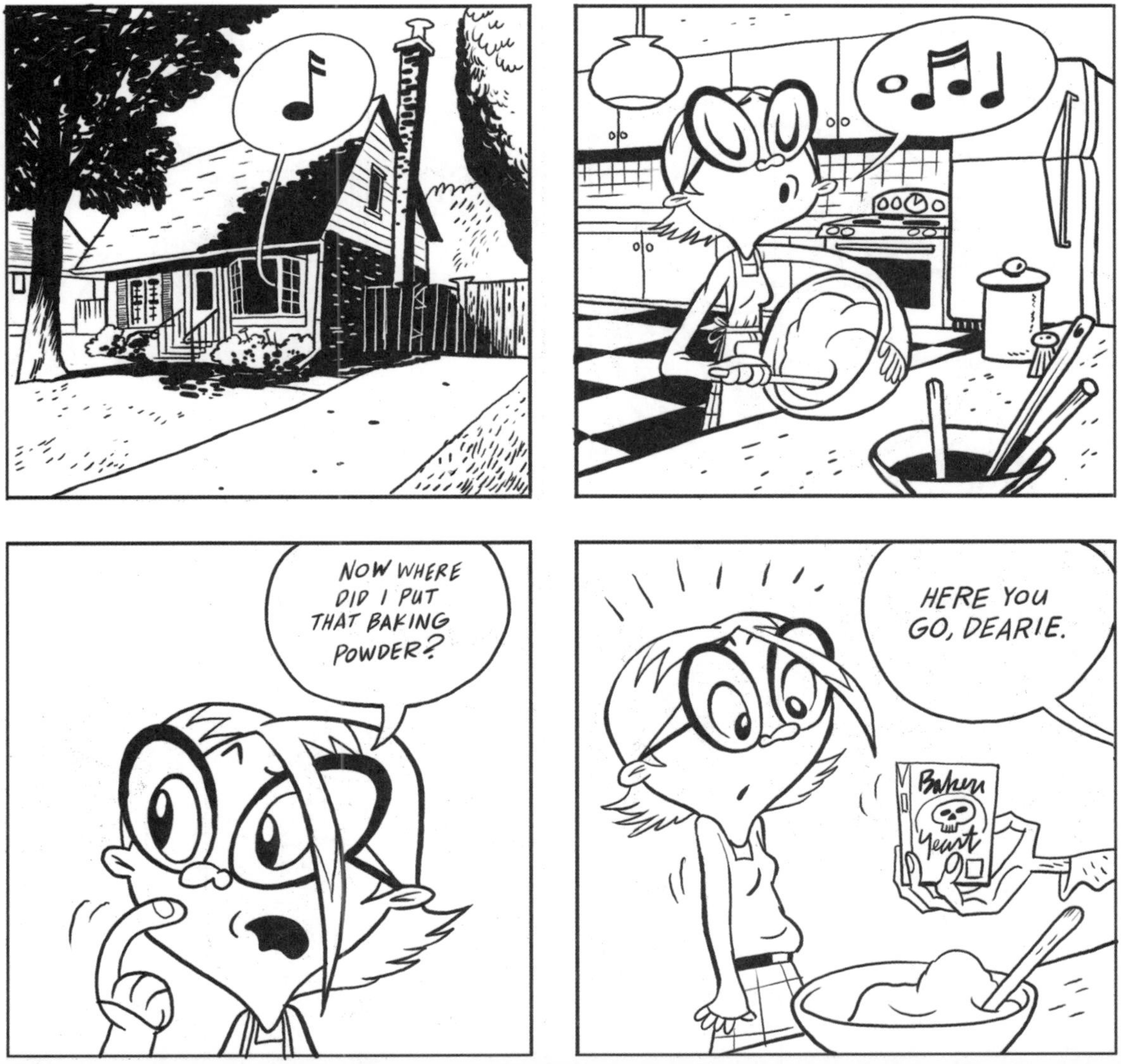
NOW WHERE DID I PUT THAT BAKING POWDER?
HERE YOU GO, DEARIE.

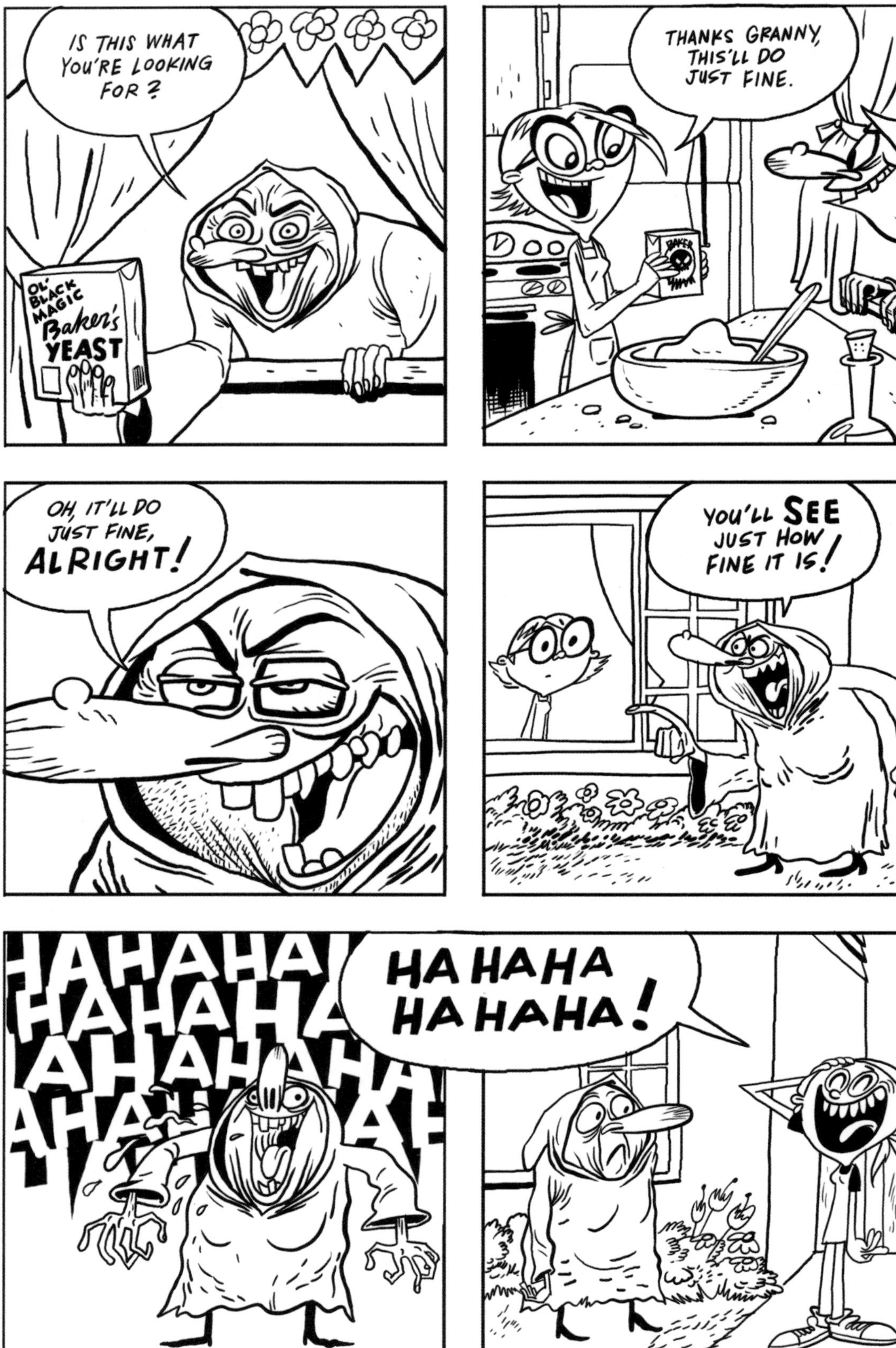
IS THIS WHAT YOU'RE LOOKING FOR?
OL' BLACK MAGIC Baker's YEAST
THANKS GRANNY, THIS'LL DO JUST FINE.
OH, IT'LL DO JUST FINE, ALRIGHT!
YOU'LL SEE JUST HOW FINE IT IS!
HAHAHA HAHAHA!

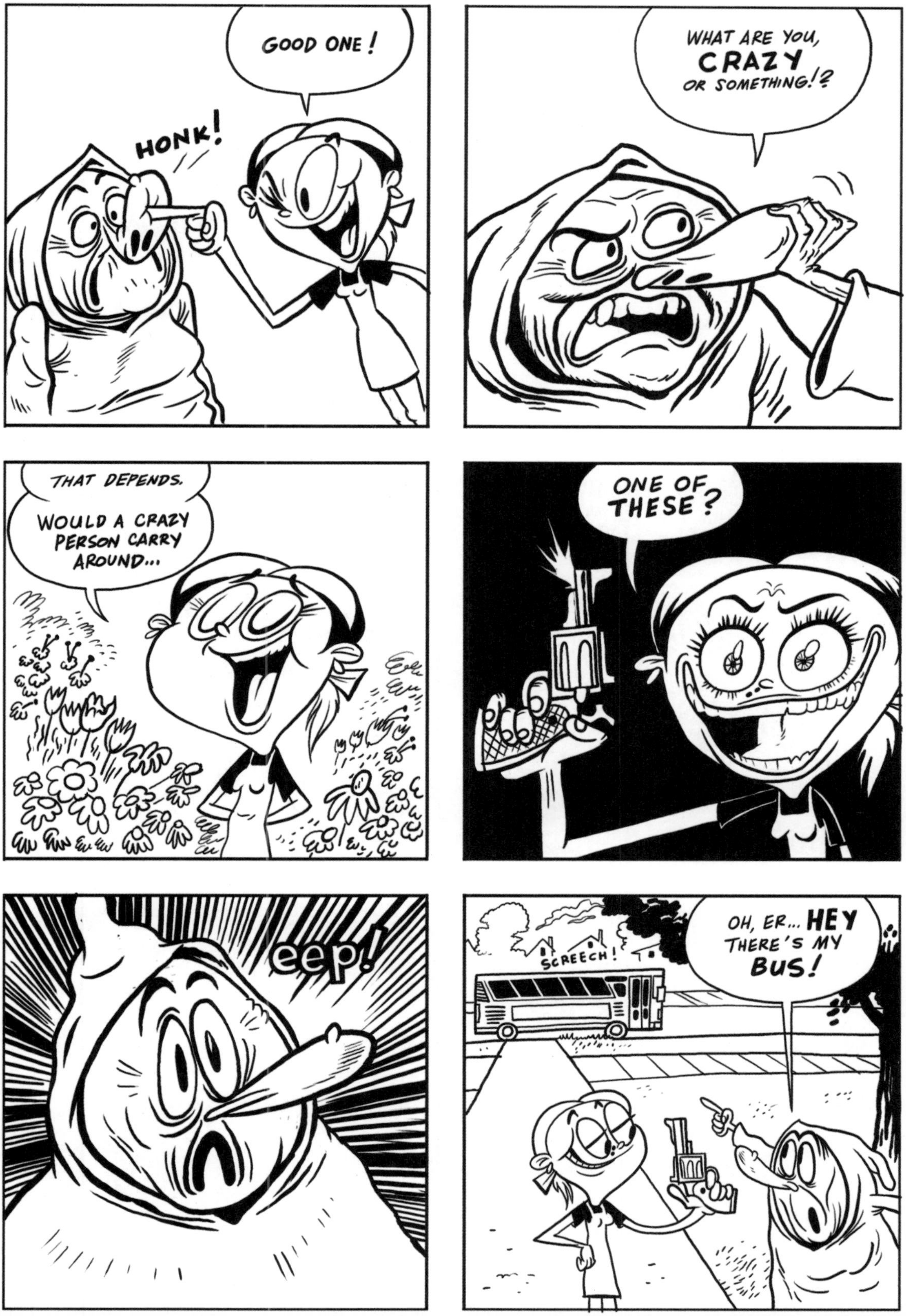
GOOD ONE!
HONK!
WHAT ARE YOU, CRAZY OR SOMETHING!?
THAT DEPENDS.
WOULD A CRAZY PERSON CARRY AROUND...
ONE OF THESE?
eep!
SCREECH!
OH, ER... HEY THERE'S MY BUS!

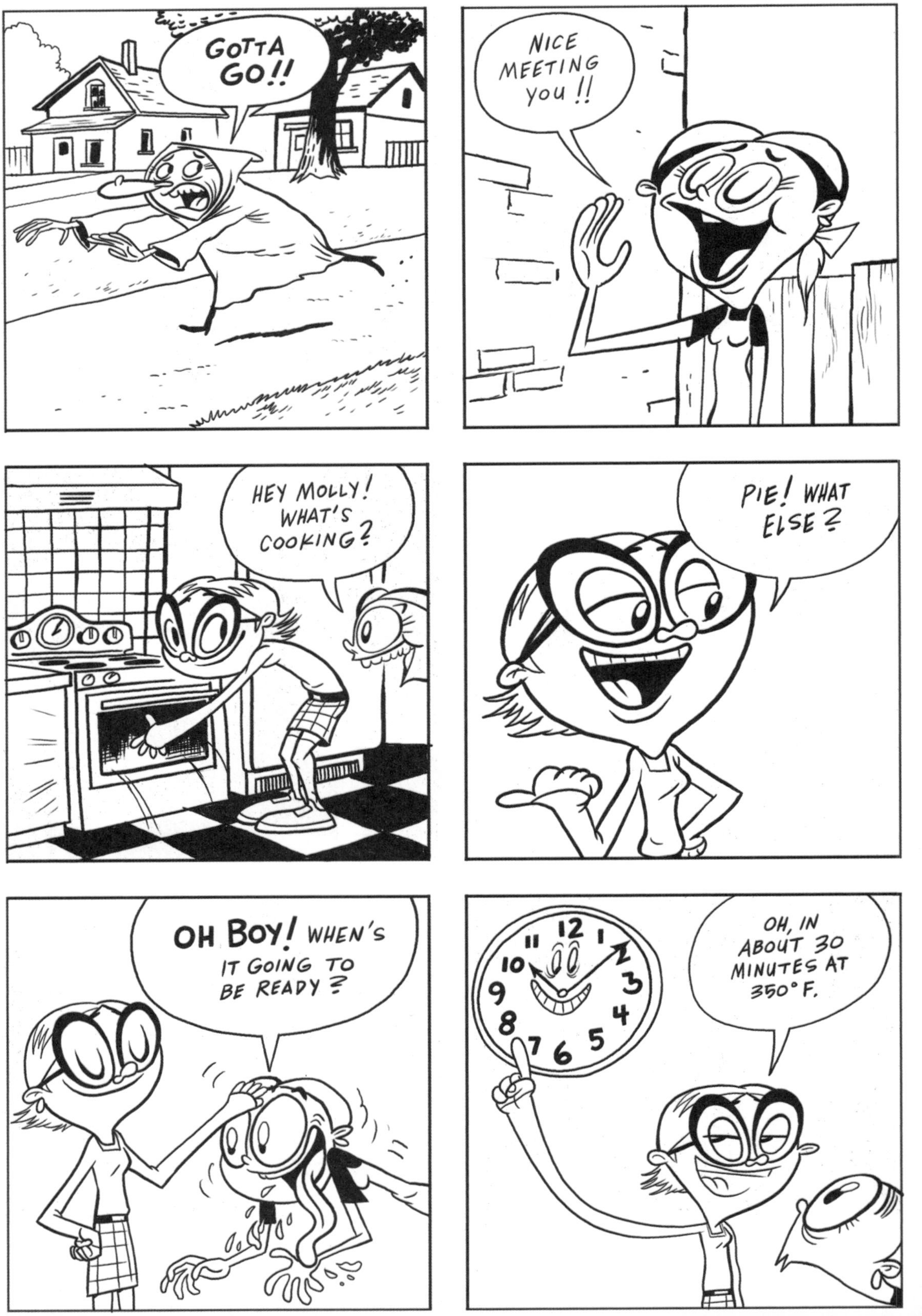
GOTTA GO!!
NICE MEETING YOU!!
HEY MOLLY! WHAT'S COOKING?
PIE! WHAT ELSE?
OH BOY! WHEN'S IT GOING TO BE READY?
12
1
2
3
4
5
6
7
8
9
10
11
OH, IN ABOUT 30 MINUTES AT 350° F.

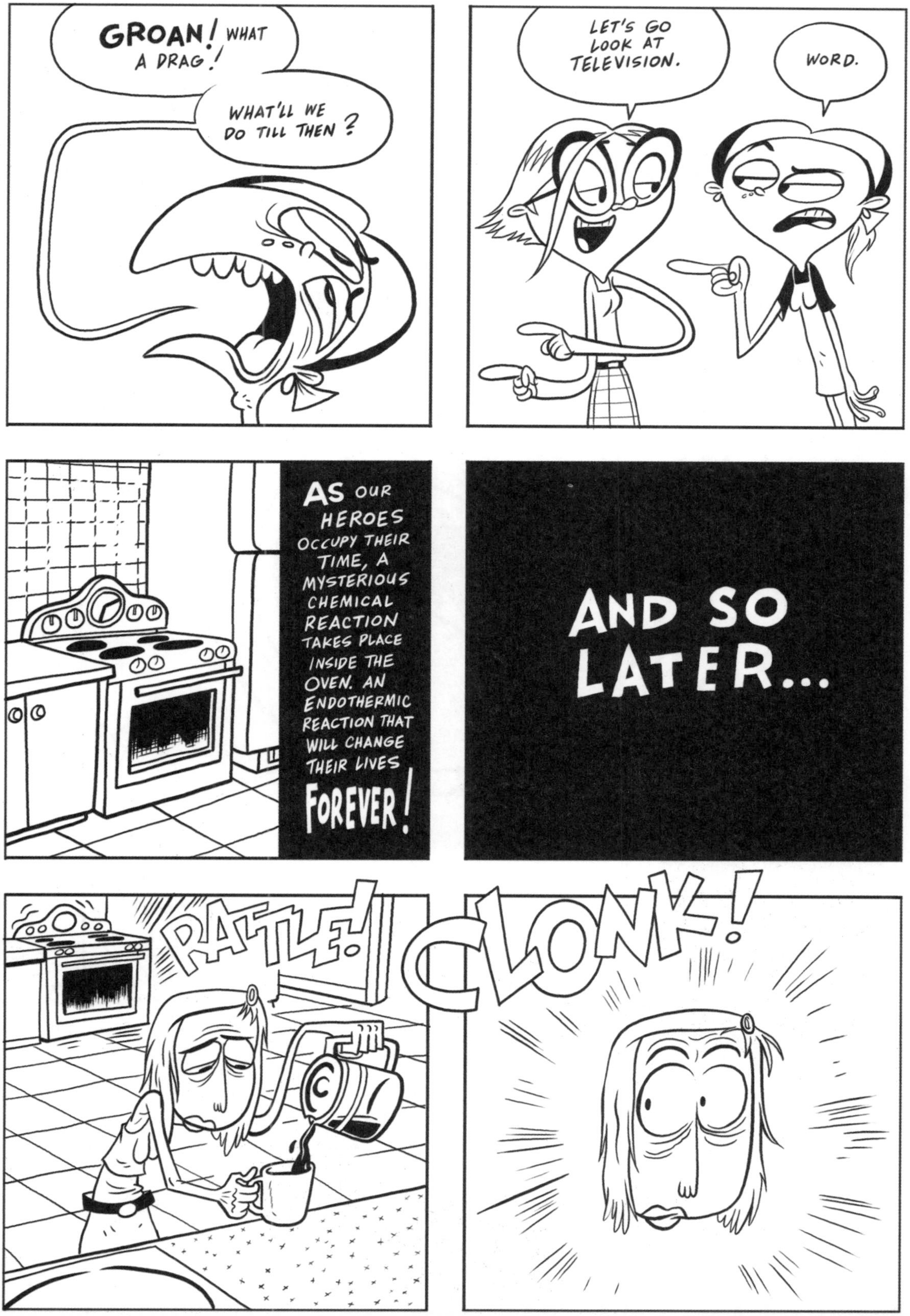
GROAN! WHAT A DRAG!
WHAT'LL WE DO TILL THEN?
LET'S GO LOOK AT TELEVISION.
WORD.
AS OUR HEROES OCCUPY THEIR TIME, A MYSTERIOUS CHEMICAL REACTION TAKES PLACE INSIDE THE OVEN. AN ENDOTHERMIC REACTION THAT WILL CHANGE THEIR LIVES FOREVER!
AND SO LATER...
RATTLE!
CLONK!

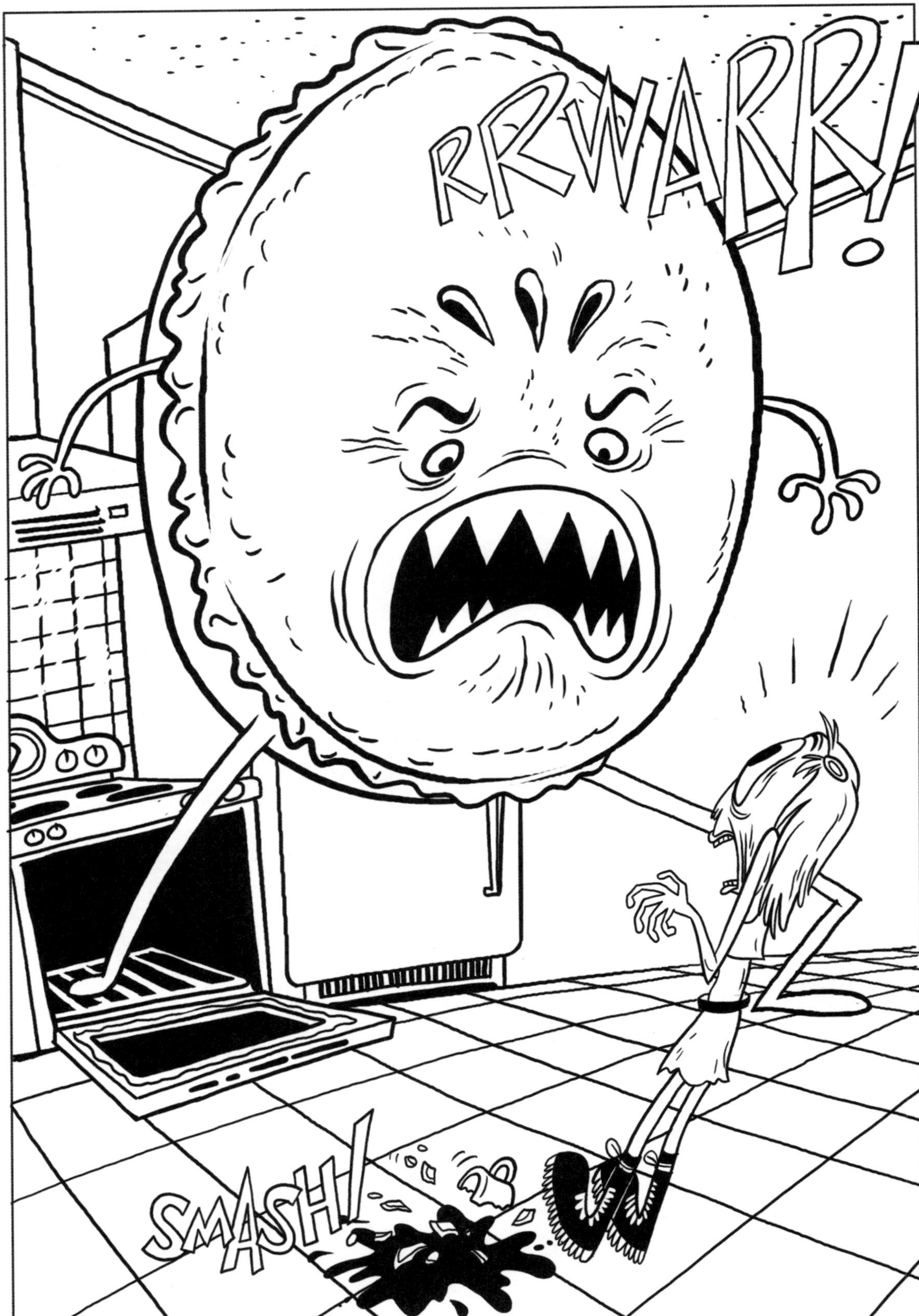
RRWARR!
SMASH!

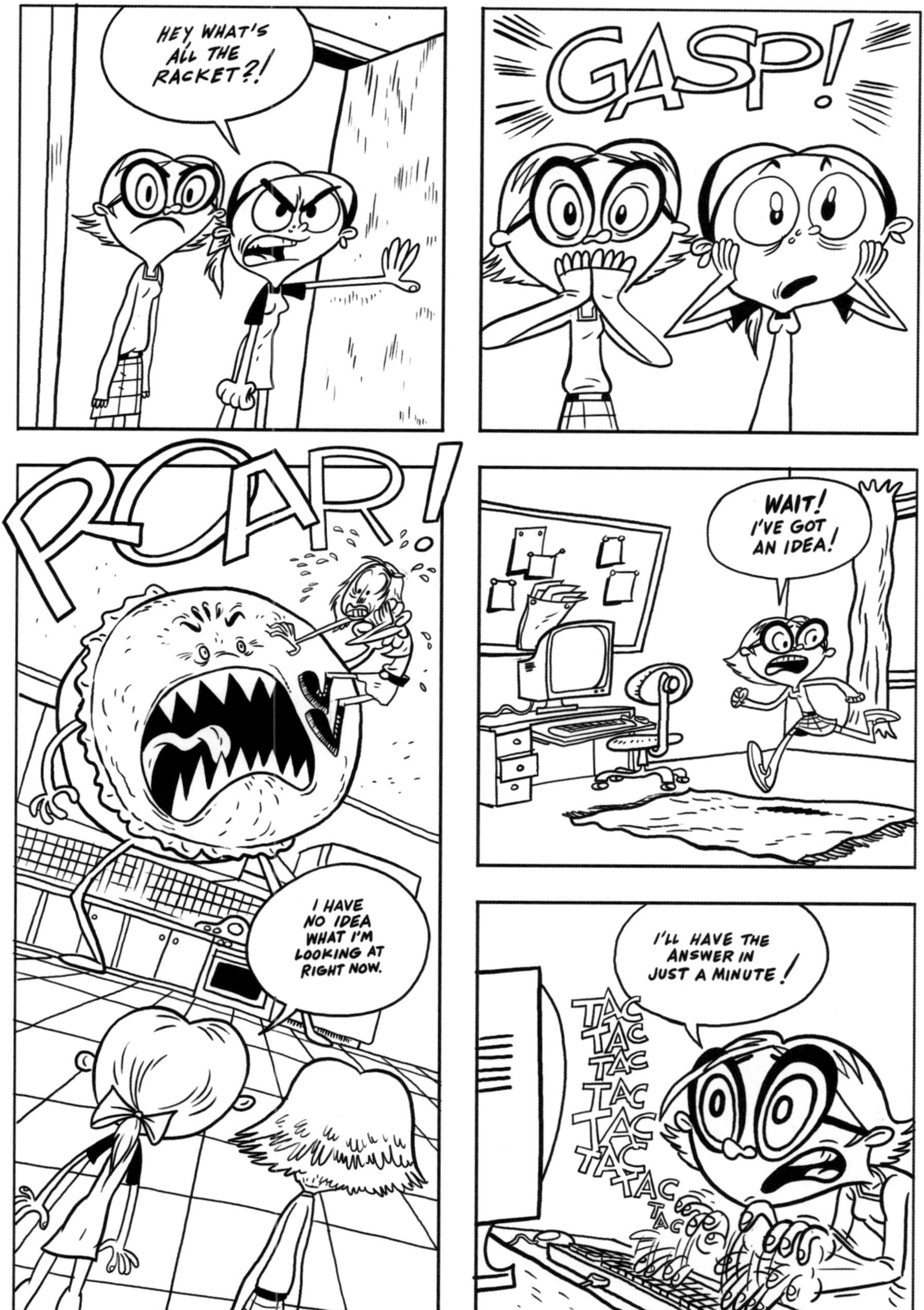
HEY WHAT'S ALL THE RACKET?!
GASP!
ROAR!
I HAVE NO IDEA WHAT I'M LOOKING AT RIGHT NOW.
WAIT! I'VE GOT AN IDEA!
I'LL HAVE THE ANSWER IN JUST A MINUTE!
TAC TAC TAC TAC TAC TAC TAC TAC TAC

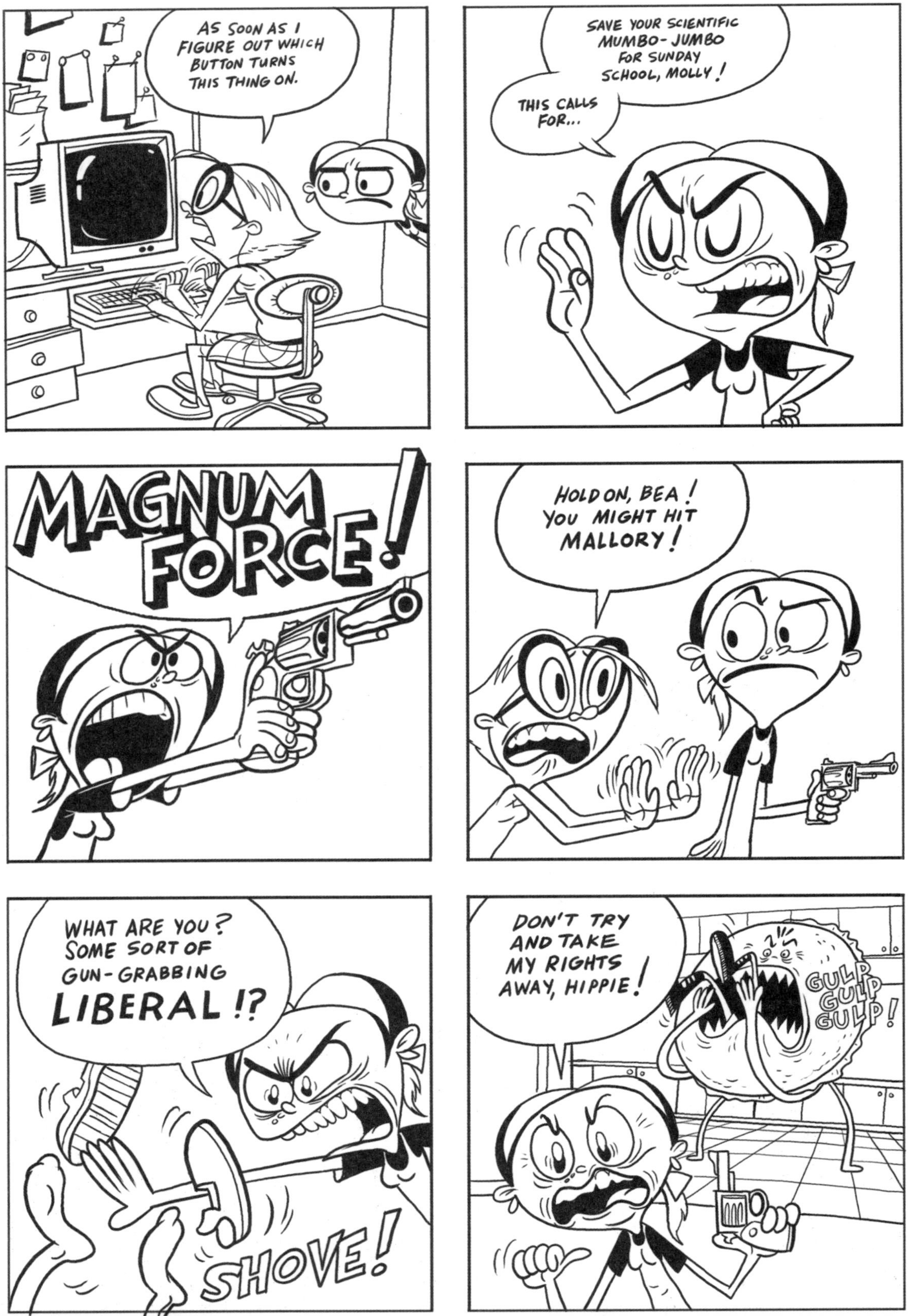
AS SOON AS I FIGURE OUT WHICH BUTTON TURNS THIS THING ON.
SAVE YOUR SCIENTIFIC MUMBO-JUMBO FOR SUNDAY SCHOOL, MOLLY!
THIS CALLS FOR...
MAGNUM FORCE!
HOLD ON, BEA! YOU MIGHT HIT MALLORY!
WHAT ARE YOU? SOME SORT OF GUN-GRABBING LIBERAL!?
SHOVE!
DON'T TRY AND TAKE MY RIGHTS AWAY, HIPPIE!
GULP GULP GULP!

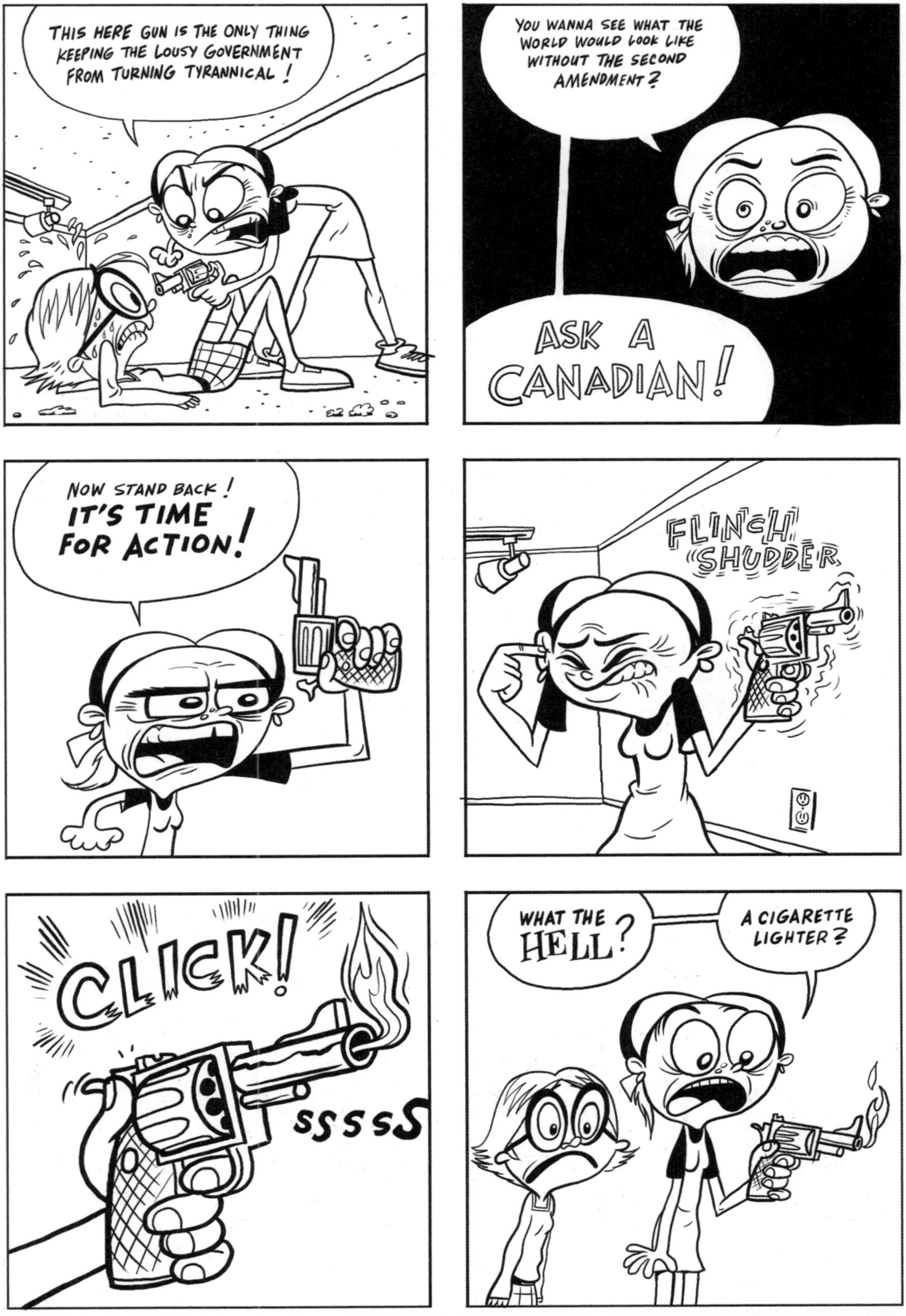

THIS HERE GUN IS THE ONLY THING KEEPING THE LOUSY GOVERNMENT FROM TURNING TYRANNICAL!
YOU WANNA SEE WHAT THE WORLD WOULD LOOK LIKE WITHOUT THE SECOND AMENDMENT?
ASK A CANADIAN!
NOW STAND BACK! IT'S TIME FOR ACTION!
FLINCH
SHUDDER
CLICK!
SSSSS
WHAT THE HELL?
A CIGARETTE LIGHTER?

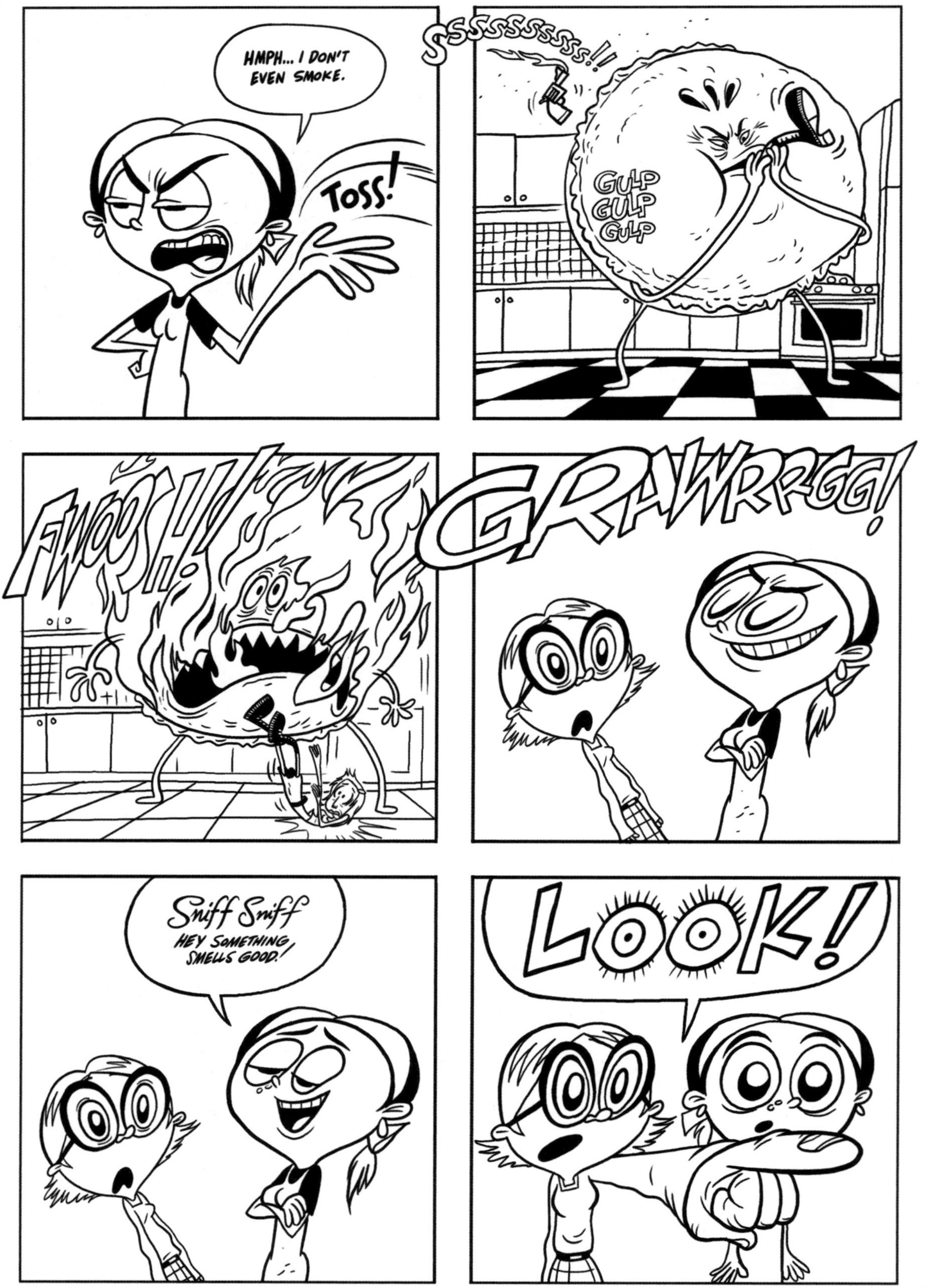
HMPH... I DON'T EVEN SMOKE.
TOSS!
SSSSSSSSSSS!!
GULP GULP GULP
FWOOSH!!
GRAWRRGG!
Sniff Sniff
HEY SOMETHING SMELLS GOOD!
LOOK!

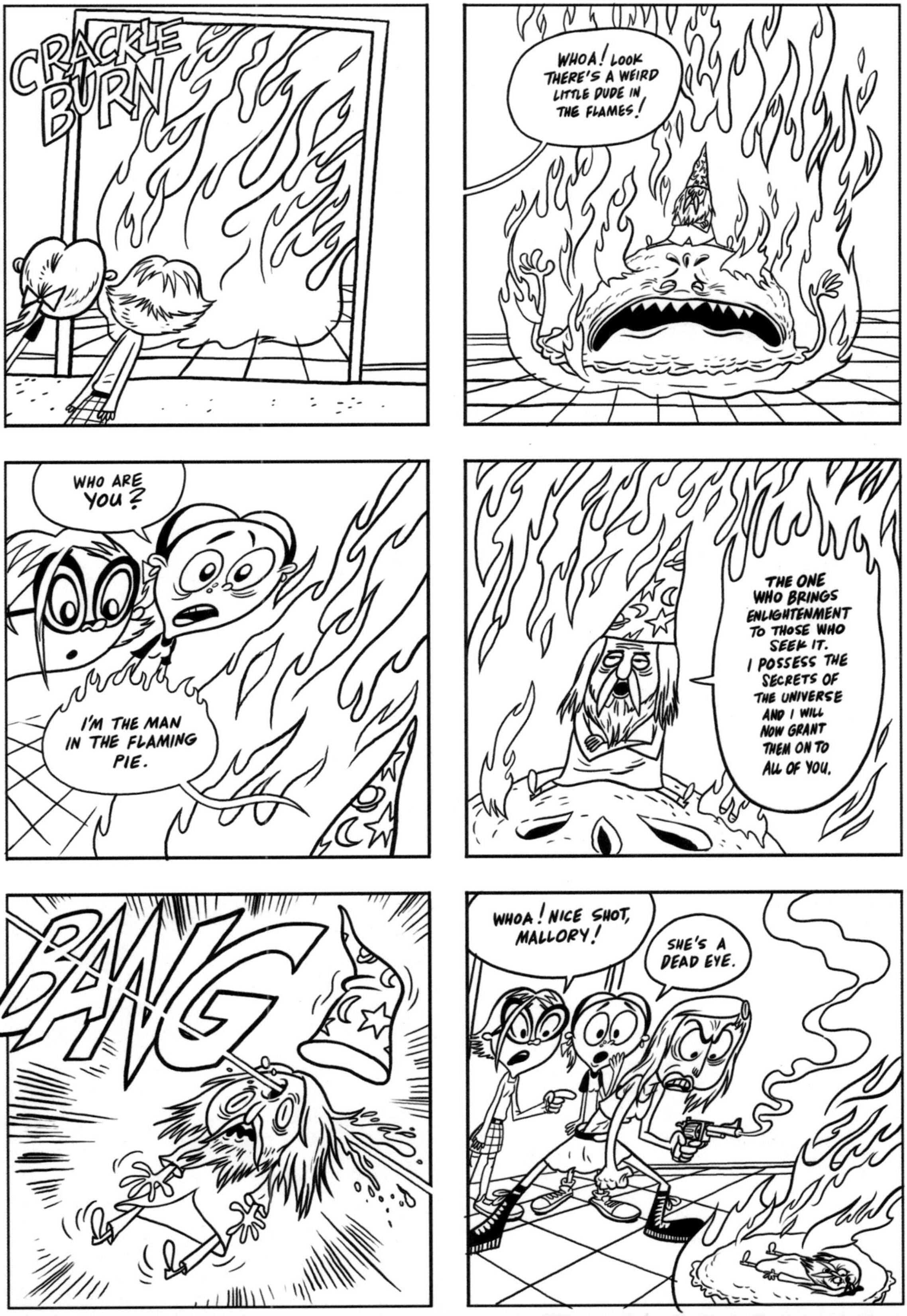
CRACKLE BURN
WHOA! LOOK THERE'S A WEIRD LITTLE DUDE IN THE FLAMES!
WHO ARE YOU?
I'M THE MAN IN THE FLAMING PIE.
THE ONE WHO BRINGS ENLIGHTENMENT TO THOSE WHO SEEK IT. I POSSESS THE SECRETS OF THE UNIVERSE AND I WILL NOW GRANT THEM ON TO ALL OF YOU.
BANG
WHOA! NICE SHOT, MALLORY!
SHE'S A DEAD EYE.

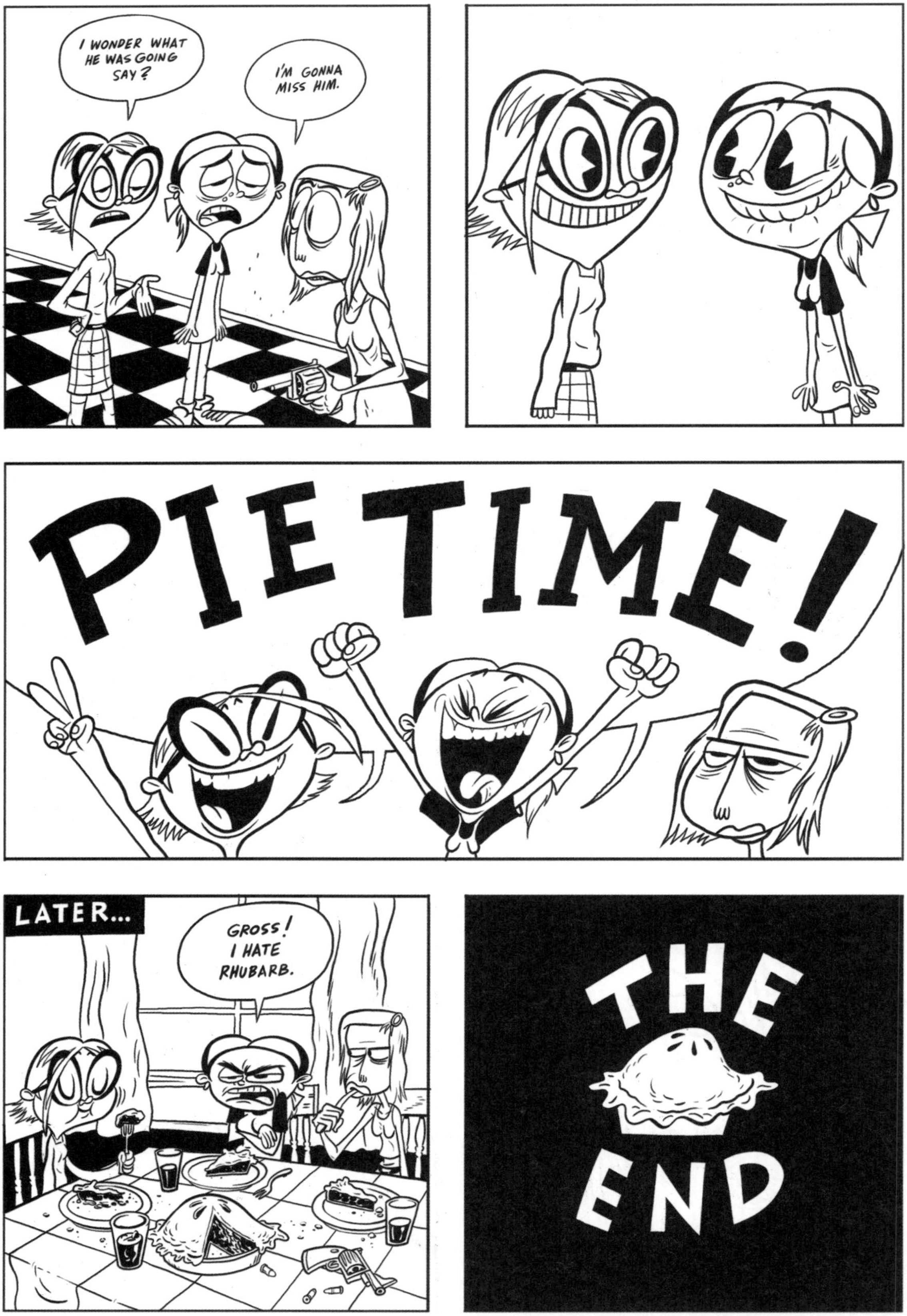
I WONDER WHAT HE WAS GOING SAY?
I'M GONNA MISS HIM.
PIETIME!
LATER...
GROSS! I HATE RHUBARB.
THE END

3ONUS OMICS

While rooting through me of the old *Angora apkin* binders I found a w more comics for your joyment! These are from a promo oklet Nick and I made in 8 for the animation pitch. I drew four of these *'il Angora"* comics, one which seems to have sappeared...

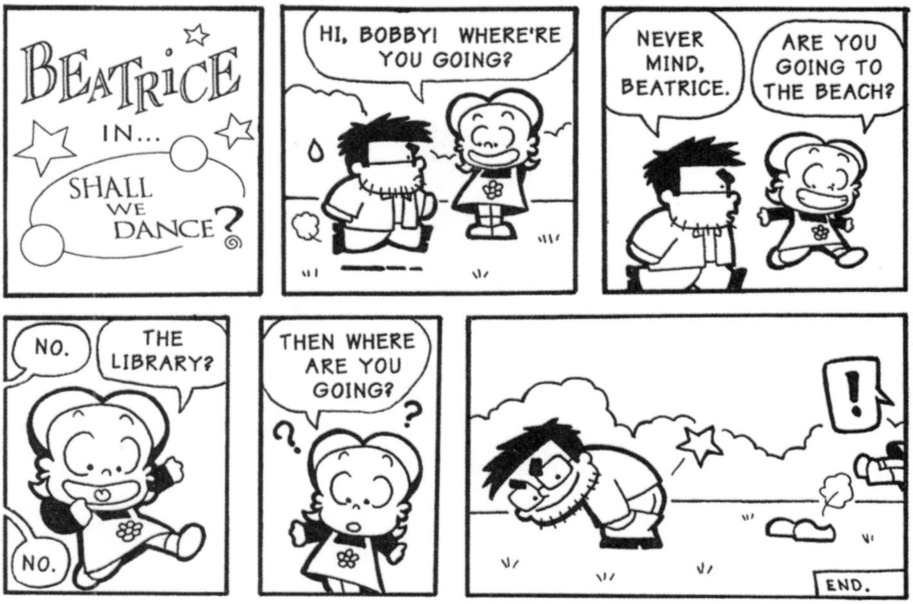
BEATRICE
IN...
SHALL WE DANCE?
HI, BOBBY! WHERE'RE YOU GOING?
NEVER MIND, BEATRICE.
ARE YOU GOING TO THE BEACH?
NO.
THE LIBRARY?
NO.
THEN WHERE ARE YOU GOING?
!
END.

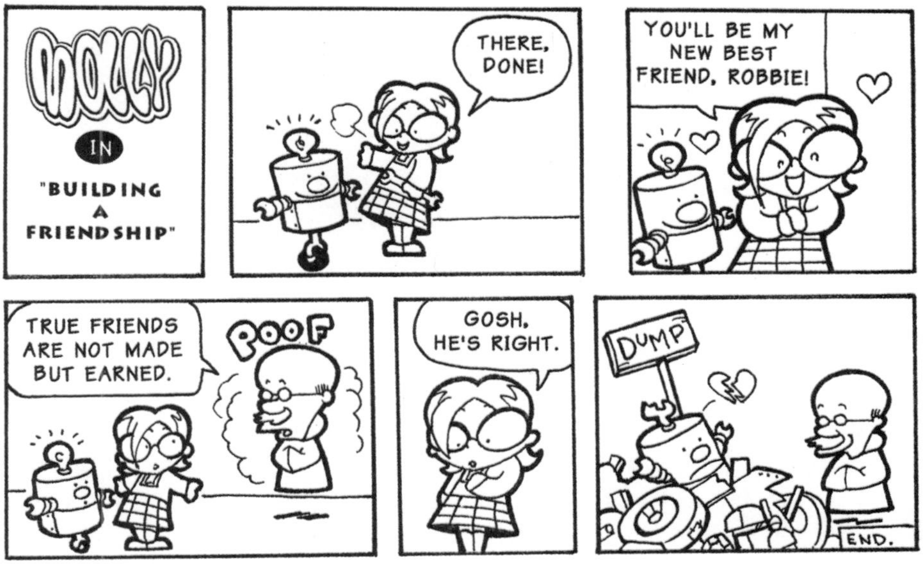
MOLLY
IN
"BUILDING A FRIENDSHIP"
THERE, DONE!
YOU'LL BE MY NEW BEST FRIEND, ROBBIE!
TRUE FRIENDS ARE NOT MADE BUT EARNED.
POOF
GOSH, HE'S RIGHT.
DUMP
END.

LIFE WITH MALLORY

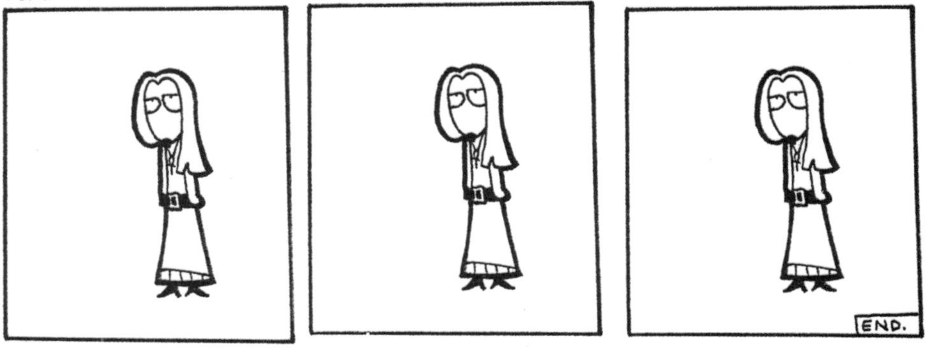
END.

Photo by Sue Marsden

About the Author

Troy Little is the author of the critically acclaimed graphic novel *Chiaroscuro*.
He lives in Prince Edward Island, Canada with his wife, Carol,
and twin daughters, Alicen & Hayden.

Troy is currently working on bringing *Angora Napkin* to life in an animated pilot.
He plans on returning to work on the next volume of *Chiaroscuro* in early 2009.